Greece & Rome

NEW SURVEYS IN THE CLASSICS No. 29

'GREEK SCIENCE,

BY

T. E. RIHLL

Published for the Classical Association

OXFORD UNIVERSITY PRESS

1999

OXFORD

UNIVERSITY PRESS

Great Clarendon Street, Oxford OX2 6DP

Oxford University Press is a department of the University of Oxford
and furthers the University's aim of excellence in research, scholarship,
and education by publishing worldwide in

Oxford New York

Athens Auckland Bangkok Bogotá Bombay Buenos Aires Calcutta
Cape Town Chennai Dar es Salaam Delhi Florence Hong Kong Istanbul
Karachi Kuala Lumpur Madrid Melbourne Mexico City Mumbai
Nairobi Paris São Paulo Singapore Taipei Tokyo Toronto Warsaw
with associated companies in Berlin Ibadan

Oxford is a registered trade mark of Oxford University Press
in the UK and in cetain other countries

ISSN 0017–3835
ISBN 019–922395–5

Typeset by Joshua Associates Ltd., Oxford
Printed in Great Britain
on acid-free paper by
by Bell and Bain Ltd., Glasgow

PREFACE

The subject of Greek science is vast. One could spend a lifetime reading and thinking about just what Aristotle wrote, and Aristotle was only one of a number of prolific authors. Surviving authors are only contributors to the subject on which they wrote, having predecessors, contemporaries, and successors. It is simply not possible to gather, absorb, and evaluate all of Greek science, and all of the research of all scholars of Greek science.

There are many excellent existing books about aspects of Greek science, which typically discuss the great men and the great discoveries, or trace, with perfect hindsight, the paths of development in a subject. A brief recitation of the same material is hardly needed, especially when space is at such a premium. Instead, what I hope to convey is a sense of the range and scope of the ancient scientific material which exists. I will not spend all of my time on the great and good, so that I can make room for some of the lesser lights. Not all Greek scientists were geniuses and not all of their ideas were brilliant. But these other works are nevertheless fascinating, and deserve to be better known. They convey more 'ordinary' science, the ancient equivalent of the TV nature programme or the coffee-table science book, which then as now was more common, and which then as now penetrated popular culture.

Consequently, I see my primary purpose in this survey as being to introduce modern readers to the ancient Greek literature which is classified loosely as science. A great deal survives, from which I shall select to give a taster of the ancient practice and practitioners of science. I hope these will be found sufficiently interesting to the reader to inspire her or him to go and read some ancient scientific text in full – for its historical value, if not for its scientific content. I also wish to draw attention to scientific matters in authors of more popular genres. My secondary purpose is to indicate the range and extent of the modern literature on ancient science. It is not from lack of interest or disapproval that I have omitted numerous ancient and modern works from this survey, but my inability to read everything relevant, and a lack of space to discuss more than a fraction of what I have read. The 'Further Reading' section at the end of each chapter is intended to guide the reader to more literature and bibliographies, old and new.

I will not discuss the philosophy of science or the philosophy of the history of science, but it is appropriate here to indicate my position on some contentious matters within those fields. I believe in a real world 'out there'; that we can perceive that world through our senses; that we do not perceive reality simply, directly, and immediately, but that our perception is filtered by our ideas and beliefs; that systems of ideas and beliefs change over time and space, so that different filters operate in different times and places. I believe that modern understandings of the real world can help us comprehend ancient understandings, as much as if not more than they may hinder us.[1] I believe that science, like every other human activity, does not take place in a vacuum, but is influenced by the social, economic, political, religious, and every other type of cultural system operating in the place and time in which the science is undertaken.

For the purpose of this survey I have focused on works in English, i.e. ancient texts with good English translations, and secondary literature in English. But it should be noted that English speakers are less well served than some others, especially in the area of the absolute essential to study: the texts.[2] Budé have an excellent range of ancient scientific texts with facing French translations.[3] Teubner also have a good range of texts, some with facing German translations (Latin in older editions). The Loeb Library is rather disappointing when it comes to the scientific tradition: the texts which have been done have been done well, on the whole,[4] but the coverage is patchy. You will not find in Loeb's library Archimedes, Apollonios, Diophantos or Euclid, bar a few short highlights selected for the two volumes of *Greek Mathematical Works*;[5] you will not find Ptolemy's *Astronomy*,[6] *Geography*, *Optics*, *Harmonics*,

---

[1] On this see Pickstone 1995.

[2] We might compare the 104 books by Galen which Hunayn ibn Ishaq translated into Syriac in the C9 A.D. (Benoît and Micheau 1995, 201) with the 30-odd available in English.

[3] They include, for example, Arrian's *Periplous of the Euxine*, Diophantos' *Arithmetic*, and the Leiden and Stockholm alchemical texts.

[4] Some editions suffer lacunae deliberately introduced in response to cultural factors prevailing when the work was published (often, a long time ago), such as Hort's omission of a section of Theophrastos' *History of Plants* 9.18, which mentions male genitalia, contraceptive drugs (for men as well as women), aphrodisiacs (including what is reputed to be an ancient equivalent of Viagra), and abortion.

[5] Edited and translated by Thomas 1939–41. These volumes are excellent as far as they go; the problem is that they have just bits of different works. Consider a hypothetical analogy: what sort of understanding could one achieve of, say, Greek tragedy, if one depended on two volumes of *Greek Tragic Works* featuring 'the best' speeches in this or that play by Aiskhulos, Sophokles, and Euripides?

[6] Better known by the title the *Almagest*, formed from the Arabic definite article *al-* and Greek *megiste*, and meaning 'The Greatest'. It dominated astronomical thinking for over a millennium. It has been translated by Toomer and published by Duckworth 1984.

Handy Tables, Hypotheses, Phaseis, Analemma or *Simple Sphere*, but only his *Astrology*;[7] you will find only one volume of the hundreds written by the prolific Galen.[8] You will find Theophrastos' *Characters, Causes of Plants* and *History of Plants*, with *On Weather Signs* and *On Odours* tucked on to the end of the second volume of the latter; you will not find other works of his, such as *On Fire, On Fish, On the Senses*, and *On Stones*. (Things could be worse: Penguin only have the *Characters*, which is his least important work.) For many of these omissions, someone somewhere has edited the text and published an English translation, but they can be difficult to find, and they can be very old.[9] For the convenience of the reader I have quoted the Loeb translation wherever possible,[10] and I thank Harvard University Press for permission so to do.

A considerable debt of gratitude is owed to students at the University of Wales Swansea and the University of Wales Lampeter who have taken my courses on ancient science and technology since 1991. Their enthusiasm for the subject has been a constant stimulus to me to develop and promote its study. I am also indebted to my husband, John Tucker, without whose help and encouragement I would probably never have got to grips with geometry, and hence astronomy and mathematical geography. He also read every chapter several times and improved the structure and clarity of the text enormously. The Institute for the History of Science and the University Library (Carolina Rediviva) at the University of Uppsala kindly allowed me to use their facilities in August 1998. It is also a pleasure to thank Ian McAuslan for his tremendous help and advice at various stages of this project.

T. E. Rihll

Perriswood, Gower
March 1999

---

[7] Known by the title *Tetrabiblos*, 'Four Books'.

[8] *On the Natural Faculties*, ed. and trans. by Brock, 1916. *Galen: Selected Works* by Singer, published by Oxford (World's Classics Series) 1997, contains 15 treatises in translation, with a good introduction.

[9] I'm thinking here particularly of Dioscorides, published by Gunther in 1933 but actually Goodyer's translation from 1655; it is not easily recognizable as English. Scarborough and Nutton have done a recent edition, translation, and commentary of the Preface to Dioscorides' *Materia Medica* in *Trans. and Studies of the College of Physicians of Philadelphia* n.s. 4 (1982), 187–227. The Preface consumes 3 printed pages; the commentary consumes 30. This gives some idea of the work which can be involved in the explication of an ancient scientific text. The whole text was done into German in 1902 by Berendes.

[10] The full catalogue is on the Internet at
http://www.hup.harvard.edu/Web_Loeb.catalog.am.html

CONTENTS

Note on Names and Citations   viii

Acknowledgements   ix

Note to the Scientifically Faint-hearted Reader   x

I   The Nature of Greek Science   1

II   Physics   24

III   Mathematics   39

IV   Astronomy   62

V   Geography   82

VI   Biology and Medicine   106

      Epilogue   137

      Bibliography   139

      About the Author   154

      Index of Names, Subjects, and Passages   155

ILLUSTRATIONS

Figure 3.1	Greek alphabetic numerals	52
Figure 3.2	Pythagoras' theorem	57
Figure 3.3	Proof tree for part of Pythagoras' theorem	58
Figure 4.1	The celestial north pole in 400 B.C.	67
Figure 4.2	Aristarchus Proposition 7: On the distance of the sun from earth	75
Figure 5.1	The Mediterranean Sea according to ancient map-makers	97
Figure 6.1	Ancient whaling gear as described by Oppian	113

NOTE ON NAMES AND CITATIONS

It is impossible to be consistent in the rendition of Greek names. Some are well known in Latinized form, but there is no consistency even among these, so we have Solon but not Platon, Themistocles but not Aristoteles. Pedantry leads to unfamiliar spellings whichever principle or tradition one follows. There are four standard letter substitutions which I have found typically lead students into errors of pronunciation, and so I try to avoid them: I normally use 'k' and 'kh' (not c and ch) for κ and χ, 'i' (not e) for ι and 'u' (not y) for υ. Nevertheless, you will still find here Pythagoras not Puthagoras, Euclid not Eukleides, and all that is usually required to turn an unfamiliar name into a familiar one is a little flexibility over these substitutions and final 'n'.

To save a lot of space in the text and notes I have used the 'Harvard system' for modern works e.g. Lloyd 1995. Full details will be found in the Bibliography.

ACKNOWLEDGEMENTS

The author is grateful to: Aris & Phillips for permission to reproduce an extract from A. Sommerstein's translation of Aristophanes' *Wasps*; Cambridge University Press for permission to reproduce extracts from J. O. Thomson's *History of Ancient Geography*; Oxford University Press for permission to reproduce extracts from E. W. Marsden's translation of Philo's *Belopoiika*; Dover Publications Inc. for permission to reproduce extracts from T. B. L. Heath's translations of Aristarchus' *On the Size and Distance of the Sun and the Moon* and Archimedes' *On Floating Bodies*; Duckworth & Co. for permission to reproduce extracts from G. Toomer's translation of Ptolemy's *Almagest* and D. Furley's translation of Philoponus' *Corollary on Void*; Harvard University Press (Loeb Classical Library) for permission to reproduce extracts from: H. Cherniss' translation of Plutarch's *On the Face of the Orb of the Moon*, T. H. Corcoran's translation of Seneca's *Natural Questions*, J. W. & A. M. Duff's translation of *Aetna*, A. Fairbank's translation of Philostratos' *Imagines*, W. S. Hett's translation of [Aristotle]'s *On Colours*, Sir A. Hort's translation of Theophrastos' *History of Plants*, H. L. Jones's translation of Strabo's *Geography*, W. H. S. Jones' translation of Hippokrates' *Aphorisms*, A. W. Mair's translation of Oppian's *Halieutica* and Aratos' *Phainomena*, C. Oldfather's translation of Diodorus Siculus' *Library of History*, B. Perrin's translation of Plutarch's *Life of Theseus*, P. Potter's translation of Hippokrates' *Haemorrhoids*, H. Rackham's translation of Pliny the Elder's *Natural History*, F. E. Robbins' translation of Ptolemy's *Tetrabiblos*, J. Rusten's translation of Theophrastos' *Characters*, W. G. Spencer's translation of Celsus' *De Medicina*, and I. Thomas's translation of Euclid's *Elements* and Vitruvius' *On Architecture*; Princeton University Press for permission to reproduce extracts from E. S. Forster's translation of [Aristotle]'s *Mechanics* and W. Ogle's translation of Aristotle's *Parts of Animals*; and Paul Bessette for producing Fig. 4.1 using Cybersky.

TO THE SCIENTIFICALLY FAINT-HEARTED READER

Understanding what is going on in most of Greek science is well within the competence of any intelligent person, as it was in antiquity. Take heart! If you read an ancient scientific text and feel, not that you are out of your depth scientifically, but more or less *bewildered* by the contents, then you are probably reading it through modern spectacles, so to speak. Assume always that the ancient author makes sense: what he wrote was considered sensible by enough people over enough centuries – more than a thousand years in some cases – for that text to have been repeatedly copied and thus survive for us to read now. The task then is to discover in what sense he makes sense. As Klein put it with respect to mathematics, 'our task consists precisely in bringing the content of Greek mathematics to light not by externally transposing it into another mode of presentation but rather by comprehending it in the one way which seemed comprehensible to the Greeks'.[1] This search for sense can apply to the structure of a work as well as its contents: our task in that case is to recognize the principle of organization at work in what otherwise appears to be a set of more or less disorganized notes, as for example in the cases of Aristotle's *History of Animals*, Theophrastos' *History of Plants*, or Dioskorides' *Herbal*.

Not knowing much modern science can be an advantage, for then you do not have to unlearn what you have been taught in order to comprehend ancient science. The unscientifically-trained modern reader can approach e.g. Aristotle with an eye which sees the world perhaps more as he saw it. Even the partially scientifically trained reader may side with the ancients on some issues, despite knowing that they were wrong. And if you never stopped to consider some of the things which these ancient scientists consider, then they may fill you with wonderment, instead of puzzlement, or worse – following a well-established pattern of ancient Greek attitudes to rival theories – scorn.

Likewise, try not to jump to conclusions over 'the obvious'. Consider the following example. Given the naturalness and commonness of pregnancy, 'it's obvious' that pregnancy lasts nine months. Obvious, because we naturally assume that a woman knows when she's pregnant,

---

[1] Klein 1968, reprinted by Dover 1992, p. 127.

because, apart from 'feelings' or other intangibles, her periods stop. But this assumption is false, because sometimes they don't (with no ill effect on the embryo, *contra* Nigidius *apud* Pliny *NH* 7.66). It is not unusual for periods to occur for the next month or two, so that a woman can be three months pregnant before she realizes it, and light periods can continue even beyond that. These days modern technology can establish beyond doubt that she is several months, and not one month, pregnant. The ancients, needless to say, had no such technology, so relied on the cessation of periods to determine the start of pregnancy. So it was not obvious to them how long pregnancy lasted in women.[2] Thus when ancient paediatricians are concerned with 'the eight-month child' and 'the seven-month child' (e.g. Hippocratic treatises on the same), do not assume that these are premature babies. The (at first sight surprising) high survival rate expected for 'the seven-month child' is to be explained by the fact that some, if not most of them, were not premature at all, but were carried full term.

For scholars and scientists there are several approaches to the subject. Some material is so technical and complex that only a professional in that field today could understand what the ancient exponent was talking about – take Archimedes' mathematics, as an example. He was one of the most brilliant mathematicians of all time, and with the best will in the world, most of us are not going to be able to understand him, however much we might like to, and however hard we try. Understanding Archimedes therefore depends on professional mathematicians working their way through his corpus. Unless they have Greek, they in turn depend on classicists translating the text. But translating a text is difficult if you do not understand what the text means – and understanding what Archimedes' texts mean requires a mathematician![3] In previous centuries and the beginning of this there were more polymaths around, who could handle both requirements,[4] hence the age of some editions of

---

[2] Aristotle *HA* 584a35–b1 comments on the difference in this regard between humans (variable 7–11 months) and all other animals (invariable by species); see also [Aristotle] *Problems* 10.41. An inscription from the healing sanctuary of Asklepios at Epidaurus records Cleo's five-year long pregnancy, *IG* 4.951. See also Pliny *NH* 7.40 on a Roman legal case, where the judge knew of no good cause to deny the possibility of a 13-month pregnancy, and so awarded a disputed estate to the child of a widow of that time's standing.

[3] The problem is particularly acute in mathematics; see chapter 3 below.

[4] e.g. Thompson on natural history, birds and fishes in particular; Heiberg, Heath, and Thomas on Greek maths; Bailey on the chemical parts of Pliny's *Natural History*; and Bennet Woodcroft, a Professor of Machinery, who became tired of waiting for some professional classicist somewhere to do Hero's *Pneumatics*, and commissioned a classicist (J. Greenwood) to translate it (1851). It is *still* the only English translation of that work (Hall reprinted this with an introduction in 1971), and the source of almost all illustrations of Hero's machines, which are published widely.

scientific texts and subjects. Some subjects have been tackled by a team, a classicist to give a 'raw' translation of the words, and a specialist in the relevant area to understand their meaning, and thus together to produce a correct translation, for example, the E. R. Caley (chemist) and J. F. C. Richards (classicist) partnership[5] for Theophrastos' *On Stones*; O. Pederson (historian of science) and M. Pihl (physicist) for *Early Physics and Astronomy*; M. R. Cohen (philosopher) and I. E. Drabkin (classicist) for *Sourcebook in Greek Science*; and recently the Pliny translation group,[6] but this is rare.[7] More commonly the classicist consults scientific colleagues on specific points of difficulty,[8] but then only the texts which interest the classicists get done.

Once the text, a technically as well as linguistically accurate modern translation, and a commentary to explain the technical matters are done, the next task is to establish the historical context of the text. This area desperately needs attention by ancient historians. Few have ventured here and it is a very underdeveloped area. Hence the current historically-abstract, philologically or technically dominated state of the literature on many ancient scientific texts. As each stage progresses, it feeds back towards the text, modifying the interpretations and understanding of it.[9] Thus there is a role and a need for 'ordinary' historians in the study of the history of Greek science, which is a land of opportunity for adventurous scholars.

---

[5] Another classicist, S. H. Weber, and a member of the Columbia University School of Mines, T. T. Read, were also involved in early stages of production of this book.

[6] On which see Rottländer 1986. The team are translating Pliny into German.

[7] Heilbron 1996 argues that it has almost become a necessity for the history of science to be tackled by teams of scholars, scientists, and support staff in IT etc. This is the published version of the opening address of the Max Planck Institute for the History of Science in Berlin, March 1995. It remains to be seen if, and if so how, this programmatic statement is put into practice.

[8] For example, Toynbee consulted a vet (R. Walker) for his *Animals in Roman Life and Art* 1973; Walker then contributed to the book an appendix on Roman veterinary medicine, pp. 303–43.

[9] For example, proper attention to the historical information contained in one of Galen's works, as well as to the MS tradition, the style, and the medical content, allowed Nutton 1997 to demonstrate conclusively that Galen died not in 199 (as traditionally believed, on the basis of an entry in the Suda), but after 204, and possibly as late as 207. An early stage of the whole process may be seen in the area of the classical tradition in Islamic sources, which are now beginning to appear in modern European language translations. For example, Saïd al-Andalusi's *The Catalogue of Nations* is now available in English. The scholars who edited and translated the text are specialists in medieval Arabic, whose knowledge of classical scientific texts is limited (but my knowledge of medieval Arabic is non-existent) and whose notes to the text are correspondingly weak. But now that they have translated the text from Arabic, many others can access the text and enlarge our general understanding of it. The Arabs were not interested in Greek or Latin literature, but translated and preserved every ancient scientific treatise they could find.

I. THE NATURE OF GREEK SCIENCE

1.1 *On science and scientists*

The essential difference between science and related forms of intellectual activity is very difficult to define exactly. A dictionary definition of science is an accurate reflection of what *some* people understand by the term 'science', and then only in the period and place in which the dictionary was written. Most people live their lives and use their language without reference to a dictionary. Even sticking to the dictionary definition, what the word 'science' has meant to different people has varied over time and cultures, and its meaning continues to change.[1] As such, the term itself can be a source of anachronism in the study of science in ancient times. For we naturally tend to find in ancient authors just those sorts of things which we recognize as science in our own times, and to ignore those things which are incomprehensible or just plain wrong – to *our* way of thinking. And we naturally tend to organize what we find into categories which reflect *our* way of dividing up the world into subjects and disciplines. Thus things that the ancients linked together, we tear apart and treat separately. In particular, some we include in the category of science, others we exclude.

In this process, Crombie has emphasized that the circumscription of subject matter – what is regarded *as* science, and what count as valid questions, pieces of evidence, types of argument and answer – is the key to opening doors to new knowledge and understanding; but that at the same time it *closes* other doors. For example, modern astronomers are expected not to engage in astrology, but that door remained open for their predecessors, from ancient Greece to enlightenment Britain, who were socially and intellectually free to study both subjects

---

[1] According to Crombie 1994 there are, and historically have been, six and only six distinct styles of scientific thinking. A scientific style is a way of thinking about the world that aims 'to advance knowledge by the identification of answerable questions and soluble problems, to devise methods of finding possible answers and solutions, and at the same time to determine what counted among these as acceptable' (p. ix). Each style focused its inquiries upon certain regular natural phenomena, decided what sort of question would be considered valid, and determined what sort of answers would be acceptable. 'A style thus opened certain routes of inquiry and closed others' (vol. 1, p. xi). The Greek style of scientific thinking, the earliest European style and a style which has continued to the present day, he calls Postulation, and discusses at length in volume 1.

simultaneously. The ancients put astrology on a par with astronomy, as two sides of the same coin.[2] Changing views of the meaning of 'science' closed this door in due course, and classical scholarship felt its influence. So, until very recently, modern scholars have highlighted the ancients' achievements in ancient astronomy, and done their best to ignore (if not positively conceal, excuse, or try to explain away) what they regarded as an embarrassing lapse of rationality.[3]

Modern intellectual traffic between the 'science' end of ancient activities and the 'superstition' end of the same, even when both were conducted by the same ancient person, tends to be one-way. Astronomy-historians, for example, can produce works focused tightly on ancient theories of the cosmos. They may extend this to include closely related matters, such as the business of actually observing heavenly phenomena, but it is not considered necessary for an intellectually sound treatment of ancient astronomy. Astrology-historians need to explain ancient astronomical theories before they can start on the real subject of their interest, which is astrological theories. And alchemy-historians need to know ancient astrology (and therefore ancient astronomy) in order to deal with their subject of interest.[4] But a historian of astronomy considers alchemy well outside the remit of his study.

For the purpose of this book, I too have divided the subject matter into modern categories, in spite of what I have said above, for three pragmatic reasons. First, because the original ancient categories are too large to serve as analytical tools. For the Greeks, all serious intellectual pursuits could be classified under the heading *philosophia*. The Greek term usually translated as 'science', *episteme*, covered cooking, amongst other things;[5] with due respect to the modern category of domestic science, that will not do for our purposes. Natural history, or more precisely, inquiry into *phusis*, nature, was the nearest phrase to the modern term 'science', but if we use this category, then we cannot sort the material, because almost everything falls into the one category, and the only obvious tool left to apply to break the mass up into manageable

---

[2] Astrology was also closely linked with medicine, chemistry (under the ancient label *phusis*, physics), botany, and anthropology. For the first, see Scarborough 1991 esp. pp. 154–63.

[3] E.g. Cohen and Drabkin 1948, pp. viii–ix: 'No one can well deny that a good deal of what may be called "pseudo-science", such as astrology and the like, can be found in the writings of such sober Greek scientists as Aristotle and Ptolemy. But it is well to remember that the intrusion of the occult can be found in modern writings such as Kepler's or Newton's and in the contributions to the early volumes of the transactions of the Royal Society down to the works of Lodge, Carrel and Eddington in our own day.'

[4] See e.g. Keyser 1990a.

[5] See Owens 1991.

chunks is the chronological one, loosely applied.[6] As W. Knorr pointed out in a mathematical context,[7] 'to explain certain aspects of modern geometry, it may become advisable, even necessary, to import notions from more recent fields, like algebra. This raises the possibility of anachronism, as is present in all analogical forms of exegesis. That risk becomes acceptable if the alternative is the learner's incomprehension.' I have taken that risk by using modern categories. A second reason why I have divided the subject matter into modern categories is that most of the existing modern literature focuses on one or another category, and since this is a survey, it seems sensible to organize it on the same principles. The third reason is that a brief survey of a vast field is not the place to try to develop a new taxonomy of ancient science. However, within each category it is my intention to include material which sits uncomfortably within it, simply in order to make clear the limitations of these categories.

A separate and serious problem with 'science' as a category is that the abstract nature of scientific ideas seems to encourage an abstraction in the study of its history. Often the ideas are presented in splendid isolation from the social, political, religious, and economic context of their formation.[8] (This problem is not confined to ancient history.) For example, when one reads the word 'school' applied to e.g. Aristotle's Lyceum, one imagines a building, at the very least. Yet there was no private building until after Aristotle's death;[9] his 'colleagues' and 'students' met him and each other in a sacred public wood outside Athens' city walls, where *ho boulomenos*[10] could worship Apollo Lukeios, or go for a stroll, or collect firewood, or hunt rabbits, or whatever.[11] Meanwhile ancient studies carried out by people now more or less anonymous in circumstances not fitting with modern notions of research can be overlooked. For example, Mithridates' immunity to all known

---

[6] This is a problem with French's otherwise excellent *Ancient Natural History*, which is sometimes frustrating, but rewards well the diligent reader.

[7] Knorr 1991 p. 122 n. 11.

[8] Needham suggested that this abstract approach arose because 'the social background of Hellenistic science and technology can be taken for granted because it is quite familiar to us from our schooldays onwards', 1962 §26 p. xxvi. This familiarity might have been true for some 30 years ago, but it is sadly untrue today, and a generation of scholars who allegedly took social knowledge for granted, and thus neglected to draw out its significance, seems to have led to scholarship which does not recognize its significance at all, typified in e.g. Barnes 1979.

[9] There was a publicly owned gymnasium there from at least the late fifth century, for public use.

[10] Any Athenian citizen who wished.

[11] See Lynch 1972. The same general point is true of Plato's Academy; see Cherniss 1945.

venoms and poisons[12] was the result of a long programme of research and development by toxicologists who worked in his service,[13] combined with empirical trials on death-row prisoners in the pursuit of antidotes. Pompey (at least) was interested in this scientific project: he ordered a Latin translation of Mithridates' written results (Pliny *NH* 25.7). These results, like those obtained by the human vivisectionists of the Hellenistic period, were incorporated into the ancient scientific knowledge base, and can now be studied in comfortable abstraction from the context of their creation. Medical ethics is not new incidentally, and, as with vegetarianism, the arguments have not changed much since antiquity.

One of the major features of Greek science is that most of its practitioners were autodidacts. Even those who studied under a philosophical giant seem, with very few exceptions, not to have been content to follow a path laid down by a predecessor. They wished to carve out their own path, citing predecessors' views when it suited them, and ignoring them likewise. They did not so much stand on their predecessors' shoulders as knock them down, step over them, and go elsewhere.[14] In this respect, the nature of the scientific endeavour today is quite different from that in antiquity. A big and related difference, with many profound corollaries, is the individualism of ancient science. Though we (and the ancients) occasionally talk of philosophical 'schools' or medical 'sects', these terms more often refer

---

[12] This prevented him from committing suicide by mouth after his capture by the Romans, and caused him to fall on his sword instead.

[13] We have one name, Krateuas. Very little is known about him, other than that he was known as a rootcutter, he lived at Mithridates' court, and he wrote a lost, illustrated, work on plants, which may have been the basis for later herbals such as that by Dioskorides; see Wellmann 1897, with Riddle's discussion 1985 pp. 180–217. Attalus III of Pergamum was also (and a generation earlier) interested in and very knowledgeable about toxic substances and antidotes, which he tested on condemned criminals (Galen, *Antidotes*, 1.1 (14.2 K)), and on 'friends' according to the hostile tradition in Justin's *Epitome of Trogus' History of Philip* 36.4.3.

[14] This observation was made first by the Greeks themselves. Diodorus Siculus 2.29.6: 'a few [Greeks] here and there really strive for the higher studies and continue in the pursuit of them as a profit-making business, and these are always trying to make innovations in connection with the most important doctrines instead of following in the path of their predecessors. The result of this is that the barbarians, by sticking to the same things always, keep a firm hold on every detail, while the Greeks, on the other hand, aiming at the profit to be made out of the business, keep founding new schools and, wrangling with each other over the most important matters of speculation, bring it about that their pupils hold conflicting views, and that their minds, vacillating throughout their lives and unable to believe anything at all with firm conviction, simply wander in confusion. It is at any rate true that, if a man were to examine carefully the most famous schools of the philosophers, he would find them differing from one another to the uttermost degree and maintaining opposite opinions regarding the most fundamental tenets' (trans. Oldfather). There are examples from the medical field and discussion of this point in Lloyd 1995 and Hankinson 1995.

to like-minded individuals, who might be widely dispersed over time and space, than to organizations of intellectual co-workers and colleagues. Someone who never set foot in the Academy might be called a Platonist, because the label reflected his philosophical inclinations and not his membership of some club, society, or association.

Moreover, it is a large and usually overlooked *assumption* that the authors of ancient scientific texts were 'professional' philosophers or doctors or teachers or people otherwise engaged most of their time in thinking or writing about their subject. The same point can be made for other producers of literary works, e.g. dramatists.[15] It seems to me probable that a significant number of these people undertook their studies in their (relatively ample) leisure time. As late as the last century, the men who founded ancient history and kindred subjects founded them in their spare time: for example, George Grote was a banker, MP and a few other things simultaneously, Thomas Heath was a civil servant, and James Gow was a lawyer; they were not salaried academics.

For much of Western history there is an assumption that writers belong to an educated elite. But this assumption is highly presumptuous for ancient Greece. A fair number of the Greek authors were, we can safely assume, born to farm,[16] whilst others were taught craft skills by their fathers. Sokrates' father was a stonemason; Aristotle's a healer; Theophrastos' a laundryman; Ktesibios' a barber. Apollonios of Perga was called a carpenter;[17] several creators of panaceas mentioned by

---

[15] Aiskhulos famously wanted recorded on his gravestone not that he wrote this or that tragedy, but that he fought at Marathon. As a hoplite, it is a safe assumption that he was a farmer, as were more than 90% of the population. Thoukudides wrote history when forced into exile after active (but unsuccessful, hence exile) service as general in the Peloponnesian war; Xenophon was a professional soldier, again largely because he was exiled and thus prevented from engaging in farming and politics; Cicero was a professional politician first, and author of diverse subjects second; Plutarch was a politician, priest at Delphi and much else besides; the list could be as long as the authors about whom we have biographical information. Why then should we suppose that those who wrote what we call 'scientific treatises', about whom we usually have little if any reliable biographical information, were fundamentally different, a class apart from authors of all other types of literary work? For example, later Greeks knew so little about Euclid that they confused the Euclid of *Elements* with another philosopher called Euclid who came from Megara. See also Authier 1995 on Plutarch as creator of the (false) archetypical image of the scientist, and its perseverance in the face of any and all evidence to the contrary.

[16] Nutton assumes the same of 'most doctors resident in a small town' and points out that 'doctors were regularly encouraged to grow their own simples' [simple drugs], 1985b quotes from p. 140. All those Greek scientists who played a part in the politics of their local poleis (e.g. Arkhytas, Empedokles, Eudoxos, Hippias, Philolaos) may confidently be assumed to have owned farms. Polubios (3.59.3–5) thought that many Greeks of the Hellenistic and Roman periods pursued an intellectual life because political domination by Macedon, the successor states, and then Rome, 'relieved' them of the ambition to pursue a life in war and politics when not managing their farms. Polubios himself was a case in point.

[17] By Saïd al-Andalusi in the *Book of Categories of Nations*, 1991 p. 26. The association is not

Galen are labelled tradesmen (or worse) of one sort or another;[18] and Archimedes was apparently at Hieron's beck and call.[19] Demetrios of Phaleron governed Athens before organizing the Library at Alexandria;[20] a number of Greek intellectuals appeared on the Roman scene first as civic officials, ambassadors for their poleis;[21] Frontinus was consul and governor of Britain (amongst other things), whose interest in hydraulic engineering arose from his (important political) appointment by Nerva to the office of overseer of the water supply to the city of Rome;[22] and Pliny was Commander of the Fleet at Misenum when he died, famously observing Vesuvius from too close quarters. If this point is not convincing, consider, as the implied alternative, the plausibility of an ancient Greek boy (still less a Roman) telling his father that he wanted to be a professional philosopher when he grew up.[23]

accidental: the geometer's tools are the carpenter's tools – compass and set square or gnomon. Hahn (1995, p. 126 n. 25) drew attention to 'a kind of applied geometry with technological innovation' which characterizes the real or attributed achievements of Thales, Anaximander, Rhoikos, Theodoros, Khersiphron, and Metagenes. Although only the first two are generally thought of as presocratic *philosophers* (the other four being labelled architect/engineers) I believe that the kind of employment specialization these labels imply is inappropriate for the period.

[18] Namely, Celer the centurion, Diogas the trainer, Euskhemos the eunuch, Flavius the boxer, Orion the groom (which indicates an overlap between human and veterinary medicine), and Philoxenos the schoolmaster, all cited by Nutton in his hugely entertaining, as well as very informative, article on 'The drug trade in antiquity', 1985b, p. 145.

[19] Cicero, nearest in time of those remarking on his origins, described Archimedes as 'a humble little man', *Tusc.Disp.* 5.23, which can hardly refer to his personality as revealed in his surviving works, and therefore ought to be read as a reference to his socio-economic status. Silius Italicus thought likewise, calling Archimedes destitute (*nudus*), *Punica* 14.343. This, however, did not fit at all with Plutarch's image of the scientist induced only by Roman soldiers besieging the city to tear himself away from contemplation of abstract mathematics and get his hands dirty in an occasional bit of mechanical engineering, so Plutarch *Marcellus* 14.5 says he was a relative (unspecified) and friend of Hieron.

[20] Aristeas, *Epistle* 10, 29–30. He too was 'not well-born' according to Diog. Laert. 5.75.

[21] e.g. Poseidonios of Apameia and famously Karneades, who so irritated Cato (Plut. *Cato* 22–3). Similarly the historian Polubios, who went to Rome as a political hostage for the good behaviour of his home community, the Achaian League, after they lost the battle of Pudna.

[22] His treatise on the *Aqueducts* was completed under Trajan. Before that he had written military treatises for Domitian, and a work on surveying.

[23] Absence of evidence is not evidence of absence, and the primary sources (prior to the C2 A.D.) are notoriously uninterested in biography and autobiography, so we must be content with probabilities. Greek scientists did not leave memoirs – even Galen did not leave a memoir as such. On his many autobiographical comments scattered through his works, it is essential to understand the context, for which see Nutton 1972, to whose points we should add one more, concerning forgeries. 'Forgers' might not simply be in the business of trying to make sales of their own works by passing them off as Galen's; they might rather be medical opponents in the business of trying to discredit him, as Anaximenes of Lampsakos 'forged' one of his rivals, the historian Theopompos, to damage him (Pausanias 6.18.2). There are of course secondary sources written in antiquity, by men like Diogenes Laertius (*Lives of the Famous Philosophers*), Philostratos (*Lives of the Sophists*) and Eunapios (*Lives of the Philosophers*), but they are all late (C3–4 A.D.) and generally unreliable – they are mentioned frequently in modern scholarship because we are beggars for biographical information and have no other choice. On the hypothetical Greek boy, my feeling is that the

The abstraction of ancient science from the people and the context of its creation misses the most important question in any historical study, which is not *what* happened, but *why* did it happen? And even the 'what' question is going to be inadequately handled if it is uncontextualized. Lloyd has long argued that it is precisely the socio-political context which explains why Greek science emerged in the first place,[24] and this contextualizing approach needs to be extended to all aspects of ancient science, not just its beginnings.[25]

Contextualization will not just benefit historians of science. 'To study what passes for science in a society is to go to the centre of the values of that society', as Lloyd has pointed out forcefully.[26] The ancient historian with little or no interest in ancient science can learn a great deal about 'ordinary' history from the scientific texts produced in any particular place and time. They contain a large amount of incidental information concerning every-day life and ideas at the time the texts were written. Nutton (1972 p. 50) described Galen's *Prognosis* as 'the finest contemporary account of society in Rome during the reign of Marcus Aurelius'. Consider a selection of 'scientific' texts from just one century (the fourth B.C.), and from one place (Athens): in Theophrastos' treatise *On Fire*, one discovers that there were entertainers eating fire and performing the fire-walk; from his *Metaphysics* that puppies were kept in quail cages to produce small dogs; from his *On Stones* that coal was mined and used as fuel; and from the Aristotelian *Problems* that sponge divers were using diving bells. None of this is obvious from the dramatists, historians, orators, novelists, large pile of inscribed stones, and other sources typically used by ancient historians. The primary sources for any period consist not just of the well-known and well-ploughed texts: there are a lot of grossly underutilized 'scientific' texts too, which cast a different and sometimes brilliant light on ancient society.

more 'elite' the father considered himself and his family to be, the more opposed he would have been to this idea.

[24] Much of what he has written since 1979; see e.g. Lloyd 1992. See further below §2.

[25] For examples illustrating the importance of this type of approach for reaching a fuller and deeper understanding of the scientific context of such texts, see e.g. Klein 1968 on mathematics (*arithmos* means a number of *things*, not just an abstract quantity); Osborne 1987 on the importance of the literary context in which fragments of the presocratics appear in later authors; Solmsen 1975 on presocratic and Socratic ways of thinking evidenced in history and drama (and other forms of non-philosophical/scientific literature); Rihll and Tucker 1999 on the socio-economic context of theories of matter; Cosens 1998 on the importance of practicals in Galen's treatises; and Shapiro 1994 on seventeenth-century scientists' adoption of practising artists' ideas on colour mixing (this has much interesting material on ancient theories of colour).

[26] Introductory essay to the reprint of his Inaugural Lecture (1985), in 1989, p. 353.

This incidental information is also important to the historian of science, for the society in which the science was created shapes the science itself, and neither can be properly understood in isolation from the other. This will be a theme throughout this book.

1.2 *On the methods and assumptions of Greek science*

Geoffrey Lloyd, more than any other modern scholar, has highlighted the *variety* of theories, ideas, and opinions which co-existed in ancient Greece, and their interdependence. We moderns may, quite naturally, alight on one or two which seems to be 'on the right track' or to be 'predecessors' of modern theories or methods, but the ancients did not know which way natural history or medicine or philosophy or technology would develop after them; they did not know which theories were 'right' – or at any rate 'less wrong' (as judged by today's beliefs and standards); and they did not know which theories would 'fit' into a modern concise history of a particular discipline. They did not, in short and of course, have hindsight.

As a result, ancient society as a whole did not give the kind of precedence *we* might give to one theory or sect over another: Hippocratics over herbalists, for example. If we write histories which focus only on those theories which complement or are consistent with modern theories (as was usual for previous generations of scholars), and ignore those ancient theories which can be so inconsistent with modern thinking that it is almost embarrassing to discuss them (akin to drawing attention to a friend's *faux pas*), then our histories will give a very distorted view of ancient science and ancient society.

Ancient theories developed in competition with one another. The agonistic nature of Greek culture penetrates their science too. Developing as a response to a pre-existing theory, modified in response to new theories or new arguments or new evidence, shaped by those debates rather than by a systematic and 'objective' programme of research into some type of natural phenomenon, the various theories should not be seen as free-standing intellectual systems developed in an intellectual vacuum. Their content and form is shaped partly by the content and form of other, pre-existing and contemporaneous, theories and ideas. To quote Lloyd (1989, pp. 431–2), '[the Greeks] created, they invented, their own distinctive and divergent ideas, often in direct and explicit confrontation with their rivals. The concept of nature was forged in controversy, notably as the underpinning to the claims made by new styles of wisdom in their attempts to outbid more traditional kinds.' No area of ancient scientific work was free from such dispute, not even Euclidean geometry.[27]

Lloyd is also responsible for advancing the idea that the Greek 'scientific' spirit grew out of the socio-political environment, where decisions were made by debate not by fiat, in non-monarchical systems of government, where an idea was tested by reasoning and not accepted as given. This idea[28] has been picked up widely by historians of Greek science, and has much to commend it as an explanatory factor for the extraordinary emergence of 'scientific thinking'. It does not dovetail neatly with the standard view on socio-political development in the Greek poleis,[29] but in my opinion,[30] it is the standard view which needs serious revision rather than Lloyd's hypothesis.

I think that another factor in the Greeks' unusual independence of mind is their slaveholding. Freedom, in all its aspects, was a highly cherished possession amongst the free, and acute awareness that it could be lost made it all the more precious. Hence their passion for autonomy. Autonomy does not sit well with the notion of a higher authority of any kind, political or intellectual. The atomists (beginning with Leukippos and Demokritos) pushed this to the extreme in side-lining even the authority of the gods, by thinking up a wholly materialistic, deterministic cosmos which had no place for gods at all. The independence theme

[27] For example, Zeno of Sidon launched what he thought was a damaging attack on Euclid's axiomatic method. Poseidonios (amongst others) argued the toss with him; see Proclus, *On Euclid's Elements Book* 1, especially 199–200, 214–18.

[28] Which originated with the French scholars Gernet, Vernant, and Detienne, who argued for an association between rationality and the polis, but which has been developed by Lloyd.

[29] This envisages an 'aristocratic' stage in the (crucial) archaic period, with a very gradual assumption of responsibility by the *demos* (the people), and presumes that what debates were held in this period were dominated by a few 'great and good' whilst the *demos* stood around and said or did little or nothing. This is hardly compatible with the general atmosphere of argument and debate presumed by Lloyd. He has been criticized for this reason in Hurwit 1985. The details needed to try to dovetail social and intellectual histories are also unexplicated at the moment: since the intellectual revolution started in Ionia, does Lloyd suppose that the Ionian poleis were more 'democratic' earlier than the mainland poleis? Is there any correlation between constitutional type and philosophers' home towns? Although Athens is the most famous and most well-known ancient democracy, her only homegrown critical thinkers of great stature were Sokrates and Plato. Many people from other poleis found this polis a congenial place to live and think critically – at least some of the time (Anaxagoras and Aristotle, amongst others, both felt compelled by fear to skip the country at a certain point in their residencies). Which conjunction leads to the question: is there a connection between being a *metic* rather than a citizen, and being a free thinker? Metics, by definition, were excluded from the political environment, so if there is a connection here, it would considerably complicate Lloyd's hypothesis. It would however tally with Polubios' view on political and intellectual life (see n. 16 above).

[30] I speak not as an historian of science but as an 'ordinary' ancient historian who cut her professional teeth on Greek political and constitutional history, especially in the archaic period.

continues even in Roman times: Seneca, for example, comments with reference to various leaders of and ideas within Stoicism, 'we are not ruled by a king. Each is his own man' (*Epistle* 33.9).

All ancient theories on nature were part and parcel of theories on god, the good, and much else besides. The ancient emphasis on the good, the perfect, the form, or similar notions might be compared with the modern hankering after the god of quantification: in both cases there is a tendency to try to import into everything something highly valued in the society which produces it. For some Greeks, such as the elderly Sokrates, what really mattered was how one lived one's life, and all other matters were subordinated to ethics. Most of us moderns have been brought to believe that what really matters is measurement and accountability (in many senses of the word, but especially the literal one), and all other matters are subordinated to number, even intrinsically incommensurable things such as the artistic element in a performance of ice-skating. For us, numbers seem to lend an aura of objectivity, solidity, and reliability which mere opinion lacks. But if you allocate a number to a weightless opinion, then you can amass opinions, and get a supposedly objective number; thus the world is quantified. For the ancients, the virtues (especially goodness and justice) seem to have had a role similar to our numbers, providing an idealized scale against which all real things could be measured, a conceptual rock in a real sea of shifting sand, a familiar comfort-blanket in a world in flux.

Ancient atomism had no place for deities and argued for atheism. Competing theories required gods somewhere, e.g. creator (Plato) or unmoved mover (Aristotle), but otherwise tried to keep them out of explanations for natural phenomena. Atomists argued for chaos and randomness as the fundamental principle at work in nature, others (teleologists) argued for purpose and direction, and still others (sceptics) argued for a suspension of judgement on the grounds that the senses are unreliable and, despite everybody's best efforts, nobody really knows what is or why.[31]

What they all assume, except the sceptics who assume only that they can know nothing, is that natural phenomena occur in regular, ordered ways which are susceptible to analysis. Patterns can be recognized, studied, and explained by reasoning, preferably working from observation of particulars to first principles and then from those first principles

---

[31] See Sharples 1996 for a discussion of the main schools in Hellenistic times, arranged around their answers to various types of question rather than a traditional historical narrative or description of each school's philosophical tenets.

to the general case. The imperative for a theory to fit with observation, and the theory's basis in observation, is clear from the methodological aim to 'save the phenomena'.[32]

Pattern recognition seems to have started with celestial phenomena, which are the most regular, if complex, motions in all of nature, and are observable everywhere. Hesiod, for example, is full of folklore on the risings and settings of certain stars and what agricultural jobs should be started or finished by them, and the astral significance of certain days in the calendar. By Aristotle's time, patterns of an altogether more down-to-earth form were being sought, and he attempted to sort e.g. the animal kingdom into coherent subsets. Dioskorides sought patterns in the therapeutic effects of different medicines,[33] and Galen sought patterns in the structure and function of e.g. various tubes and pipe-like tissues in the body. In such cases the investigator made more or less effort to collect information to analyse. Aristotle's systematic approach is evidenced better in the area of political science than natural science (but this serves to remind us of the polymathic nature of ancient philosophy and philosophers). He tasked students to find out about the different political constitutions and constitutional histories of well over 100 different poleis, as a preliminary to writing his synthesis of the subject, the *Politics*. It seems natural to assume that he followed a similar procedure as a preliminary to his syntheses of other subjects, such as the *History of Animals*.

It is worthwhile to point out, when discussing this issue and almost inevitably making implicit comparisons with modern practice, that the ancient Greeks had limited access to data – raw, or cooked by a predecessor. I should say 'opinions' rather than 'data'. Theophrastos learnt about odours by talking to perfumers, about charcoal by talking to charcoal-burners, and about fish by talking to fishermen, for example. He questioned or disputed some of the things he was told or read in a predecessor's work, but usually had no way to refute or confirm them by personal autopsy and 'examination of the evidence'. There was no encyclopaedia to consult,[34] no museum to check specimens,[35] and no

---

[32] On which see Lloyd 1991, chapter 11.

[33] See Riddle 1985.

[34] After a couple of hundred years of such data-gathering and processing it became possible for others to write the first encyclopaedias, which suited the Roman temperament of the times.

[35] The 'museum' at Alexandria was not a museum in the modern sense, but a home of the muses, that is, a place where the muses' arts were practised. The main facilities were the library and a zoo. Little zoological work of consequence was done there and I believe that it functioned more for the entertainment and adornment of Ptolemy's court than for any investigative study of animal life.

library but the collection of scrolls put together over the years by Aristotle and himself. Even then it required a certain determination to try to find and compare an opinion/assertion concerning a specific subject in a scroll with no contents, index, or even gaps between words. Finally, if he was *really* interested in obtaining a true and accurate answer, there was no obvious source of funds to sponsor a field-trip to wherever the disputed claim arose or concerned.[36] Φασί, 'they say' is as common in the scientific texts as it is in the historical ones like Herodotos' – and it should not be read in a disparaging sense, as it sometimes is with Herodotos, for this was the main way in which anyone knew anything. Moreover, it is part of the standard language of knowledge: to take an extreme example, when the mathematicians advance a theorem, they usually state it in the form 'I say (λέγω) that X'.[37] Centuries later, aspiring doctors had no medical schools to attend and no pathology laboratories in which to learn about and practise on the human body; if they had heard of and could obtain a manuscript of a treatise written by the emperor's physician, then they would find Galen encouraging them to grab any opportunity to acquire a body to dissect, or watch a dissection being performed by someone else, since such opportunities were so rare. Galen had the debatable advantage of an early career start as repairer of gladiators in the local arena; he avoided surgery after about three years in that business, but this evidently unpleasant experience surely gave him a head start on knowledge of human anatomy.

Another very important aspect of the scientific enterprise in Greece is that audiences needed to be persuaded. They did not – sometimes *could not*, for reasons just mentioned – judge the validity of a scientific claim

Pickled specimens are recorded in e.g. Demostratos *apud* Aelian 13.21, but these are oddities or curiosities – in this example it is a supposed Triton (half man, half fish), preserved at the *inland* town of Tanagra.

[36] Even on the most pro-active hypothesis about how Theophrastos obtained his information (Maxwell-Stuart 1996), it is supposed only that he 'took notes of the places through which he passed in the course of his everyday life, as events directed' (p. 266). There is no suggestion that he travelled to find answers. He did, however, start a garden (according to Diogenes Laertius' life – written over 400 years after Theophrastos' *floruit*) in which he might have grown and studied a number of plants, but he could not possibly have grown the vast majority of the plants mentioned in his botanical works, the information for which surely came from oral, and to much lesser extent written, sources.

[37] E.g. Archimedes, *On Plane Equilibriums*, prop. 7 (principle of the lever): 'If the magnitudes be incommensurable, they will likewise balance at distances reciprocally proportional to their magnitudes. Let (A+B) and C be incommensurable magnitudes, and let DE, EF be distances, and let the ratio of (A+B) to C be the same as the ratio of ED to EF; then I say that the centre of gravity of the magnitude composed of (A+B) and C is E' (Thomas trans. slightly modified).

on content alone, and they were not in the habit of accepting things on authority, for which the Greeks had a healthy disrespect. So scientists, like politicians, needed to *persuade* people that they were right and their opponents were wrong. This is true even in mathematics, which also is 'an art which secures its effects through speech' according to Plato (*Gorgias* 451a–c). Style of writing is still today an important factor in the reception of ideas in scientific discourse between scientists, never mind in conversation or communication between scientists and the general public, for example, in a court of law dealing with forensic evidence, or media coverage of a scientific breakthrough.

In choosing between rival hypotheses, the best scientists showed a marked desire for simplicity: what is usually called Ockham's razor ought to be called Aristotle's razor, according to Derkse.[38] Simplicity in a theory is not the same thing as a simple theory or simplification of the problem. As Derkse says (p. 187), 'it often needs genius (in some degree) to find the simple and convincing solution of what before was only dimly understood', and 'the evident simplicity of a solution and its elegant derivation seem to be impossible to overlook *only in retrospect*' (emphasis added).

1.3 *On science and technology and science and philosophy*

In modern times there is a clear distinction between science and technology. Science has occupied an elevated intellectual position in recent history, with technology seen very much as a poor relation; science is pure, technology is applied; science is thinking, technology is doing; science is academic, technology is vocational; and most recently in an age of gender-awareness, science is male, technology is female.[39]

Now the ancient Greeks distinguished between *logos* and *techne*, and

---

[38] Derkse 1993 p. 203. 'Ockham's razor' is the methodological view that in the formulation of explanations, 'it is better to use *the most limited* set of explanatory elements (hypotheses, assumptions, variables) *wherever possible* and *if adequate*. Superfluous explanatory elements should be shaved away', Derkse 1993 p. 10, emphases added. When choosing between competing explanations the same principle can be followed. Derkse argues strongly that Aristotle uses simplicity as a constant concomitant in the inductive process of intuitively grasping first principles, and that it could itself be labelled a principle on Aristotle's theory of knowledge. '[Aristotle's] abundant use of some form of the principle of parsimony, economy and simplicity is to be found in many domains and has many characteristics: as a principle of minimal ontological assumption (*Physics*), as a rule of method (*Post. Anal.*), as a criterion for theory evaluation (*On the Heavens*, *Physics*), as a heuristic device (in the biological writings), as a surprising feature of the workings of nature, which gives aesthetic satisfaction and intellectual joy (biological works)', p. 203.

[39] See e.g. Cowan 1996 or Wertheim 1997.

until recently it has been commonly assumed, without much ado, that *logos* = reason or word and *techne* = technology or deed. We might add the parallel assumption that the Greeks were the thinkers of antiquity, and the Romans the doers. But even a brief glance at some of the ancients' surviving texts is enough to raise an eyebrow to this quick and dirty equivalence assumption. For example, in the bible of mathematical astronomy, the *Almagest*, Ptolemy tells his audience how to make various pieces of more or less complicated equipment for sighting celestial phenomena. Meanwhile in the handbook of the Roman building trade, *De architectura*, Vitruvius discusses the relevance of an Archimedean theorem on the sphericity of water to the functioning of a waterlevel used to ensure that a floor, stair, lintel or whatever was horizontal. The Stoic polymath Poseidonios bothered to describe the nuts and bolts of e.g. weaving, ploughing, and baking.[40] In another field, a renowned physician (Andreas, court doctor to Ptolemy IV) devised a machine for reducing fractures and dislocations.[41] It is relevant here to remember that the doyens of modern 'hard' science, e.g. particle physicists, can be and sometimes *must be* dab hands at wielding their hi-tech equivalent of saws and screwdrivers, for experimental research on innovative ideas sometimes demands innovative equipment. Innovative equipment, by definition, cannot be bought ready-made, so they must and do make it themselves. By contrast, as Lloyd pointed out (1997b, p. 44), the ancient scientists sometimes emphasized the superiority of theory over practice 'to make a virtue out of a necessity' because 'their work often had little chance of practical implementation'.

As Whitney 1990 showed well, technological knowledge was viewed

---

[40] Seneca *Epistles* 90.20–23. Poseidonios' attention to 'banausic' arts may have disappointed Seneca, but Poseidonios clearly thought these subjects worthy of serious intellectual effort.

[41] Celsus 8.20.4. See also Drachmann 1963 pp. 171–85 with translations of relevant parts of Rufus, Heliodoros, and Galen *apud* Oreibasios, citing devices invented or improved upon by a number of named individuals who by implication were doctors. For in 49.23, when Oreibasios mentions the *trispastos* invented by Apellis or Archimedes, he distinguishes them by saying 'First let us bear in mind that neither Apellis nor Archimedes was a doctor, but they were mechanics'. He continues that 'the doctors of that time reduced the dimensions of the construction and made out of the triple pulley a surgical spanner for resetting dislocations and fractures'. Other examples of the point: Knorr 1991 argues that the *Elements* has a strong basis in practical applications, and Høyrup 1997 argues that (i) 'Hero's geometry depends to a greater extent than [is] usually assumed on Near Eastern practical geometry or its descendant traditions in the classical world'; (ii) that the conventional image of Hero 'as the transformer of theoretical into applied mathematics is only a half-truth'; and (iii) that 'much of what is shared by Hero's *Metrica* and the pseudo-Heronian collections assembled by Heiberg as *Geometrica* are shared borrowings from the same [practical geometry] tradition' (quotes from p. 67). O'Neill 1998 argues more generally that the distinction between 'practical' (problem-solving, constructing) and 'theoretical' (seeking after truth, discovering) mathematics is overplayed and not helpful.

by the ancients as part of a – *one* – spectrum of knowledge, which ran from the humblest craft activity to the speculations of astronomers. The modern dichotomy between 'science' and 'technology' did not exist, and the different types of knowledge on this spectrum were classified differently by different philosophers. For example, Plato ordered and ranked them on the basis of their perceived contribution to the development of the moral good of the person pursuing them. This did not stop him, however, from commenting that the proper astronomer would admire the night sky 'as a geometer might admire diagrams exquisitely drawn by some consummate artist like Daedalus' (*Republic* 529d–e). He stops short of saying that Daedalus does geometry, but this needs to be taken in his context that the 'proper astronomer' will use the visible heavens only as a guide to aid in the study of the abstract perfect reality. Aristotle produced a less value-laden, broadly tripartite division, consisting of (i) theoretical knowledge, concerned with being and truth (physics, maths, metaphysics), (ii) practical knowledge, concerned with human action (politics, economics, ethics), and (iii) productive knowledge, concerned with making something (house, poem, shield).[42]

Seneca, disputing Poseidonios' attribution of the invention of mechanical tools and arts and crafts generally to philosophers, differentiates between *sapientia* and *sagacitas*, wisdom and ingenuity,[43] personified for him by Diogenes the dog (Cynic) and Daedalus (§14). Cicero earlier had linked man's ability to change his environment through technology with human dignity, a very important Roman virtue, and power, an even more important concept for the Romans.[44] And Augustine later saw technology as an expression of man's natural genius, *even* in those cases where its purpose 'may seem superfluous, perilous and pernicious'.[45] This echoes Pliny's constant complaints about the vast expenditure of effort on the acquisition or production of such superfluous, perilous, and pernicious things as gold and pearls, whilst simultaneously being filled with admiration and wonderment at what people could do.

---

[42] Whitney discusses these points fully, with ample references to the primary sources, in chapter 2.

[43] *Epistle* 90.7–13, esp. 11.

[44] *De natura deorum* 2.50. Cicero follows his teacher Poseidonios in crediting philosophers with the creation of civilization, even if he disagreed with him on much else; see e.g. *Tusc. Disputations* 5.2.

[45] *City of God* 22.24. Whitney thinks that Augustine is being ironic in this passage. Identifying irony in writing is always a contentious issue, but in the area of scientific texts I agree with Scarborough and Nutton 1982 p. 214 that 'irony is always the last refuge of the baffled translator'.

As regards science and philosophy, the Greeks' concern with episte-mology, with thinking about how they were thinking about a subject, as well as the subject itself, is one of the hallmarks of their work (and is what Crombie emphasizes). Nevertheless, the two are distinct, and as there exist many excellent works by philosophers which focus exclu-sively on the philosophical aspects, so may we focus here on the science. Ideally, the two aspects would be fully integrated, but this is not the place to attempt it. Similarly, cosmology is philosophy, and will be omitted from the chapter on astronomy.[46]

1.4 *On why it is said that the Greeks 'invented' science*

In short, because they introduced the notions of natural causality and rational proof: because they tried to eliminate what they considered to be supernatural elements from their explanations for natural phenomena, because they made (often unobserved and sometimes unobservable) connections between phenomena, and ordered them into parts and wholes or causes and effects (rather than just amassed observations), and because they tried to think their way rationally (which does not mean logically or sensibly to modern tastes[47]) through the perceived order of observed phenomena.[48] The belief in natural causation with consequent natural effects was matched by the belief that knowledge proceeds by reasoning from intellectual premise to rational conclusion.

For some reason[49] a few Greeks living on the margins of the Greek

[46] The distinction between and mutual independence of cosmology and astronomy in the ancients is clarified and emphasized by Hanson 1973.

[47] See Frede and Striker 1996.

[48] Lloyd 1983 emphasized that 'scientific' writings (particularly the life sciences, on which he was focused) sometimes do little more than repeat folklore, but then there is an attempt to rationalize those traditional beliefs, which sometimes involves examining them critically and testing them. He also stresses the difference between what the scientists say they should do or are doing and what they actually do, which usually falls short of these ideals to greater or lesser extent.

[49] Many hypotheses have been advanced to explain this. Farrington 1944 and 1947 emphasized the role of technology. A contributory role for technology has also and recently been argued by Hahn 1995. I concur fully with his view of the influence of then current technology on ancient philosophers, at least in the Greek period – before the sort of attitude exhibited by Plutarch set in, and which Plutarch anachronistically attributed to earlier men about whom he wrote, e.g. Archimedes (*Life of Marcellus*) or Plato (*Convivial Questions* 8.2.1). Goody and Watt 1968 pp. 27–68 emphasized the role of literacy. Most recent views take Lloyd's socio-political context as a starting point. Many add what might be termed cultural hybrid vigour (Sarton argued this long ago): those living in the Ionian communities, exposed to more than one cultural influence (Greek and Lydian/Median/Persian), were presented with radically different explanations of the world. I would emphasize that this circumstance was compounded by the developing slave culture which forcibly moved and rapidly assimilated different Greeks and non-Greeks into new societies and cultures. As such, faced with a choice of different, competing, traditional, 'received wisdoms', they were prompted to sort and criticize them, from whatever quarter they came.

world (and thus simultaneously on the margins of other worlds) began to think that natural phenomena, such as the seasons, eclipses, rainfall and so on were physical consequences or effects of other physical phenomena or causes. Bit by bit, Zeus was relieved of thunderbolt duty, Poseidon of earthquakes, Apollo of epidemic disease, Hera of births, and the rest of the pantheon of gods were pensioned off or abstracted, to become symbols of natural phenomena rather than the wilful and larger-than-life but all-too-human characters which populate and sometimes dominate Greek literature.[50] The cause-effect relationships were believed to follow one another in a regular, comprehensible, and (if one's theories were right) predictable way.

Experience provided observations of particular phenomena, and induction provided a staircase to rise from cases of particulars to higher level generalities. This was the Aristotelian method,[51] and was followed on the whole by the Peripatetics, or Pedestrians.[52] The Platonists and Neoplatonists, however, gave more weight to some of the problems connected with sense-perception and preferred not to rely on the senses; they just thought their way through to generalities, sometimes erecting their hypothetical staircase on an implausibly small empirical rock. Many Platonists, as a result, are not often counted amongst ancient scientists, but are labelled philosophers and metaphysicians.

The Greeks did not themselves claim to be doing anything significantly different from what their predecessors did and contemporaries in other cultures were doing. They did not claim to have started a revolution in history: on the contrary, they sometimes even invented traditions which gave the credit for intellectual developments to older cultures, especially Egypt or Babylon. For example, Herodotos credited the Egyptians with the invention of geometry, the Sages of Greece were said to have gone to seek wisdom in far-off lands (usually Egypt and the Near East), and it is commonly observed in modern works that presocratic philosophy/science began in Ionia, the Hellenized coast of modern day Turkey, variously in close contact or conflict with the great cultures of the Near East: Assyria, Lydia, Media, Persia, and Mesopotamia. However, as Jones (1996, p. 154) observed in the context of astronomy: 'I do not think that the competition [between Ptolemy's tables and Babylonian arithmetical schemes] would have been seen at the time as one between 'Babylonian' and 'Greek' science; it is even far

---

[50] See e.g. the discussion about Jupiter in Seneca *N.Q.* 2.42–6.
[51] See e.g. *Topics* 1.10, *Posterior Analytics* 1.31.
[52] 'Pedestrians' is Saïd al-Andalusi's translation of the term peripateic, *Categories of Nations* p. 29.

from obvious whether Ptolemy and his contemporaries had as clear a notion of the separate Greek and Mesopotamian components in their astronomy as we think we have. At any rate, Ptolemy never speaks in national or linguistic terms, but only of sound or unsound deductive methodology.'

The mathematical fact that we call Pythagoras' theorem was known to the Babylonians at least 1200 years before Pythagoras was born.[53] Why then do we call it Pythagoras' theorem? Because facts and theorems are different. The mathematical fact antedates him, but the *theorem* is his. And herein lies the difference between Greek activities, which we are calling science, and what went before or elsewhere, which we do not call science. The Babylonians observed a mathematical regularity, and compiled or calculated tables of similar regularities. The Greeks, or rather (as *later* tradition asserts) a Greek called Pythagoras, observed this mathematical regularity, and proved geometrically that it holds for all particular cases.

The search for the general, the abstract, case, and the process of arguing rationally about the case: these are the hallmarks of science, which are absent from non-scientific knowledge and understanding.

1.5 *On great men and others in the history of science*

There is a strong and understandable tendency in the history of anything to simplify the story in order to clarify it. This applies to academic histories as well as to the popular consciousness. We tend to remember who was first to do something, but not who was second, and we mark some small changes in thought or equipment as 'innovations' whilst others are 'improvements'. Typically the labels are and can be applied only with hindsight. Normally, no-one can tell *at the time* what ideas or inventions will be significant, hugely significant, or insignificant, to future generations and hence to history. And unfortunately, in the history of science as in other things, the best person does not always win; the fame (very rarely is there any fortune involved) sometimes goes to the 'wrong' person or thing. More commonly, the 'winner' gets all the fame, and the people on whose shoulders he (or very rarely in the ancient world, she) stood get forgotten, and become members of an army of anonymous, industrious, intelligent nobodies.

These nobodies were an essential element in the story, even if, as in

---

[53] See Aaboe 1964.

most cases for the ancient period, they are anonymous and will always be so, because history, that is our sources, have omitted[54] or never knew their names, and exactly what they did. The same problem faces constitutional historians, when they recognize that all sorts of laws attributed to, say, Solon, were not and in some cases *could* not have been proposed by him, but must have been introduced by some anonymous other man[55] (and in the political field, it is always 'man'). It seems to be part of human nature to attribute great deeds to great men, and great deeds fly though time and space like moths to a candle, a great man. But that is *not* how science or technology develops. It is *not* a series of great leaps with a few small steps in between. It is a swarming mass of small steps, with an occasional and often unintentional hop, skip, jump, or trip along the ways (for there are many).[56]

Heroes seem to be necessary to all cultures. Certain individuals are widely perceived – rightly or wrongly – to stand head and shoulders above the rest on some culturally determined scale of things, such as, in modern times, kicking a football around, making music, driving fast, or helping others. Different subcultures have different heroes, and heroes exist at all levels, from the school playground to the world stage, past and present. Science is no different. Indeed, modern scientists seem to feel an acute need to indulge in this game, privately and publicly creating and keeping 'top ten' lists by subject, by papers, by citation, by era, by any way they can think of to identify and rank the heroes of their profession.

The ancient Greeks liked to create heroes too. For them, it was typically the top seven rather than the top ten (the symbolism of 7 being profound in Greek, Roman, and Hebrew cultures): the 7 Sages, on the

---

[54] It is quite noticeable how often ancient critics of axial rotation or heliocentric theory omit the names of Herakleides, Hiketas, Aristarkhos and Seleukos, and refer anonymously to 'some people' or similar such terms. Anonymity does not just affect the 'little people'.

[55] For example, the story that Solon introduced laws 'reforming' the coinage. Athens almost certainly did not adopt coinage until after Solon's *floruit*.

[56] See e.g. Boas 1959 p. 499 on Lavoisier and modern chemistry: 'As usually happens when one examines a dramatic event in the history of science, it turns out not to have been so simple. Seventeenth-century chemists had tried to have both a rational system of nomenclature and a rational theory of combustion: had tried, and had failed'. Or Ihde's comments on the same paper in the same book, p. 522, 'this period [was] one which was essential for the clearing out of a great deal of rubbish which had accumulated during the previous centuries and which was serving as an obstacle to progress in chemistry. Actually a study of this period is a confusing one because, as so often happens with the clearing out of rubbish, it is not destroyed but is tossed aside where it can again serve as an obstacle to progress'. The rubbish in question is Empedokles'-Aristotle's four-elements theory, by the way.

science side, and the 7 Wonders, on the technology side.[57] The story is easier to tell when there are heroes. As Homeric battles are apparently won by a few outstanding warriors, so the development of human understanding of and ability to manipulate the world was apparently dominated by a few intellectual and mechanical geniuses. By contrast, a rich description of the story including all known figures tends to be hard for audiences to follow. But in truth, science and technology do not advance by a series of great leaps forward any more than battles are won by duels between champions.

Besides heroization, the Greeks also liked to make links between individual heroes, to spin continuous threads out of discrete strands, to join the dots to make a coherent picture. The Seven Sages were roughly contemporary and were all in at the beginning of the Greek Renaissance, so they were made into friends and acquaintances. For the rest, in the same way that the gods were united in a genealogy, clever men were linked in an educational lineage, master A taught pupil B, who became a master and taught pupil C, and so it goes on down through the generations. Sometimes such lines of influence have a basis in history, such as Aristotle-Theophrastos-Strato, though even here it is misleading. Theophrastos was a contemporary and close friend of Aristotle; their books were not distinguished by one author or another until centuries later, and Theophrastos was a successor only in so far as he outlived Aristotle by about a generation.[58] Sometimes lines of purported educational lineage indicate nothing more than a similarity in outlook between the predecessor and his alleged pupil.

1.6 *On hindsight and teleology in the history of science*

The main problem with Cohen and Drabkin's essential *Sourcebook in Greek Science* is that it is teleological. What one finds in this book is, on the whole, a collection of ancient writings on various subjects which reveal a method that happened to coincide with what scientists thought about the world and their role in it at the time Cohen and Drabkin were writing (1940s). Their selection was based on material 'which would generally be regarded today as scientific in method, i.e. based, in principle, either on mathematics or on empirical verification'.[59] A

[57] There are many examples of sevens in Greek thought: see Byl 1980 pp. 252ff. for its appearance in Aristotle.
[58] Aristotle died first (aged 60-something) whilst Theophrastos enjoyed another 30 years or so of vigorous intellectual life, continuing to study, teach, and write into his 90s.
[59] Theories 'that are now known to be false or even ridiculous' were referred to in notes only as

sourcebook is a selection, not a collection. This can be said of the entire surviving corpus of ancient texts: what has survived has done so precisely because it has been selected as worth preserving (and sometimes translating) by generation after generation of priests, scholars, and scientists down through the ages. And those ancient texts which still survive in medieval or Renaissance, Greek, Latin, or Arabic MSS but have yet to be edited – never mind translated – are still unedited because no-one who has known of their existence in manuscripts over the last few centuries has deemed them worth the effort.[60]

Cohen and Drabkin chose the best from antiquity, where 'best' meant nearest to modern (1940s) ways of thinking. Here we find the 'greatest' achievements of Greek science where 'great' is again defined by reference to us, and what we think is 'right', or at least, on the right track. This is what some people want from a history of Greek science, and there is a place for it in the modern world, especially for modern practitioners of some science who are interested in the history of their own particular subject. But it gives a very distorted view of Greek science to those who are interested in Greek history and culture, or Greek science as a whole. For example, despite its profound influence on all sorts of topics from alchemy to zoology, four-elements theory as developed by Empedokles and Aristotle is omitted from the contents because it is 'wrong'.[61] As a sourcebook, it naturally omits context. It focuses tightly on the 'significant' scientific idea – significant to us, that is. It gives little or no clue of how much else is in the treatise in question, and typically edits out any 'irrelevant' material within the crucial passage with a series of . . . (dot-dot-dots).[62]

---

necessary to make sense of a passage quoted. They omitted entirely anything which 'encroach[ed] on the field of Greek magic, superstition, and religion' (all quotes from p. viii). Lines have to be drawn somewhere, deciding what to include and what to exclude. We would draw them differently today, and 50 years from now they would be drawn differently again. For example, a contemporary sourcebook might include as (superficially) an apparent antecedent to gene theory, Seneca *NQ* 3.29.3: 'In the semen there is contained the entire record of the man to be, and the not-yet-born infant has the laws governing a beard and grey hair. The features of the entire body and its successive phases are there, in a tiny and hidden form'.

[60] And the effort is very considerable. See for example Touwaide 1991. About 5% of the collection of Greek veterinary treatises which make up the *Hippiatrica* have yet to be edited, according to Fischer 1988 p. 195.

[61] Of course it becomes necessary to explain what this theory was in order to understand reference to it (actual or implied) in passages which are selected for inclusion in the sourcebook, and Cohen and Drabkin provide such an outline in the form of notes. But they do not include any source specifically on this theory or its main ancient competitor, atomism.

[62] In this respect Lewes 1864 stands apart from most scholars for his decision to retain the 'essential or incidental absurdities' thus 'preserving, as far as may be, the historical colouring derived from the inherent weakness of early science and the individual weakness of Aristotle' (p. ix).

And yet those 'irrelevancies' are fundamental for reaching a proper understanding of Greek science. For example, many Greek 'scientific' treatises could be used as exemplars in a modern course on rhetoric; a wide range of rhetorical devices are used liberally (in most disciplines), because the author has to persuade his audience (see above §1.2). All this is lost when texts are epitomized or gutted and stuffed into source-books. On the other hand, few of us have the time required to read all the texts from cover to cover, and some subjects interest us more than others. So sourcebooks (like surveys) are starting points, giving quick glimpses of a broad range of subjects. The reader can then decide which subject(s) to pursue in more depth.

FURTHER READING

A good brief introduction to the subject as a whole is G. E. R. Lloyd's *Early Greek Science: Thales to Aristotle* and *Greek Science: Aristotle and After* (both 1982). R. French's *Ancient Natural History* (1994) ranges widely across topics and time, organized loosely around the chronological development of ideas about nature and how to approach it. It has a thought-provoking introduction which, in a nutshell, argues that the word science is inappropriate in the ancient context. D. Lindberg's *The Beginnings of Western Science* (1992) provides a more traditional type of overview.

Another wide-ranging work on Greek science is M. Clagett, *Greek Science in Antiquity* (1955) which, despite changes of emphases in the philosophy and history of science during the 45 years since it was written, is still worth reading to get an overview of the subject. Slightly older, but also still valuable, are B. Farrington's *Science in Antiquity* (1936) and *Greek Science* (2 vols, 1944 and 1949). T. Africa offers (in his own words) 'not a history of science but a study of scientists', which concentrates on context, and which foreshadowed many current debates[63] about Greek science back in 1968: *Science and the State in Greece and Rome*.

More detailed treatment of the nature and beginnings of Greek science can be found in Lloyd's four books *Polarity and Analogy* (1966), which is concerned above all with method in ancient scientific thought, *Magic, Reason and Experience* (1979), *Science, Folklore and Ideology* (1983) and *Aristotelian Explorations* (1996), which all have special reference to the life sciences, but the arguments have wider application. A number of his articles on specific topics (again mostly but not exclusively concerned with the life sciences) have been

---

[63] For example, the competitiveness of ancient scientists and their theories, the continued inclusion of folklore within the 'scientific' tradition, and the status of astrology and other practices now considered occult or hokum.

collected and reprinted in convenient form in *Methods and Problems in Greek Science* (1991). This reprint includes very useful introductions which 'take stock of work done subsequently on the problems discussed' (p. xiii) and which thus point to the directions in which some of the arguments have moved and the changing emphases which Lloyd and others have put upon each of them. His *Adversaries and Authorities* (1996) compares and contrasts ancient Greek and ancient Chinese approaches to science, illuminating all sorts of issues concerning the practice and practitioners of science in these societies.

There are a number of useful electronic resources and web sites for the history of science. The Virtual Library for the History of Science, Technology and Medicine at **http://www.asap.unimelb.edu.au/hstm/hstm_ove.html** offers a gateway to many of them.

There are entries on many ancient scientists in the *Dictionary of Scientific Biography* (*DSB*), 18 vols (New York, 1970–90).

II. PHYSICS

2.1 *Introduction*

Physical theories underlie all other theories in Greek science, for physics concerned the nature of stuff. If offered answers to the question 'what is it made of?', where the 'it' could be anything and everything. Consequently, all other subjects looked to one or another theory in physics for understanding of the nature of the stuff of *their* study, be it heaven, earth, soul, or whatever. Consider two examples.

1. The author of *On Colours* ([Aristotle]) tries to explain what is going on when a mineral's streak colour[1] is different from the external colour of the stone or metal by reference to his theory of matter and the formation of minerals:

> Some objects, when smoothed by rubbing or by other forces, exhibit varied and different colours, like silver when it is rubbed and gold, bronze and steel. Some kinds of stones show different colours, like ★★★[2], for though black they draw white lines, because they are originally composed of small elements which are thick and black, and by the dyeing process which takes place when they are made, all the passages through which the dye passes are coloured, so that a different appearance is given to the [overall] colour . . . But in the process of rubbing each of them to a homogeneous and smooth surface, as in treating on a touchstone, they lose their blackness, and recover their colour, the dye showing through when there is contact and continuity (793a20–b3, Hett trans.).

Now a modern geology book will explain the concept of a streak colour, but will not normally explain *why* the streak colour may differ from the colour of the stone.[3] [Aristotle] *was* trying to explain it, and

---

[1] 'The streak colour of a mineral is the colour of its powder obtained by scraping or rubbing the specimen on a streak plate made of unglazed china, or other material harder than the mineral to be tested. The streak of a mineral may be quite different from its colour', Rosenfeld 1965 p. 38. This is a technical definition of something familiar: graphite is a soft mineral with a grey streak colour – so soft that it leaves a streak on paper. Hence graphite is used to make pencils.

[2] There is a lacuna in the text, long enough for a word of about 6 or 7 letters, which was probably the name of the stone. There is insufficient detail here for a positive identification of this stone, but Augite would fit (a common pyroxene which is black to a dull dark green and has a white to murky green streak colour).

[3] See n. 1. Rosenfeld's general discussion of colour in rocks makes an interesting comparison with [Aristotle]'s quoted in the text: 'When the colour of a mineral depends on its chemical composition it is said to be *inherent*. Many minerals have no inherent colour in the pure state, they are colourless or white. Such minerals may be coloured by minute inclusions of an impurity in chemical combination, or disseminated as small particles in the mineral. This type of colouration is called *exotic*. The exotic colours of minerals vary quite widely according to the type and amount of colouring material. The opaque white colour of many colourless minerals

explanation at this level in any field ultimately rested on the author's beliefs about matter and change.

2. Philo's explanation of why solid bronze plates can be springy enough to fire missiles includes the statements that, on the one hand, heating softens metal because the particles become less densely packed, while on the other tempering and hammering harden them. Of the latter he says, 'for both processes cause the particles to become tightly packed, because the minute pieces of matter run together and the interstices of void are removed', and thus the bronze plates from which the springs are made have hard faces on a soft middle, producing resilience.[4]

In the modern world physics is a diverse subject covering all sorts of things, from theoretical particles with rum names (e.g. gluons which, as their name suggests, stick other particles together), through mechanics and optics, to forces of nature such as gravity and magnetism. I shall divide the discussion into two parts: matter, and forces acting on matter, though this leaves subjects like optics difficult to place.[5]

With regard to matter, the ancients' non-recognition of a clear distinction between organic and inorganic matter, together with their habit of drawing analogies and examples from the animal, vegetable, and mineral kingdoms, means that in ancient sources there is no obvious dividing line between what we would call physics and what we would call biology or chemistry.[6] The history of chemistry as usually written seems to be almost unique in having no ancient component, as if it did not exist.[7] This is perhaps because ancient ideas about the combination and separation of bits of matter were usually dealt with in treatises entitled Physics, or, in the case of the most important ancient treatise on this subject, in a work entitled *Meteorology* (Aristotle's work of that

such as quartz, gypsum, and talc is usually due to reflection of light from countless minute cracks or bubbles of fluid in the mineral, and rarely to the inclusion of white impurity, such as kaolin in some feldspars', p. 37f.

[4] *Belopoiika* 71. He closes the discussion shortly after this 'in case we inadvertently digress too far and enter deeper into physical arguments' §72.3–4.

[5] For this subject and its interconnections with much else in ancient physical thinking, see Berryman 1998. Smith 1996 has recently translated and commented upon Ptolemy's *Optics*.

[6] Note the difference with modern Physics, which is defined in the *OED* as being 'the science, or sciences, treating of the properties of matter and energy, or of the action of the different forms of energy and matter in general (excluding Chemistry and Biology)'. Since the discovery in the last decade of life-forms on earth, in deep caves and in the abyss of the ocean, which are based on direct chemical synthesis (not photosynthesis), the nature of life itself is open to question, and many of the relevant definitions will need reconsideration.

[7] Thorndike's volumes stand as a massive and valuable exception: volume 1 of a *History of Magic and Experimental Science* 1923 starts with Pliny, and fills nearly 300 pages with the Roman period alone.

name, book 4).[8] However, this may soon change: C. Anne Wilson argues convincingly that distilling of wine can be traced back to the fifth century B.C.,[9] and by pushing back some 500 years the invention of this chemical process and the equipment needed to achieve it, at least a small outburst of activity on the subject may be expected.

With regard to forces, some texts adopt a more mathematical bent, such as Archimedes' *On Floating Bodies*, while others adopt a more practical bent (and go under the name Mechanics) such as Hero's *Artillery-construction*. It is becoming increasingly clear that ancient technology could reach extraordinary degrees of sophistication, matching and sometimes surpassing the complexity found in treatises on mechanics. Various Archimedean, Ktesibian and Heronian machines which are described more or less fully in surviving texts[10] were formerly considered by some scholars either to be purely theoretical constructions or as 'gadgets' or 'toys'. But the Antikythera mechanism[11] and the south-pointing chariot[12] make it abundantly clear that ancient technology was not exclusively low-tech, and should not be treated in isolation from ancient ideas and practices in mathematics and physics, a good understanding of which must have been necessary to make these machines.[13] Nor were machines unusual in ancient society. They were to be found in every home, many public buildings and spaces, on and under the ground and sea, for work and for pleasure. From looms and olive presses, locks and keys, hoists and windlasses, to water-clocks and thunder-makers, machines were a familiar part of life for the ancient Greeks and Romans.

This inevitably leads some to question why there was no scientific revolution, and no industrial revolution, in antiquity. I believe that this is the wrong question,[14] but nevertheless offer an answer to it. In my view,

---

[8] Düring tried to overcome this problem by entitling his commentary on *Meteorology* 4 as *Aristotle's Chemical Treatise* 1944. But like the ancients, most moderns discussing this subject tackle it in works with Physics, rather than Chemistry, in the title. Ancient chemical ideas may also be discussed in works with alchemy in the title, e.g. Keyser 1990a.

[9] 'Distilling, sublimation and the Four Elements: the aims and achievements of the earliest Greek chemists' in Tuplin and Fox 1999, to appear. My thanks to the editors for allowing pre-publication access to the MS.

[10] Hero's *Automatopoietikes* (Automaton-making) has recently been translated into English by Murphy 1995. It gives a wonderful impression of the backstage activities which went on during the performance of dramas.

[11] See de Solla Price 1974.

[12] See Lewis 1992.

[13] The role of applied geometry in such things is noted by Proclus, *Comm. on Euclid's Elements Book 1*, Prologue Part 2, 63–4. His late antique [C5 A.D.] view on pure geometry is well summarized in §§49–56.

[14] For many reasons, the most important of which is the general methodological principle that it

one reason is this. These modern revolutions depended on continuity of effort: many people building on many predecessors' work. Years, decades, even centuries of intellectual and financial investment in research and development – this is what was missing in Greece.[15] Babbage conceived the analytical engine (the first mechanical general-purpose computer) before 1834; a long and winding set of paths (some dead ends), travelled by a lot of people, spending a lot of money, separate Charles Babbage and Bill Gates. As for the related idea that there was technological 'stagnation' in antiquity, this rests on two oversights. First, it more or less completely ignores the development of a technology, and second, it maintains an unelucidated and apparently unbridgeable chasm between 'innovation' and 'improvement'. It is tantamount to saying that the internal combustion engine to be found in, say, a transit van (never mind a Formula 1 racing car), is the same as that designed by Diesel in the 1890s, which was bolted to the floor and had a cylinder 10 feet long.[16]

2.2 Theories of Matter

Ancient physical theories attempted to identify and explain the nature of body and soul, of space and time, of generation and destruction. The apparent constant flux in nature was explained either as an illusion (by e.g. Parmenides), or as real change (by e.g. Aristotle), in which case further hypotheses were needed and were developed to explain how stuff of type A, e.g. water, could turn into stuff of type B, e.g. ice. Physicists strove for a reduction in the number of types of stuff in the cosmos, from the apparent bewildering countless varieties to some small set of basic ingredients. Four-elements theorists reduced the number of types of stuff to four, which when mixed would account for all that

is revolution, not the absence of revolution, which needs explaining. For a discussion of related points see White 1993 and Greene 1994.

[15] See Lennox's remarks to the same effect with respect to Aristotle's zoological works, 1994. Occasional and brief periods of financial support, such as in early Ptolemaic Alexandria, are the exceptions which prove the rule, and were appreciated as such at the time. See, for example, Philo's comment upon the great leap forward in mechanical technology, in *Belopoiika* 50.24–6: 'Alexandrian craftsmen achieved this first, being heavily subsidized because they had ambitious kings who fostered craftsmanship', Marsden trans. pp. 108–9.

[16] On Diesel see Nitske and Wilson 1965. There is perhaps an analogous situation in the modern scholarly habit of tracking back a scientific idea to the earliest source one can find, crediting that person with the 'discovery' or 'creation' of the idea (however hazily it might then have been expressed), and playing down its development and transformation in later authors. The tendency to create heroes (see chapter 1 §5) plays a part here too.

variety. Atomists reduced the type of stuff to one, but allowed for numerous different shapes and sizes of indivisible bits (atoms) of that stuff, and made the mixture of shapes and sizes explain the variety. Both of these basic and competing views on the nature of matter were developed early, before Plato and Aristotle: four-elements by Empedokles, *fl.* 495–35, atomism by Leukippos (dates unknown) and Demokritos, *fl.* 465–400 (a contemporary of Sokrates).

Aristotle developed Empedokles' four-elements theory to explain how the elements are built up to form all the things that we see, hear, smell, taste and touch. The four elements – elemental earth, air, fire and water[17] – combine to form homoiomers. These are homogenous substances such as blood, bone, bark, sap, sand, or gold. Homoiomers of different types are combined[18] to form parts, such as a hand, a leaf, or a piece of ore. Different parts are joined together to form wholes, such as a human body, a tree, or a rock.

For Aristotle, matter was continuous. Everything in the universe was connected in a plenum. There might be spaces between homoiomers, parts or wholes, forming passages or gaps, but those spaces were filled with air or other substances – recall e.g. the excerpt from *On Colours* quoted in the introduction to this chapter. Through such passages one substance might interpenetrate another, as in the dyeing process in that example, but such a juxtaposed mixture of two or more substances was distinguished from a synthesis of two homoiomers to create another homoiomer. Aristotle abhorred the notion of void, and spent about half of his time in the *Physics* arguing against atomism, which presupposed void. Although four-elements theory remained the more popular physical theory in antiquity, atomism was never ousted. It was developed by Epikouros and written about in Rome by Lucretius. Some of Aristotle's colleagues and students put both theories to the test, and seem to have blurred the distinctions between them as a result. For example, Theophrastos investigated the nature of fire, and raised some very serious objections to the idea that fire could be an element (see his *On Fire*); for example, he pointed out that fire requires fuel, and that man can make fire, neither of which facts sits happily with the idea that fire is a first principle and elemental substance. Similarly Strato did a lot of work on void, and showed in a number of simple but telling demonstrations that

---

[17] These are distinguished from terrestrial earth, air, fire and water in being utterly pure, whereas terrestrial earth, air, fire and water are always subject to mixture with other elements.

[18] In the sense of juxtaposition rather than chemical synthesis.

void does exist, or at least can be created artificially: for example, take a small-mouthed small jar, put it to your lips, suck the air out, and it will stick to your lips, trying to draw them into itself to fill the vacuum.[19]

One of the most famous stories from antiquity is all about the discovery of a fundamental idea in physics: specific gravity (though this term itself is not used). We are fortunate in this case in having not just the popular version of the discovery, but also the full text of Archimedes' own published results of the same discovery. And the contrast between them is interesting and significant. Let us first hear the story as Vitruvius tells it in *On Architecture* 9:

Archimedes made many wonderful discoveries of different kinds, but of all these that which I shall now explain seems to exhibit a boundless ingenuity. When Hiero was greatly exalted in the royal power at Syracuse, in return for the success of his policy he determined to set up in a certain shrine a golden crown as a votive offering to the immortal gods. He let out the work for a stipulated payment, and weighed out the exact amount of gold for the contractor. At the appointed time the contractor brought his work skilfully executed for the king's approval, and he seemed to have fulfilled exactly the requirements about the weight of the crown. Later information was given that gold had been removed and an equal weight of silver added in the making of the crown. Hiero was indignant at this disrespect for himself, and, being unable to discover any means by which he might unmask the fraud, he asked Archimedes to give it his attention. While Archimedes was turning the problem over, he chanced to come to the place of bathing, and there, as he was sitting down in the tub, he noticed that the amount of water which flowed over the tub was equal to the amount by which his body was immersed. This indicated to him a means of solving the problem, and he did not delay, but in his joy leapt out of the tub and, rushing naked towards his home, he cried out with a loud voice that he had found what he sought. For as he ran he repeatedly shouted in Greek ηὕρηκα ηὕρηκα [I've found it, I've found it].

Then, following up his discovery, he is said to have made two masses of the same weight as the crown, one of gold and the other of silver. When he had so done, he filled a large vessel right up to the brim with water, into which he dropped the silver mass. The amount by which it was immersed in the vessel was the amount of water which overflowed. Taking out the mass, he poured back the amount by which the water had been depleted, measuring it with a pint pot, so that as before the water was made level with the brim. In this way he found what weight of silver answered to a certain measure of water.

When he had made this test, in like manner he dropped the golden mass into the full

[19] Reported in the preface to Hero's *Pneumatics*. Gottschalk 1965 concludes that this preface is 'a jumbled but otherwise faithful version of an extract from a book by Strato, almost certainly the περὶ τοῦ κενοῦ [*On the Void*] included in Diogenes' catalogue of his works (5.59). Strato's most important proofs of the existence of discrete void are given substantially as he wrote them; of the other material in Strato's book, which was of less interest to the engineers, something survives in the digression on pp. 110.3–112.6, but this part has evidently suffered much more severely from condensation and rearrangement. No doubt a good deal has also been omitted . . . but except for the paragraph pp. 114.14–29 nothing of importance has been added from any other source'.

vessel. Taking it out again, for the same reason he added a measured quantity of water, and found that the deficiency of water was not the same, but less; and the amount by which it was less corresponded with the excess of a mass of silver, having the same weight, over a mass of gold. After filling the vessel again, he then dropped the crown itself into the water, and found that more water overflowed in the case of the crown than in the case of the golden mass of identical weight; and so, from the fact that more water was needed to make up the deficiency in the case of the crown than in the case of mass, he calculated and detected the mixture of silver with the gold and the contractor's fraud stood revealed. (Pref. 9–12, Thomas trans.)

There are several things to note here. First, Vitruvius' book *On Architecture* contains much more than one might expect from the title. Indeed, apart from several scientific discoveries which he understands and discusses well (see e.g. 7.8.3 on the comparative specific gravities of mercury and gold), this book is a mine of information on all sorts of ancient ideas and practices, from the sphericity of the earth and how to make a sundial at any particular location, to the identification of good and bad water sources and many different ways to make the colour black.[20] Second, Hiero, despite his tyrannical power, and apparently taking this as an insult to himself (rather than to the gods), does not jump to the conclusion that the rumour about the goldsmith is true, or have the man tortured or tried or any other standard method available to Greek states to try to establish the truth, but asks the resident genius to apply his mind to the problem. Third, Vitruvius gives us much incidental information on daily life in Archimedes' Syracuse, for example that the customer supplied the raw material and the craftsman was paid for his labour upon it[21] (also true for Roman times); that domestic houses lacked bathing facilities (also true for most houses in Roman times); and that Greek baths were tubs not pools (not true of most Roman baths). Fourth, what we have here is a story of discovery. It explains in ordinary language a simple experiment, and draws out the crucial distinction between the weight of a body and its density (here in the sense of 'mass', lump or size). What it does not do is offer any general statement of the principle at work, nor any proof of it.

If we turn now to Archimedes' own words on the same subject, we find a very different sort of story. The relevant work is entitled *On*

---

[20] That part of his book concerned with private building was epitomized in the late empire by Faventinus (*c.* A.D. 300) and then Palladius. For Faventinus' text with commentary see Plommer 1973, who thinks that they are better than the average epitomes produced in this period (pp. 2–3).

[21] Which was the general practice for all but the simplest and cheapest items, such as domestic pottery, or the most expensive imported regional specialities, such as cloth made of a particular fabric or colour.

Floating Bodies which, despite the title, is as much about bodies which sink, like the crown, as those that float. It deals with both matter and forces acting upon it, but since it is most famous for the discovery concerning matter, I include it in this section. It begins with one postulate (Heath trans.):[22]

Postulate 1.
Let us assume that a fluid has the property that, if its parts lie evenly and are continuous, the part which is less compressed is expelled by that which is more compressed; and each of its parts is compressed by the fluid above it perpendicularly, unless the fluid is shut up in something and compressed by something else.

From this very modest beginning he moves on to the propositions, which are proved geometrically one by one.

Proposition 1.
If a surface be cut by a plane always passing through a certain point, and if the section be always a circumference [of a circle] whose centre is the aforesaid point, the surface is that of a sphere.

Proposition 2.
The surface of any fluid at rest is the surface of a sphere whose centre is the same as that of the earth.

Proposition 3.
Of solids those which, size for size, are of equal weight with a fluid will, if let down into the fluid, be immersed so that they do not project above the surface but do not sink lower.

Proposition 4.
A solid lighter than a fluid will, if immersed in it, not be completely submerged, but part of it will project above the surface.

Proposition 5.
Any solid lighter than a fluid will, if placed in the fluid, be so far immersed that the weight of the solid will be equal to the weight of the fluid displaced.

Proposition 6.
If a solid lighter than a fluid be forcibly immersed in it, the solid will be driven upwards by a force equal to the difference between its weight and the weight of the fluid displaced.

Proposition 7.
A solid heavier than a fluid will, if placed in it, descend to the bottom of the fluid, and the solid will, when weighed in the fluid, be lighter than its true weight by the weight of the fluid displaced.[23]

---

[22] The translation of the postulate is from his little book *Archimedes*, 1920, which reads more easily than his translation of the same in *The Works of Archimedes*, 1912. The rest of the translation is from the latter work.

[23] After the proof of this proposition follows the second and last postulate for the entire work; as Thomas says of this in the Loeb (*GMW* 2 p. 245 n.a.) 'if the object of mathematics be to base the conclusions on the fewest and most self-evident axioms, Archimedes' treatise *On Floating Bodies*

The seventh proposition is Archimedes' own version of the discovery. Instead of a tale about crowns and kings, about sploshing around in a tub and the excitement of discovery, about dropping things in pots of water and measuring the volume of water required to refill the pot after removing them again, we have a completely general assertion of a fact about the weight of a solid in air and in water, and a proof that it is true. Note that it does not go on to say that different materials have different ratios of weight in water to what Archimedes calls its 'true' weight, i.e. weight in air, yet it is only by *that* fact that the alloyed nature of the crown could be proved, since silver and gold have different ratios. But the specific gravity of anything is something which can only be found by empirical means, and I think that Archimedes could not have made any general statements about it which he could have proved, so he said nothing.

When we look at the crucial set of experiments, they work on volumes in Vitruvius' version, but the principle is expressed in weights in Archimedes'. Translated into modern mathematical formulae[24] both methods end up with equivalent results, but in terms of practice they involve significant differences. For the method described by Vitruvius requires a waterproof pot big enough to hold the crown, the acquisition of a lump of gold and a lump of silver each equal in weight-in-air to the crown, and a jug. It is much more simple than the method implied by Archimedes, which requires in addition a balance or set of scales, with (at least) a bowl-type pan for the scales for weighing the water displaced. Archimedes' method, however, would be much more exact, since ancient scales could weigh very finely indeed, whereas fluid measurements were much more rough and ready.[25] It is possible that Archimedes made the discovery by the volume method, but then developed the more accurate and more complete weight method.

The concept of specific gravity became so well and so widely understood by Nero's time that Seneca, in his popularizing work on natural science, considered it obvious, and discussed it without reference to Archimedes, the bath, crown, or any other element in the tale:

---

must indeed be ranked highly'. There follow two more propositions in book 1, then book 2, which is described by Heath as a geometrical *tour de force*.

[24] Such formulae are given whenever this subject is discussed, e.g. in Thomas *GMW* 2 pp. 38–9 and 250–1, Heath 1912 pp. 260–1; given the constraints of space here, it seems superfluous to repeat them.

[25] And removal of the mass from the water without displacing more fluid in the process would demand further equipment and considerable care of execution.

It is well known that there are certain lakes which support people who do not know how to swim. There used to be a pond in Sicily, and there still is one in Syria, where bricks float and no objects thrown in sink no matter how heavy they are. The reason for this is obvious. Weigh anything you like and compare it with water, provided the volume (*modus*, measure) of both is equal. If the water is heavier it will support the object which is lighter and lift it as high above the surface as it is lighter. Objects heavier than the water will sink. But if the weight of the water is equal to the weight of the object you measure it against, the object will neither go to the bottom nor stick up. It will be in balance with the water and in fact will float but almost submerged and without any part sticking up. This is why some logs are elevated almost entirely above water, others are half-way submerged, others go down to the point of equal balance in the water. For, when the weight of both is equal neither yields to the other, but objects heavier than the water sink, the lighter objects are supported. However, heavy or light derives not from our own estimate but from a comparison with the water in which the object is to be carried. So, when water is heavier than a man's body or a stone it does not permit anything to sink which does not overcome the water's own heaviness. (*NQ* 3.25.5–6, Corcoran trans.)

It is worth noting, finally, that the fact of the displacement of water was known, long before Archimedes lived, to a slave called Aesop. His fables were widely known, and one in particular may have played some small and perhaps subconscious role in this discovery. It is as follows:

A thirsty crow found a pitcher with some water in it, but so little was there that, try as she might, she could not reach it with her beak, and it seemed as though she would die of thirst within sight of the remedy. At last she hit upon a clever plan. She began dropping pebbles into the pitcher, and with each pebble the water rose a little higher until at last it reached the brim, and the knowing bird was able to quench her thirst. (Vernon-Jones trans.)

The essential difference between this and Archimedes' behaviour – between being a wise old bird and being a scientist – is that Archimedes measured the amount of water displaced (by weight, volume or both), dropped lumps of different materials of the same weight into the water, and compared the amount of water displaced in each case.

2.3 *Forces*

The earliest theories on forces were propounded in the context of cosmologies, for example Empedokles' notions of 'Love' and 'Strife' as the forces which bring the elements together and rend them apart respectively, or Anaxagoras' 'Mind' which controls the world. In due course theories developed two separate strands, one for sub-lunar phenomena (terrestrial and atmospheric), and another for celestial bodies, which were thought to be composed of something else and to behave in a different way, in keeping with their perfection (unlike the imperfection of the earthly world). Our interest here is in their ideas about sub-lunar phenomena.

For Aristotle, it is the primary qualities or properties of Hot and Cold which act on passive Moist and Dry matter to change it. Change was understood very broadly, to include e.g. change of place, change of colour, and change of food into blood and excreta. The principal motive forces were innate heat and natural motion. Innate heat 'concocted' or cooked matter to bring it to more or less perfect form.[26] Imperfections arose from a disproportion in the type and ratio of matter to heat. The heaviest things were in the centre of the universe, the lightest at the edges. Natural motion drove heavy things, e.g. earth, down, and drove light things, e.g. fire, up, until they reached their proper place, or were obstructed from reaching it by something else. Things could also change place by forced motion, being pushed or pulled by something outside the thing itself. And living beings could exert voluntary motion by moving themselves intentionally. On this basis Aristotle built an elaborate theory of dynamics, and his ideas were dominant for over 1,500 years, despite some acute and powerful criticisms advanced against them in antiquity. Philoponos, for example, to a large degree anticipated Galileo by pointing out that:

if you take two weights differing from each other by a very wide measure, and drop them from the same height, you will see that the ratio of the times of their motion does not correspond with the ratio of their weights, but the difference between the times is much less. Thus if the weights did not differ by a wide measure, but if one were, say, double, and the other half, the times will not differ at all from each other, or, if they do, it will be by an imperceptible amount, although the weights did not have that kind of difference between them, but differed in the ratio of one to two. (*Corollary on Void*, 683.17–25, trans. Furley)[27]

Ancient ideas on forces operating on bodies at rest (statics) were a lot stronger than their ideas on forces operating on bodies in motion (dynamics). Archimedes' law of the lever, for example, is just one of the many outstanding contributions he made to statics. The forces operating on bodies at rest were amenable to then current mathematical analysis (as was the presumed perfect circular motion of the heavenly bodies), but those operating on moving objects, such as thrown stones,

---

[26] Lloyd has an extended discussion of Aristotle's views on *pepsis* (concoction) with reference to the biological works in 1996a chapter 4.
[27] Galileo knew and cited Philoponos' works and, like many of his contemporaries, was clearly influenced by him. See Wolff 1987.

were not. Although ancient engineers made significant progress with torsion catapults and other ballistic machines,[28] they worked with empirical arithmetical ratios based (usually) on the weight of the missile to be thrown, and theoretical understanding of the forces involved was relatively poor.[29] Mechanics had numerous practical applications, from lifting massive masonry blocks into place in temple pediments to regulating the flow of water through a pipe, and was often more amenable to experiment and demonstration than it was to mathematical analysis.

Ktesibios, who lived in Alexandria probably in C3 B.C., was the son of a barber who started making mechanical aids for his father's shop and went on to develop all manner of machines powered by water or compressed air, from his famous water-clock and equally famous force pump[30] to an air gun. He was followed by Philo and Hero, who improved on some of his designs and added some more – particularly war machines – and the three are known collectively as the great Hellenistic Mechanicians.[31] Some scholars have thought some of the machines described in their surviving texts to be fanciful – even 'Heath-Robinson' – designs.[32] But these scholars ignore other ancient literature which takes for granted the existence of such machines as real, working, and familiar to their audience. For example, the author of *Aetna* mentions a water-powered Triton horn, a water-organ, and a force-pump as analogies to explain how the blast from a volcano can be sustained for as long as the author claims it sometimes is.[33]

In [Aristotle] *Mechanics* one finds lots of mathematical proofs of mechanical principles presented as answers to problems. For example, in §1 we are offered an explanation with geometric proof for why bigger balances are more accurate than smaller ones, with a summary in plain language, and ending with a warning about purple traders' methods of deceiving customers by rigging the balance in their favour. In §21 the

---

[28] On which see Marsden 1971.

[29] See e.g. Philo *Belopoiika* §50.26–9: 'The fact that everything cannot be accomplished by the theoretical methods of mechanics, but that much is to be found by experiment, is proved especially by what I am going to say' (Marsden trans.).

[30] Known in antiquity as the Ktesibian pump, and the sort of pump used in Roman fire-engines. See Oleson 1984 for full discussion of this and other pumps.

[31] Drachmann 1948 focuses on their work on pneumatics. Also useful is Drachmann 1963, which contains a translation from the Arabic of much of Hero's *Mechanics* with relevant passages from other authors. On Archimedes' machines see Sleeswyk 1990 and Simms 1995.

[32] See e.g. Green 1986, who uses this phrase of Ktesibios' water-organ.

[33] *Aetna* 294–9, and 328 respectively. In a completely different time and context the Christian author Tertullian referred to God playing the water-organ, *De baptismo* 8.

question 'why do dentists find it easier to extract teeth by using forceps rather than the bare hand?' is explained with reference to the lever, as is the shadoof (a very simple water-lifting device) in §28. That theory is following practice and trying to explain why mechanical things are the way they are is sometimes very obvious, for example in §25 we find the question 'why do they string beds the way they do?' Abstract science and everyday life are inextricably mixed here.

Problems §§32–4 ask questions which Newton answered more satisfactorily with his Laws of Motion, while the author recognizes explicitly that he's groping here.[34]

§32 Why is it that an object which is thrown eventually comes to a standstill? Does it stop when the force which started it fails, or because the object is drawn in a contrary direction, or is it due to its downward tendency, which is stronger than the force which threw it? Or is it absurd to discuss such questions, while the principle escapes us? §33 How is it that a body is carried along by a motion not of its own, if that which started it does not keep following and pushing it along? Is it not clear that in the beginning the impelling force so acted as to push the thing along, and this in its turn pushes something else? The moving body comes to a standstill when the force which pushes it along can no longer so act as to push it, and when the weight of the moving object has a stronger inclination downwards than the forward force of that which pushes it. §34 Why is it that neither small nor large bodies travel far when thrown, but they must have due relation to the person who throws them? Is it because that which is thrown or pushed must offer resistance to that from which it is pushed, and whatever does not yield owing to its mass, or does not resist owing to its weakness, does not admit of being thrown or pushed? A body, then, which is far beyond the force which tries to push it, does not yield at all; while that which is far weaker offers no resistance. Or is it because that which travels along does so only as far as it moves the air to its depths, and that which is not moved cannot itself move anything either? Both these things are the case here; that which is very large and that which is very small must be looked on as not moving at all; for the latter does not move anything, while the former is not itself at all moved' (Forster trans.)

Not surprisingly, physics remained a subject of lively debate. In Roman times the same sort of problems and the same sort of answers were offered, though generally with a more rhetorical and less mathematical edge to them. For example, Seneca says:

How could water be in tension without air? Take the jet of water that grows from the bottom of the centre of the arena and goes all the way to the top of the amphitheatre – do you think this happens without air tension? Yet neither the hand nor any sort of mechanical device can emit or force water out the way air can. The water responds to the air. It is raised up by the air, which is inserted in the pipe and forces it up. Although

---

[34] Even the real Aristotle occasionally ventured out of his depth, for example on astronomy. Lloyd takes him to task for this (1996a chapter 8), perhaps a little unjustly; Aristotle was no mathematician. See Heath 1949.

water naturally flows down, it struggles mightily against its nature and rises. How about ships laden with cargo? Do they not show that it is resistance of air, not water, that keeps them from sinking? Water would give way and be unable to maintain the weight if it were not itself sustained by air. A discus hurled from a higher position into a pond does not sink but bounces back. How could it do this unless it were beaten back by air? (*NQ* 2.9.2–3, Corcoran trans.)

Seneca is engaging with theory, and his argument is replete with examples from Roman daily life – the theatre, shipping, and the perennial simple entertainment of making stones skip across water. Producing a jet of water high into the air was far from simple however, and a similar project preoccupied the great physicist and mathematician Leibniz in later times (at Wolfenbuttel). As we move into the late empire, a number of scholars, notably the Aristotelian Alexander of Aphrodisias (late C2–early C3 A.D.) and the Neoplatonists John Philoponus (a Christian) and Simplicius (a pagan; both first half of the C6 A.D.) engaged much more deeply with the theories of the ancient Aristotle,[35] but still the arguments about space and time, matter and void, static and dynamic forces were unresolved.

FURTHER READING

G. Freudenthal, *Aristotle's Theory of Material Substance* (Oxford, 1995) and L. Judson (ed.), *Aristotle's Physics* (Oxford, 1991) offer good recent discussions of Aristotle's ideas on matter. For the atomists see D. Furley, *Two Studies in the Greek Atomists* (Princeton, 1967) and *The Greek Cosmologists: the Formation of the Atomic Theory and its Earliest Critics* (Cambridge, 1987). For the debates in late Antiquity, see R. Sorabji, *Time, Creation and the Continuum* (London, 1983) and *Matter, Space and Motion* (London, 1988). Older works provide good overviews but are prone to implicit translation of technical, especially mathematical, ideas.[36] Some of the best amongst them are F. Solmsen, *Aristotle's System of the Physical World* (Ithaca, 1960) and O. Pedersen and M. Pihl, *Early Physics and Astronomy* (London, 1974). The latter contains more than one would expect from the title and has a very useful biographical appendix which includes Arabic and mediaeval writers as well as Greeks and Romans (by 'early' they mean up to Copernicus). S. Samburksy's *Physical World of the Greeks* (London, 1956), *Physics of the Stoics* (London, 1959), and *Physical World of Late Antiquity* (London, 1963) are still worth reading. On

---

[35] The 15,000 pages of Greek texts by the late (*c.* A.D. 200–600) commentators on Aristotle are the subject of a large programme of English translations (over 60 volumes planned) under the general editorship of R. Sorabji, published by Duckworth.

[36] On implicit translation see Chapter 3.1 below.

forces a good overview is provided by J. Lindsay, *Blast, Power and Ballistics: Concepts of Force and Energy in the Ancient World* (London, 1974), which also contains a great deal more than one might expect from the title. A. G. Drachmann, *Mechanical Technology of Greek and Roman Antiquity* (Copenhagen, 1963) and K. D. White, *Greek and Roman Technology* (London, 1984) provide good overviews of mechanics and machines in antiquity.

Principal primary sources in English translation:

Archimedes, *The Works of Archimedes*. Trans. in modern notation by T. B. L. Heath (Cambridge, 1897); the 1912 ed. has a supplement *The Method* of Archimedes.

Aristotle, *Meteorology*, Loeb trans. Translation of book 4 with detailed introduction and commentary in I. During, *Aristotle's Chemical Treatise* (Goteburg, 1944). Alexander of Aphrodisias' commentary on the *Meteorology* has recently been translated by E. Lewis in the Duckworth Late Commentators on Aristotle series, ed. R. Sorabji.

Euclid, *Optics*. Trans. H. Burton, in *Journal of the Optical Society of America* 35 (1945), 357–72.

Hero, *Pneumatics*, by B. Woodcroft, facsimile reprint ed. M. B. Hall (London, 1973).

Hero, *Belopoiika* and *Kheiroballista* in Marsden, 1971, vol. 1.

Philo, *Belopoiika* in Marsden, 1971, vol. 1.

Philoponus' commentaries on Aristotle's *Physics* are published in many volumes in the Duckworth Late Commentators on Aristotle series, ed. R. Sorabji.

Ptolemy, *Optics*. Trans. and comm. by A. M. Smith, *Trans. American Philosophical Society* 86.2 (Philadelphia, 1996).

Simplicius' commentaries on Aristotle's *Physics* are published in many volumes in the Duckworth Late Commentators on Aristotle series, ed. R. Sorabji.

Strato's fragments await an English translation. For the Greek text and commentary, and translation of the fragments surviving in Arabic, see Gottschalk, 1965.

Vitruvius, *On Architecture* is translated in Loeb (in 2 vols) and Dover (in 1 vol.).

III. MATHEMATICS

3.1 *Introduction*

Mathematics probably ranks as the Greeks' greatest achievement, in the eyes of many modern scientists. And amongst the general public it is fair to say that some Greek mathematicians are better known than *any* other figures from antiquity, with the possible exception of Alexander the Great. For example, Pythagoras, Euclid, and Archimedes are household names two thousand years after they lived and wrote their mathematics. The Greek alphabet, or some of it anyway, is widely known today because modern mathematics uses it by preference for symbols. For example, α, β and θ for angles, the amazing[1] π, Σ as the summation sign, and the χ-square test. The Greeks gave us 'square' and 'cube' numbers, e.g. 2^2 and 3^3. 'Squaring the circle' is modern English idiom for an impossible task – the original task, set by the Greeks, being the mathematical problem of constructing a square with the same area as a given circle.[2] Aristophanes mentions this problem.[3] Famously, Plato forbade the geometrically-challenged to enter his Academy.[4] He also found mathematically interesting numbers for his ideal Republic.[5] Greek mathematical texts are rich in mathematical concepts, methods, and results. Like Greek plays, they contain timeless insights and truths. Also like literary works they require analysis and interpretation.

The influence of Greek mathematics continues through the ages. For example, arithmetic, music, geometry, and astronomy – pure number, applied number, stationary magnitude, and magnitude in motion respectively – began life in Plato's ideal Republic[6] and constituted the quadrivium of sciences for the late Roman and Middle Ages.[7] The

---

[1] For an enjoyable, as well as educational, book on this, see Blatner 1997.

[2] Using only ruler and compass and a finite number of steps, to keep within Euclidian terms. This was proved to be impossible to do in 1882 (when Lindemann proved that π was a transcendental number).

[3] *Birds* 1001–5, Meton speaking, production date 414 B.C.

[4] Famously but probably not accurately, for this story comes from an author who wrote 1400 years after Plato lived, Tzetzes, *Khiliades* 8.972–3 (on whom see also chapter 6 n. 22).

[5] E.g. 5040 citizens, a number with 59 divisors including all the numbers from 1 to 10, as he observes, *Laws* 737e, 738a.

[6] 7.521c–31c, on which see Fowler 1990 chapter 4.

[7] On which see Stahl 1971. The other three subjects (the trivium) were grammar (which covered language and literature), dialectic (logic), and rhetoric (expression).

dramatic discovery of a proof of Fermat's last theorem in 1993–4 shows how even current mathematical activity originates in Greek mathematical activity.[8]

There are essentially three approaches to the study of Greek mathematics. The traditional approach, which might be called *implicit translation*, is to seek the mathematical facts discovered by the Greeks, and to present them in a way which is easily comprehensible to moderns. T. B. L. Heath's and B. van der Waerden's works are of this type.[9] The second approach is to try to understand what the Greeks were saying in their own terms (with careful attention to the manuscript tradition), which might be called *explicit transliteration*. J. Klein's, W. Knorr's and D. Fowler's works are of this type. We will come back to these two approaches in a moment. The third approach is to treat the mathematical texts as any other surviving literary work, and engage in *source criticism*: to ask questions of the aims and motives of the author in writing a particular work, in a particular genre, and for a particular audience. W. Knorr began to explore these questions explicitly in his later studies.[10]

There is a debate between implicit translation and explicit transliteration that is akin to the debate between doing classics in translation and doing classics in the original language. Mathematics is a language, a highly symbolic one. In translation, some ideas are lost and others are implanted. If Greek mathematics looks familiar to us, it is at least partly because it has been translated from ancient into modern mathematical concepts and notation. The preponderance of studies based on implicit translation has made Greek mathematics *more* understandable and familiar to us than it should be.[11] This implicit translation extends even to what we consider the most basic feature of mathematics:

---

[8] Fermat's famous last theorem was written in 1637 in the margin of his copy of Diophantos' *Arithmetica*, book 2, next to Problem 8: 'to divide a square number into two other square numbers'. This inspired Fermat to assert that 'It is impossible to divide a cube into two other cubes, or a fourth power or, in general, any number which is a power greater than the second into two powers of the same denomination'. Or in modern symbolic terms, the equation $x^n + y^n = z^n$ has no integer solution when n is greater than 2. This is in contrast to Pythagorean triples, where $x^2 + y^2 = z^2$, of which there are, as Euclid proved (in words not algebra), an infinite number of solutions. On Wiles's proof of Fermat's theorem, see Singh 1997.

[9] E.g. Heath 1897, van der Waerden 1983. Anglin and Lambek 1995 continue this tradition with the dubious defence that 'a presentation faithful to the original sources, while catering to the serious scholar, would bore most students to tears' (p. vi). Even if true for students of mathematics – for whom the book was written – the opposite is more likely to be true for students of Greece and Rome.

[10] See e.g. Knorr 1986.

[11] See for example Heath's chapter in Livingstone 1921. Unguru's complaint about this sort of implicit translation, made 20 years ago (1979), is repeated and developed by Knorr 1991.

number. In any ordinary ancient text (i.e. not mathematical treatises) where a number appears, that number will often appear in translation in numerical form, e.g. 100, when it usually appears in the original in verbal form, one hundred.[12] As de Ste Croix commented with respect to Heath's assumption that the Greeks performed arithmetical operations in columns, '[Heath] was trying in effect to smuggle into Greek arithmetic (of course without the slightest intention to deceive) a partial substitute for the place-value which is missing from the numeral notation, involving the use of a blank space corresponding to our zero. The whole conception, however, is fundamentally wrong, both on factual grounds and because it is based on a misconception of the functioning of the alphabetic numeral notation'.[13]

To take a less subtle example, in most modern translations of ancient mathematical texts algebraic notation is conspicuous in the notes – or worse, the text – whereas in the Greek text it is conspicuous by its absence.[14] Even in mathematical texts, in the original there is no +, or –, or ×, or ÷, or =, or even $\sqrt{\ }$.[15] This last is despite the fact that the Greeks spent a lot of time and effort on the problem of incommensurable quantities (e.g. $\sqrt{2}$), which they discovered. They conceived and spoke about 'roots' in terms of the side of a square: given a certain area – pictured as a square – what is the length of one side? That length is what we call the square root. (And if the number cannot be pictured as a square, but forms a rectangle or a triangle for example, then it cannot have a square root.)[16] Those readers who are uncomfortable with

[12] In fact this statement applies even to some mathematical texts, but these are rare cases; see Fowler 1990 p. 221. See Pliny *NH* 33.133 on the increase in the magnitude of numbers needed during Roman history ('in the old days there was no number standing for more than one hundred thousand'). The same thing happened before and after: Homer calls ten thousand just that, *deka khilioi*, but later Greeks used *myrioi* (which hitherto meant countless) for ten thousand. The word million appeared in fourteenth century Italy. Now we have billion and trillion. Greek and Roman methods of measuring and numerating are well treated in Richardson 1985, which is especially useful for people reading ancient texts in the original, as it explains all the common forms of expression of mathematical ideas and technical usages, with the focus squarely on non-mathematical texts such as the Athenian orators, Cicero, and the Greek and Roman historians.

[13] de Ste Croix, 1956, p. 56, with full defence of this charge on pp. 56–9.

[14] The same problem dogs Mesopotamian mathematics. For an excellent discussion of that, with frequent, relevant, and important reference to Greek mathematics, see J. Høyrup 1996. As Høyrup showed elsewhere, the operations performed in so-called Babylonian 'algebra' are not (and could not be) arithmetical operations with numbers. They are analytical operations on geometric figures.

[15] All these symbols are post-antiquity. The symbol + is first used as an abbreviation for Latin 'et' (and) in a MS dated 1417. The symbols + and – first appear in print in 1489, where they refer to surpluses and deficits in business problems, not as operations or positive/negative numbers. The symbol $\sqrt{\ }$ is first used in 1525. The equality sign first appears in print in 1557. The multiplication symbol × first appears in print in 1618, and the division symbol ÷ was first used in 1659. See Cajori 1928–9.

[16] Figured numbers are well discussed in Heath 1921, pp. 76–84.

mathematics might find the Greek way of talking and thinking about these things more comprehensible than the modern way.[17]

For addition, subtraction and so on, what we find in the Greek text (instead of +, − and so on) is either nothing to indicate the operations to be performed on the numbers, or a preposition such as 'with' or 'from'. How the operations are described varies from author to author. There is no completely standard word, number or operation order, so that one sometimes has to work out from the mathematical context what is meant in any particular part of a calculation: in an example given by Thomas in the Loeb[18] one could read $10/71^{ths}$ or $10 + 1/71^{ths}$. It is not mere pedantry to insist on the difference between these ways of referring to mathematical operations and our own. For modern mathematicians, for whom exactness, accuracy, and clarity are the highest virtues, the ambiguities of some Greek mathematics would be a nightmare.

On the other hand, in order to reach understanding of something unfamiliar, we have to manipulate that unfamiliar thing with familiar concepts until we *can* understand it and see the differences and similarities between the two.[19] It is like the word *polis*, used by some ancient historians in preference to any English word or phrase in order to try to avoid importing conceptual baggage from our time and language into Greek times and language. Nevertheless, when we try to explain to students what *polis* means, we have to use English words and phrases. Transliteration is not translation, but to understand a trans- literated word does require discussion in one's own language and concepts. In my view there is a place and a need for both approaches in the history of mathematics – and science in general – in the same way that there is a need for classics education in translation and in the original. There is much of mathematical interest here, as well as of historical interest.

Increasing specialization is the boon and the bane of modern

---

[17] As Fowler points out (1990 p. 21), the Greeks think and talk about their geometrical figures literally, as if the shapes were in front of them, being manipulated by hand. We, by contrast, turn geometry into arithmetic and then turn arithmetic into algebra, and think and write about the subject abstractly. See also his comments p. 68.

[18] *Greek Mathematical Works* vol. 1 p. 45. This example from Archimedes, and the text (to which Thomas does not refer) is *Measurement of a Circle*, given on pp. 316–32, with the offending text on p. 332. Fowler p. 240 f. contrasts his own similar but more literal translation of this part of the text with Heath's description of the same proposition (there reproduced for convenience), which well illustrates the 'maths in translation' versus 'maths in the original' debate.

[19] Bunt, Jones, and Bedient 1976 put the familiar and unfamiliar side by side for Greek, Egyptian, and Babylonian mathematics; see esp. §6.12 on 'The difference between the Euclidean and the modern method of comparing areas' and chapter 7, 'Greek mathematics after Euclid: Euclidean versus modern methods'.

intellectual life: boon because it advances understanding of a topic; bane because that topic is microscopic in scale relative to intellectual life as a whole, which grows out of control. We need syntheses[20] to prevent the world of learning disaggregating into a kaleidoscopic image of shattered fragments. If the advances of any topic are to be communicated outside an increasingly tiny field of scholars working on it and capable of understanding it in its own terms,[21] then they must be made comprehensible to people outside that specialist field; they must, in short, be translated, whether from an ancient language such as Greek or Akkadian, or from a technical concept such as multiplication,[22] of which there are four different types in Babylonian mathematics.

Recent studies on ancient literacy have emphasized that the non-existence of gaps between words, of punctuation, of contents, of index, and even the practicalities of handling papyrus rolls rather than sheets of text, must have had an impact on the reading habits of the ancient Greeks.[23] In like manner the use of letters for numbers[24] and the lack of symbols for mathematical operations – on top of the usual literary habits – must have had an impact on numeracy.

I will first discuss numbers in everyday life, then how numbers were written, and then geometry. I am starting with low-brow mathematics,

---

[20] Hakfoort 1991 tries to explain both the absence of syntheses over the last generation and the sort of synthesis which might now be written in a 'post-positivist philosophical vacuum'. Lindberg 1992 is a traditional type of synthesis and has been well received, though is better on medieval science than on ancient. Serres 1995 is a synthesis in the French style, which rejoices in the variety of philosophical and disciplinary views held by its various contributors. It is well worth reading, but poorly referenced for the Greek chapters.

[21] For example, Høyrup admits (1996 p. 22) to being the sole representative of a certain approach to ancient mathematics, namely, 'recasting theories about the transmission of Babylonian mathematical knowledge and techniques to later cultures (with appurtenant transformation) and about the relation between practitioners' mathematics, scribal mathematics and "scientific" mathematics'. Most of the 'recasting' concerns the contextualization of mathematics in the culture which produced it.

[22] 'Multiplied by' is often expressed by ἐπί plus dative in a mathematical context. This is the term used in expressions of interest rates (τόκοι), for example. The Greeks were more likely to add than multiply, even for a sum as simple as 5 lots of 9: see Gow 1884 p. 51, where there is also a concise explanation of the ancient way of conceiving division, or Fowler 1990 pp. 14–16. There is an excellent explanation of technical terms in Greek mathematics (with special reference to Apollonios) in Heath 1896 pp. clvii–clxx.

[23] There is a demonstration of Greek writing habits in Fowler 1990 p. 205. On literacy in general see e.g. Harris 1989 or Thomas 1992.

[24] Thus letters could be mistakenly read as numbers and vice versa. In the Codex Constantinopolitanus, for example, some scribe took the word 'lemma' for a fraction ($\lambda\eta = 1/28^{th}$ $\mu = 1/40^{th}$ $\mu a = 1/41^{th}$) and included it in a computation. See Bruins 1964 vol.3 p. 221 on fol. 77r. Apollonios of Perga (amongst others) even played with the double meaning of letters, by adding up the values of the letters in a poem to demonstrate his method of expressing large numbers (in the tradition of Archimedes' *Sand-reckoner*); Heiberg 1922 p. 65. This dual meaning of letters offered an easy method of coding (and mystifying) information, expressing words as numbers.

such as practical computation, because our evidence for this kind of maths is a lot earlier than that for high-brow mathematics, which does not really get going until the Hellenistic period. Practical mathematics is also tied intimately to the history of the period which created and used it.

3.2 *Ready reckoning and logistike*

Historians of Greek mathematics tend to concentrate on what might be called 'high mathematics': the geometrical wizardry and axiomatic certainties of e.g. Euclid. In this they are following a long established tradition. The study of mathematics has long been influenced by the quest for general concepts and results – since Euclid, in fact. Practical computation was looked down on by Plato[25] and by some others henceforth, and philosophers held a more or less dismissive attitude toward the men who actually counted or calculated things. The distinction was recognized in ordinary Roman life. For example, the *calculatores* were explicitly barred from the tax exemptions granted to some teachers and healers in the Roman empire.[26] This type of mathematics was the type which was most used in everyday life, however, and it may have had an influence on the development of 'pure' mathematics too.[27] A few ancient historians with interests in financial matters have discussed the type of reckoning used for official (state) and private purposes.[28]

A certain level of numeracy was required not just by traders and money-lenders calculating yields.[29] Citizens serving as state officials needed to be able to measure, count, or compute figures which were relevant for their office, and other citizens serving as state auditors

[25] See e.g. *Philebus* 56d–57d, where a distinction is drawn between the calculation and measurement employed in building and commerce and the calculation and geometry practised by philosophers, the latter being described as 'far superior'. He takes a different view in *Laws* 817e–820 (esp. 819c).

[26] See e.g. *Digest of Roman Law* 27.1.15.5 (Modestinus on immunities). It is however interesting that enough of a case for their inclusion had been made to warrant the writing into the law that they did not qualify! For discussion of the privileges in question, see Duncan-Jones 1990 pp. 160–3.

[27] As Fowler notes, 1992 p. 134 n. 4, commercial practice certainly affected mathematics in Renaissance Italy, and a treatise on decimal numbers which is now considered fundamental was dedicated to a lively assortment of trades and professions using calculations in 1585.

[28] The best of which is still de Ste Croix 1956, on which see also Macve 1985. Also Tod 1950 and references there to his earlier papers on Greek numeral systems and notation.

[29] This is how we should normally think of returns on loans, rather than as 'interest', which is expressed (and calculated) with reference to time, since Greek returns are not intrinsically tied to the passage of certain lengths of time. See Cohen 1992, esp. pp. 44–6.

needed to be able to check those figures. The most primitive type of reckoning, namely keeping tallies, began with notched sticks, and continues with the chalk marks on slates and five-bar-gates on paper we still make today. Darius used such a tally device when he left with the Greek force guarding the bridge over the Bosphorus a leather thong with 60 knots in it, and told them to undo one knot each day (Hdt 4.98). If he was not back by the time they untied the last knot, they could leave. With a method such as this, one does not need to be able to count beyond 1; one simply needs to 'accumulate' or 'tick off' notches, marks, strokes, knots or any other kind of marking system on the principle of a one-to-one correspondence. In the developed democracy, treasurers of all sorts and officials such as the *logistai*, *poletai*, booty-sellers on campaign – even the juror concerned with his pay – all knew how to use more sophisticated methods of reckoning. In Aristophanes' comedy about jurors, the main characters perform a quick calculation on stage:[30]

ANTIKLEON: First of all reckon up roughly not with counters but just on your hands, the amount of tribute that comes in to us altogether from the allied states, and apart from that the taxes, one by one, and the many one-hundredths, court fees, mines, markets, harbours, rentals, confiscations. We get a total for all these of nearly two thousand talents. Out of this now put down pay for the jurors for a year, six thousand of them (never yet have more this land inhabited): we get, I think, a hundred and fifty talents.
PROKLEON: You mean our pay doesn't even come to one tenth of the revenue!

'Roughly, on your fingers will do' suggests that finger-counting is merely a second-best method available to the ordinary Athenian in the street, who can also handle very large numbers with relative ease. Unfortunately, whilst the answers to sums are often given in literary or epigraphic sources – as in the Aristophanes passage just quoted, or the Athenian Tribute Lists – the methods by which the sums were calculated are not.

   Given the size of the numbers and the preponderance of 60s as well as 10s in Athenian financial units, the finger-counting method involved was perhaps that which uses the 3 bones of each finger (but not the thumb which does the pointing operation) on one hand, so that one can count to 12 using one hand, and then use each (whole) finger of the other hand to record the powers of 12, leading to a total of 60 when all fingers and thumb of the second hand are employed. The number 12 is a much more useful base for practical purposes than 10, for, as Galen

---

[30] *Wasps* 656–64, Sommerstein trans., slightly modified.

remarked,[31] 12 has four divisors (2, 3, 4, 6), in contrast to base 10's two (2, 5), and is not less convenient anatomically than the decimal base. Or perhaps Prokleon used a much more complicated system of finger-counting of the type explained by the Venerable Bede in the C7 A.D.,[32] which seems to have a long pedigree, at least for the smaller numbers (Bede stops at a million).

Besides magistrates, significant numeracy was needed by anyone involved with state dues. The obvious categories are traders, tax-farmers and litigants. Traders paid (normally) 1/50th as a tax on all imports and exports (the *pentekoste*, normally subject to implicit translation and called the 'two-percent' tax). Tax-farmers needed to estimate fairly accurately what they could collect before submitting their bids for e.g. the *pornikon telos*[33] or the *metoikion*[34] (or risk financial ruin). Numeracy was needed by litigants to calculate fees, fines, and rewards. Most people using the Athenian courts had to pay court fees. In private cases the fees were called *prytaneia*, and were set at rates reflecting the value of the case.[35] In public cases there were two sort of fees, *parastasis*, about which we know no details, and *parakatabole*, which was a deposit of 1/5th or 1/10th of the value of the case (depending on the type of case), which was forfeited by the litigant who lost or the prosecutor who failed to secure 1/5th of the votes of the jury. Some penalties for the convicted and rewards for the plaintiff were also set as a portion or multiples of the total value of the case. An example of the first is the *epobelia*, a fine of 1/6th of the value of the case.[36] An example of the second is the reward for the successful prosecutor of 1/3rd of the value of the property confiscated from the convicted defendant in an *apographe* lawsuit.

The Athenians of Perikles' day were familiar with computations involving six. For example, there were 6 obols in a drachma, 60 minas in a talent, 6,000 drachmai in a talent, and 1/60th of imperial tribute was dedicated to Athena. This does *not* mean they worked on base 6, or base 60 (the sexagesimal system) in ordinary life. They worked in base 10, as

---

[31] *Affections and Errors of the Soul* 2.5 (5.83–4 K). As I pointed out in chapter 1, ancient scientists were polymaths and their works do not fit neatly into modern disciplinary categories. One would not today expect discussion of this point in a text about the soul, written by a physician.

[32] *De temporum ratione* 1, which concerns calculating and speaking with the fingers.

[33] The prostitutes' tax, paid by prostitutes.

[34] The metics' tax, paid by resident aliens.

[35] If the case was worth less than 100 drachmai, there was no fee. For a case valued between 100 and 1000 drachmai, the fee was 3 dr. payable by each party; for over 1000 dr. the fee was 30 dr. per party. See Harrison 1971 p. 93 for details.

[36] The name refers to the obol, because this penalty is calculated at one obol fine per drachma value.

we do. Just because sixes and sixties feature strongly in their system of units for money and financial thinking, it does not follow that they used a base 6 or 60 counting system.[37] It is easy to recognize what system is at work by looking at which number names are abbreviated in the acrophonic system: five, ten, one hundred, one thousand, ten thousand, and no others; or at the groups in the alphabetic system: the first nine letters represent 1–9, the next nine letters represent 10–90, and the third nine letters represent 100–900 (on which see further below §3). The fact that the monetary units used in Athenian financial inscriptions involve multiples and fractions of 6 (*and* 100) is incidental to the base system in operation and the way they counted and recorded quantities.[38]

The Athenian tribute lists, which record the monies given to Athena, specify the amounts given by the different allies down to obols: it is debated whether these apparently very precise figures were arrived at by computation of $1/60^{th}$ of what was given, or merely reflect conversion into Attic currency of monies paid in foreign staters or darics, or even in plate, which could have been weighed and then recorded in Attic currency figures.[39] Quantification in antiquity was a problem only for those interested in comparisons, like us. Across the Mediterranean there were numerous different systems of weights and measures in operation simultaneously. But most people lived and worked in one area with one system, and were probably as, if not less, interested in foreign weights and measures as most of us are. The variety presents a problem for the historian, however, especially those seeking to compare ancient with modern answers. For example, the various different lengths of the stade is a notorious crux in Eratosthenes' computation of the circumference of the earth: take one particular length of stade, and his answer was very close to ours; take another, and his answer is a lot less accurate.[40] The same problem could have troubled the ancient reader of any text referring to a specific quantity of a specific measure, if accuracy was important, especially if a measure by a certain name was not in use in their area. 'Handful', on the other hand, would give a rough idea to

[37] *Contra* Nixon and Price 1992.

[38] We can also look at the small denominations: the *khalkous*, *krithe* and *lepta* were 1/48th, 1/72th, and 1/336th of a drachma respectively. None of these fractions are obvious ones to choose in a sexagesimal system (and there is no coin representing 1/60th), but all are divisible by 6.

[39] See Vickers 1992. Greek coins had bullion value, they were not tokens, so precious metal objects could serve as large denominations.

[40] Stades about which we have reliable information and which were in use in Eratosthenes' time vary from about 7.5 to 10 stades to a Roman mile. On the scale of the circumference of the earth, the difference is very significant.

anyone reading it, and would do for most purposes. Consequently such approximate measures, usually based on body parts, tend to dominate in texts with practical applications.

Alexander the Great was very concerned with logistical matters: he needed to be, to keep his army alive. Any number of men, moving through enemy territory, were able to carry not more than 7 days' supplies (at most 5 if required to carry their own water too, even on half-rations).[41] They depended for their survival on securing sufficient supplies from urban centres with stored food, or being able to live off the land, which was possible only at certain times of year.[42] Alexander did not normally depend on supply lines, but relied on capturing adequate supplies as he moved forward. For this purpose he sent out reconnaissance parties, gathered intelligence from the natives, and sometimes split his army into two or more smaller units following different routes to reduce the logistical demand on the routes chosen. Troop numbers were fluctuating constantly as some died, some veterans were settled or sent home, and some reinforcements arrived. And these changing logistical demands had to be worked out at least several days in advance to be of any use. Someone amongst his advisors, if not he himself, was performing the required calculations during the entire expedition. Troops were also paid, and got into debt, records of which were kept with the army on the move, e.g. his troops were said to have been indebted to the tune of either 10,000 or 20,000 talents by the time they got back from India to Susa in 324.[43]

One of the best sets of accounts that de Ste Croix could find in all surviving Greco-Roman documentary evidence was two soldiers' pay sheets, dating from 83–4 A.D.[44] In the late empire the military again seems to have been more precise and accurate than most other groups in life, or so Vegetius opines in his *Epitome of Military Science* 2.19: 'The administration of the entire legion, including special services, military services, and money, is recorded daily in the Acts with one might say greater exactitude than records of military and civil taxation are noted down in official files' (Milner trans.). The officers responsible were called the *librarii* (§2.7), and since soldiers might receive single pay, pay and a half, or double pay, some computations were required. We also

---

[41] 'The ratio between the army's consumption rate and its carrying capability remains constant no matter how many personnel or pack animals are used to carry supplies', Engels, 1978, p. 21.

[42] See Engels op. cit., esp. chapter 1.

[43] The lower figure is given by Curtius and Plutarch; the higher by Arrian and Justin.

[44] de Ste Croix 1956 pp. 39–40, with accompanying Plate III and Figure IV.

hear, in §2.20, details about the keeping of accounts of soldiers' savings deposited 'with the standards'. Calculations of a different sort were needed for pitching camp: 'the general does not go wrong when he knows what space can hold how many fighting men' (§3.15, Milner trans.). The *mensores* paced out the square footage for the camp and the parts within it, every time they set camp (which was frequent). Further calculations were sometimes required during the actual fighting: for example, Vegetius gives us an empirical and a calculated method to find the height of a city wall (§4.30): fire an arrow with a thin thread at the top of the wall, then measure the length of the thread. Or measure the wall's shadow, and a ten-foot rod's shadow, and compute the wall's height from the ratio. This is to find the solution to the perennial problem of ensuring that scaling ladders are neither too long nor too short for the job in hand.[45]

The mention of pebbles in some literary contexts, such as Herodotos 2.36.2,[46] implies the use of abacus, but the nature of such an abacus in Greek society is very uncertain. It is debated wither the Salamis stone (and similar slabs found in Greece) is an abacus or a gaming table.[47] All certain surviving ancient examples of abaci are Roman in date. Pebbles (*psephoi*) feature in C5 and C4 Greek society most strongly in political contexts, for voting in the assembly or the courts, giving rise to the term *psephisma* for 'decree', something decided by vote. In the C4 pebbles were replaced by official bronze disks, which nevertheless retained the name and thus extended the meaning of *psephoi*. In early Greek mathematics pebbles are most obvious in the context of figured numbers, where their use laid out in regular patterns explains the notion of square, triangular, rectangular, or any other shape numbers.

Simple lines in the dust and any old token or markers, such as pebbles lying to hand in the same dust, can serve as an abacus or calculating tool.[48] All that is needed is some straight lines to make rows or columns, and something to put in those columns. Labels for each row or column are handy but not necessary if the user is familiar with the practice of

---

[45] A problem on which Polubios had expounded at some length, 9.19, having criticized Philip of Macedon for making mistakes in this area (5.97.5–6).

[46] 'In writing and reckoning with pebbles the Greeks move the hand from left to right, but the Egyptians from right to left'.

[47] See Lang 1964, Pritchett 1965, Lang 1965. Pullan 1970 (which is well illustrated with archaeological evidence and diagrams) follows Lang but is not always reliable.

[48] Alan Turing showed in 1936 that *any* calculation can be made with just 2 tokens, symbolically represented by 1 and 0 using a Turing Machine, which is nothing more than a set of simple rules. Modern computers work with just these two symbols, translated for practical purposes into electrical 'on' and 'off'.

using an abacus and has a regular method of working (left to right, or right to left, top to bottom, or bottom to top; start with the smallest unit and progress to the largest, or vice versa). The Salamis stone is very big (5′ × 2′5″), very heavy (solid marble), and must have been very expensive to make (apart from the cost of transporting the stone, it is carefully chiselled). It was sited in a sanctuary.[49] It is dated to the C6 or C5 B.C., and I find it difficult to imagine a social, economic, historical, or even mathematical context for a marble abacus which is almost the size of a bed. On the other hand, it is no easier to picture it as a gaming board.

Lang tried to show that some errors in surviving Greek arithmetic in literary and epigraphic sources could have arisen more easily through careless use of an abacus than through mistakes in written calculations. Personally, I do not believe we have enough evidence to decide the matter. Herodotos, for example, may or may not have used an abacus of some sort to compute the number of *medimnoi* of grain consumed per day by Xerxes' army (for which he failed correctly to divide 5,283,220 by 48).[50] As for Athenian financial documents, the problems are legion. Most stones are incomplete; where they are sufficiently complete, rarely is there any totalling; when there are totals that we can check, errors are not uncommon.[51] If the purpose of these records was to assert the honesty of the officials responsible for the monies concerned, and if they were 'checked' by the auditors whose function it was to check them, one wonders whether it is incompetence, lack of interest, or fraud that is preserved in these errors. I think it unduly optimistic to assume that all errors are accidents of calculation or chisel, and that if we 'correct' here and there the sums will add up: some of them may not add up because they never did add up.

3.3 *Numbers and arithmetike*

Our number symbols 0, 1, . . ., 9 are called Arabic numerals, and they mean nothing but numbers to us. They also meant nothing but numbers

---

[49] This is true of other tables thought to have been either abaci or gaming tables, such as that found at the Amphiareion.

[50] 7.187. Note that the Grene translation in the Chicago 1987 edition has an error here: the result should be 110,340 not 1,100,340. Numbers are as prone to error now as they were in Herodotos' time, it seems, whether arising from innumeracy or copying/typographic slips. Even though he apparently got it wrong, it is interesting that Herodotos thought of performing this calculation.

[51] Errors are very common in literary texts, including those originals which have survived on papyri and in which errors cannot thus be attributed to poor transcription by uncomprehending copyists, as they may be with medieval MSS. Byzantine scholars, at least, not infrequently corrected errors in the original rather than introduced them.

to the Arabs, who got them from India, which was an area of many mutually foreign languages and alphabets. The Greeks did *not* have dedicated symbols for numbers. To understand the significance of this, consider letters: for us, as for the Greeks, alpha is just alpha. For an ancient Semite, however, it was 'ox' badly pronounced.[52] So it is with numerals: in the society which first uses them, they have meaning beyond number. Abstracted from that context, they can take on new meaning. So Ptolemy's use of 'o' as an abbreviation for *ouden* (nothing) in a particular context[53] could be read as a symbol for zero in India.[54]

The earliest Greek formal method of representing cardinal numbers (one, two, three etc.) is the acrophonic system.[55] Besides | for the unit, the first letter of the word for five different numbers is used as an abbreviation for that number. The five are:

Π for *pente*, five (the right leg is drawn somewhat shorter than the left);
Δ for *deka*, ten;
H for *hekaton*, one hundred;
X for *khilioi*, one thousand; and (a relatively late arrival)
M for *myrioi*, ten thousand.

Compound numbers for 50, 500, 5,000 and 50,000 were made up of small versions of the ten power being drawn inside a large *Π*. Numbers in between were additive, so that one thousand two hundred and thirty-four, for example, was written XHHΔΔΔ||||. This is how numbers appear on the many official stelai from C5 and C4 Athens.

This was replaced in due course and in mathematical contexts by the alphabetic system, which used a slightly modified Greek alphabet of 27 letters – the ordinary Greek alphabet has only 24 letters, so another 3 were adopted from the Phoenician alphabet.

---

[52] 'Aleph'. ∀ was the symbol for ox: it is clearly the head and horns. In Greek hands, abstracted from ox, it fell over, and then came to be drawn upside down, as A. The original aleph symbol is revived in modern mathematical logic, where it is the standard notation meaning 'for all'.

[53] The contexts in which 'o' appears are fractions or positions in sexagesimal place-value notation, such as the 'Table of straight lines in the circle' (i.e. chords) in *Almagest* 1.11, where Ptolemy needs to indicate nothing in a particular place.

[54] Flegg 1989 pp. 106f. and 110.

[55] This system of numeration is used almost exclusively in inscriptions, and almost exclusively for cardinal numbers; ordinals (first, second, third etc.) are written out in words. The system is otherwise known as the Attic or Herodianic system, after the grammarian Herodianus who first explained it. Its use is not confined to Attika but is found in other areas too, down to about the C2 B.C., and it later continues in sporadic use, much as we still use Roman numerals sometimes. See Ifrah 1985 p. 230 fig.14–23 for the many variations in the signs used in acrophonic systems across Greece (not just the Attic version given in the text here).

α	1	ι	10	ρ	100
β	2	κ	20	σ	200
γ	3	λ	30	τ	300
δ	4	μ	40	υ	400
ε	5	ν	50	φ	500
F	6	ξ	60	χ	600
ζ	7	ο	70	ψ	700
η	8	π	80	ω	800
θ	9	ϙ	90	⋗	900

Fig. 3.1: Greek alphabetic numerals

The first nine letters represent the numbers 1 to 9. The next nine represent the tens from 10 to 90. The third nine letters represent the hundreds from 100 to 900. This is not a place-value system, and large numbers are sometimes written in ascending order, sometimes in descending. So 111, for example, could be written as 'αιρ' or 'ρια'. Since 'α' means 1, 'ι' means 10 and 'ρ' means 100 wherever they stand in the order, the order doesn't really matter. To put it another way and illustrate the point about letters serving as numbers, 111 could be written as 'air' or 'ria'. By transliterating the Greek letters into English ones I trust that 'air' will have been read as 'air' and not as 'one hundred and eleven', despite following immediately upon the statement that this is a way of writing the number 111, and being enclosed in apostrophes, as Greek letters serving as numbers were (usually) signalled by some distinguishing mark. For ancient Greek readers, Greek letters will always have been letters first and mathematical symbols second, whereas for us they are abstract symbols first and Greek letters second.

Moreover, to the Greeks, numbers themselves were less abstract than they are today, particularly the sort of small numbers used commonly in ordinary life. This is best illustrated in the existence of the dual in Greek grammar (when there are two somethings, so singular for one, dual for two, and plural for three or more), and in the fact that Greek numbers up to four (and Roman up to three) are adjectives which are declined to agree with the noun or pronoun in case and gender. Beyond four they are indeclinable,[56] but the inflection

---

[56] Some peoples of the world have had singular, dual, trial (3 somethings), quadrual (four somethings), and then plural for anythings greater than four. [Aristotle] *Problems* 15.3 claims that the Thracians 'alone among men' count in fours 'because their memory, like that of children,

is carried in the definite article which accompanies the number. This reveals how the thing and the quantity of the thing are connected in thought – they must agree. 'One' is even irregular, apparently coming from two different roots: *heis* or *hen*, when the one is male or neuter, but *mia* when it is female.

So far, we have considered some aspects of practical computation and the Greek number system that underpinned them. The number system concerns whole numbers and fractions. In practical computation for building and surveying however, quantities can be more complex. Some arise geometrically as ratios, and turn out to be irrational numbers.[57] A rational number is one which can be expressed as p/q, where p and q are whole numbers and $q \neq 0$. An irrational number cannot be so expressed, e.g. $\sqrt{2}$. The irrationals and their approximation by rationals is an important topic for historians of Greek mathematics for many reasons. Greek geometry involves irrational ratios and measurements that can be manipulated easily by geometrical methods but *not* represented in their number system and therefore in calculations.[58] These ratios arise naturally, commonly involving $\sqrt{2}$, $\sqrt{3}$, . . . or π. It is commonly held that there was a crisis in Greek mathematics caused by the discovery of irrationals, specifically of quantities inexpressible in the number system. This traditional view sees the crisis as causing a shift in the focus of mathematical activity from number (on which e.g. the Pythagoreans had concentrated) to geometry.

Recently this view has been challenged. Fowler has argued that early Greek mathematics (up to the C2 B.C.) was 'completely non-arithmetised',[59] but Knorr disagrees with him.[60] The idea of a crisis in the foundations of Greek mathematics presumes a solid body of Greek arithmetic, the existence of which Fowler disputes. This debate about exactly how the archaic and classical Greeks thought of

cannot extend further and they do not use a large number of anything'. Without counting, our ability to perceive quantities at a glance works up to four, but then quickly deteriorates; this is perhaps why in Greek acrophonic and Roman numerals the symbol for 1 may be repeated up to four times but then there is a change to a (one) new symbol for 5, so that one is not faced with trying to read (rather than count) IIIII. See Ifrah pp. 6–7 and fig. 9-7 over pp. 137–41 illustrating the same phenomenon in the numerical notations used by many early societies.

[57] I use the terms rational and irrational number with their current meanings, which are not those of Euclid. For discussion of the terms see Gow, 1884, pp. 78–9 and Heath *Euclid* vol. 3 pp. 11–12.

[58] Put simply in modern terminology, the Greeks did not construct what we call the real numbers (as with squaring the circle this problem was not satisfactorily resolved until the nineteenth century A.D.).

[59] Fowler 1990, p. 10.

[60] See e.g. Knorr 1991 (following a paper by Fowler), esp. §3.

quantities has implications for and should be related to other disciplines, e.g. architecture and astronomy, which currently presume the traditional view. In architecture, for example, de Jong 1989 argues that the proportions used in temples built before *c.* 400 B.C. are arithmetical (e.g. 1:3), whilst from *c.* 400 B.C. geometrical proportions take over (especially $1:1/2\sqrt{3}$). Meanwhile, in astronomy, Berggren 1991 says that until the mid second century B.C. perfectly adequate arithmetic methods were used in Greek astronomy, whereafter they were succeeded by geometrical (spheric) methods. He suggests that Euclid's *Phainomena* was the first attempt to provide a well-founded (geometric) method for making calculations which had previously been done by arithmetic methods. These calculations included the rising or setting times of certain stars or signs, or the length of daylight at any particular location on any particular day of the year. Berggren suggests that Euclid did this by adapting the preexisting body of knowledge on solid geometry to fit the two-sphere model of Eudoxos (one sphere for earth, with the celestial sphere around it).

3.4 *Geometry*

Geometry is arguably the Greeks' greatest scientific achievement. Unlike, say, Aristotle's physics or Galen's medicine, Euclid's theorems are still true and his methods are still admired. For millennia his books have been studied and referenced, though they are no longer used as a school text-book.[61] He entitled his principal work *Elements*, and it was intended to be a foundational work in the subject, a starting point. The same Greek word (*stoikheia*) also means the letters in the alphabet, and Euclid's elements are to geometry what letters are to language: the building blocks or basic components.

One of the most outstanding features of Euclid's work is its structure: the first book contains a number of definitions, postulates, and common notions, and the following twelve books endeavour to introduce or assume no extraneous material as they progress, but only to construct from definitions and propositions already done. Thus, for any proposition one can trace back the reasoning for a particular result through earlier propositions until one comes back ultimately to the original

---

[61] Until the latter half of the C19, Euclid's *Elements* were unchallenged as a textbook for schools in England; see Richards 1988 chapter 4.

postulates and common notions. This trace can be illustrated by drawing a proof tree, of which an example is given below in Figure 3.3, to illustrate the reasoning for Pythagoras' Theorem. Of course Euclid was not infallible, and there are occasionally holes in the arguments, but these should not be allowed to detract from the overall aim and success of his methods. Another outstanding feature is the thoroughness with which propositions are proved, as will become apparent in the example given below. Let us first review the *Elements*.

Book I builds from twenty-three definitions, five postulates, and nine common notions.[62] The definitions explain the basic terms of geometry, what is meant by words such as 'point' or 'line'. The common notions are axioms or self-evident truths; statements that any sensible person would take as true, although it is not possible to prove them. For example, Common Notion 1 is 'Things which are equal to the same thing are also equal to one another'. The postulates are unproved assertions about geometry. The first three postulates are assertions that amount to the possibility of doing geometry.

Postulate 1. [It is possible] to draw a straight line from any point to any point.
Postulate 2. [It is possible] to produce a finite straight line continuously in a straight line.
Postulate 3. [It is possible] to describe a circle with any centre and diameter.

The fourth and fifth postulates are different: they are premises which the beginner must accept as given, and their validity, and their classification as postulates (rather than as e.g. axioms), have been subjects of contention among mathematicians since antiquity.

Postulate 4. All right angles are equal to one another.
Postulate 5. If a straight line falling on two straight lines make the interior angles on the same sides less than two right angles, the two straight lines, if produced indefinitely, meet on that side on which are the angles less than two right angles.

Euclid thought that this last assertion was undemonstrable, and hence made it a postulate. The fifth (parallel) postulate is notorious. Attempts to prove it from the preceding four started shortly after, and the problem attracted mathematicians for two millennia. This research led to many postulates which are equivalent with the fifth. In Gerolamo Saccheri's

---

[62] In this I am following the manuscripts. All MSS have 9 common notions, but 4 of them are mathematically redundant, and consequently since antiquity their genuineness has been questioned. Most modern texts ignore the redundant ones and say that there are five common notions. But it is precisely their redundancy that argues in favour of the genuineness of these four notions, in my view.

Euclides ab omni naevo vindicatus of 1733 an equivalent postulate is rejected in the hope of deriving a contradiction, and thereby proving the fifth postulate by *reductio ad absurdum*. But the argument failed. Consequently Saccheri's work produced the first theorems of what is called non-Euclidean geometry.[63]

After the definitions, common notions and postulates, Book 1 discusses triangles, parallels and parallelograms. Book 2 gives two more definitions, and then carries on to the transformation of a rectilinear area of any shape into a parallelogram of any shape. Book 3 gives eleven more definitions, to deal with the circle. Book 4 has another seven definitions and moves on to deal with triangles and regular polygons which are drawn inside and around circles. Book 5 gives eighteen more definitions and introduces the theory of ratios, most of which was worked out by Euclid's famous predecessor Eudoxos. Book 6 adds four more definitions and applies the theory of ratios to plane geometry. Books 7, 8, and 9 start with twenty-two definitions at the beginning of Book 7, and then deal with arithmetic and the theory of numbers.[64] Book 10, after four more definitions, deals with the irrationals (ἄλογοι or ἄρρητοι, lit. 'inexpressible'). Books 11, 12, and 13 turn to solid geometry, introduced with twenty-eight definitions. So the entire work of 13 books, covering this huge range of mathematical topics, rests on a mere five postulates and nine common notions. On those few assertions which constitute a minimal undemonstrated bedrock, the framework of ancient geometry was constructed, in belt and braces fashion, proof by proof. It is a tremendous intellectual achievement.

Pythagoras' theorem appears as Proposition 47 in Book 1, and after giving the text I will sketch part of the proof tree, showing how each part of the argument builds upon prior material. Geometry is all about diagrams, and the text of the proposition is easily understood by consulting the diagram constantly. As in botany, a picture can speak a thousand words, and we can *see* that something is true, even if we do not understand the proof that it is so.

---

[63] The development of non-Euclidean geometry belongs to the C19 (e.g. publications by Lobachevskii 1829 and Boyali 1831). For a short review see Gray 1987.

[64] For example, Book 9 Prop. 20 'there are more prime numbers than any number' i.e. the number of prime numbers is infinite.

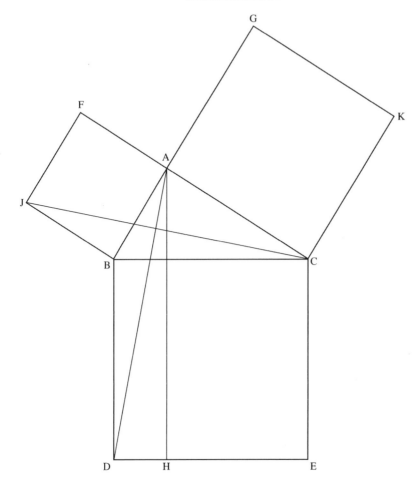

Fig. 3.2: Pythagoras' Theorem

[Proposition]
Let ABC be a right-angled triangle having the angle BAC right; I say that the square on
BC is equal to the squares on BA, AC.
[Proof]
For let there be described on BC the square BDEC, and on BA, AC the squares FB,
GC,[65] and through A let AH be drawn parallel to either BD or CE, and let AD, JC be
joined. Then, since each of the angles BAC, BAF is right, it follows that with a straight
line BA and at the point A on it, two straight lines AC, AF, not lying on the same side,
make the adjacent angles equal to two right angles; therefore CA is in a straight line with
AF.[66] For the same reasons BA is also in a straight line with AG. And since the angle

---

[65] See Prop. 46.   [66] See Prop. 14.

DBC is equal to the angle JBA, for each is right, let the angle ABC be added to each; the whole angle DBA is therefore equal to the whole angle JBC.[67] And since DB is equal to BC, and JB to BA, the two [sides] DB, BA are equal to the two [sides] BC, JB respectively; and the angle DBA is equal to the angle JBC. The base AD is therefore equal to the base JC, and the triangle ABD is equal to the triangle JBC.[68] Now the parallelogram BH is double the triangle ABD, for they have the same base BD and are in the same parallels BD, AH.[69] And the square FB is double the triangle JBC, for they have the same base JB and are in the same parallels JB, FC. Therefore the parallelogram BH is equal to the square FB. Similarly, if AE, BK are joined, it can also be proved that the parallelogram CH is equal to the square GC. Therefore the whole square BDEC is equal to the two squares FB, GC.[70] And the square BDEC is described on BC, while the squares FB, GC are described on BA, AC. Therefore the square on the side BC is equal to the squares on the sides BA, AC.

Therefore in right-angled triangles the square on the side subtending the right angle is equal to the squares on the sides containing the right angle; which was to be proved.[71]

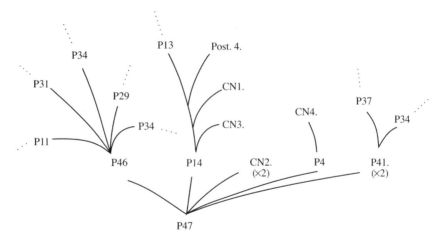

Fig. 3.3: Partial proof tree for Pythagoras' Theorem. Every branch will end, sooner or later, in a definition, postulate, or common notion.

Because of the mathematical importance of the *Elements*, the text and its debt to earlier mathematicians have been discussed in some detail in several general histories of mathematics[72] as well as in histories of Greek mathematics.[73] Such histories are usually addressed to mathematicians.

[67] See Common Notion 2.
[68] See Prop. 4.
[69] See Prop. 41.
[70] See Common Notion 2.
[71] Thomas trans. in the Loeb *Greek Mathematical Works* 1, pp. 179–85, but I have used English letters where Thomas uses Greek.
[72] E.g. by Kline 1972; Boyer and Merzback 1989.
[73] E.g. by Heath, Tannery, van der Waerden, Knorr, and Fowler.

The Greek discovery of geometrical magnitudes that cannot be expressed as rational numbers – such as the diagonal of a square with sides of size one unit – is remarkable. The fact is used twice by Aristotle as a (presumably) well-known example of argument by *reductio ad absurdum* (*Prior Analytics* 1.23.41a26 and 1.44.55.a37), and is clearly older than him. The irrationals present problems for theories of geometric magnitude such as Eudoxos' theory of proportion which underpins *Elements* book 5 and the construction of irrational magnitudes in book 10. The C5 and C4 origins of the theory of incommensurable magnitudes in the works of Pythagoras, Theodoros, Theaitetos, Arkhytas, and Eudoxos has been examined in depth by Knorr 1975.

The presumed arithmetical basis of Greek geometry has been challenged by Fowler in *The Mathematics of Plato's Academy*. For the ancient historian without sufficient maths to follow the technical arguments in detail here (and I am amongst them), we must consider the other arguments used in the debate. Fowler has a very strong such argument in the following: surviving MSS and papyri are all from the end of the C3 B.C. or later, and 99% of them (p. 219) are from the C9 A.D. or later. There are only a few isolated scraps and tatters, amounting to 1% of the total, for the period from the end of the C3 B.C. to the C9 A.D.. People of the C9 A.D. copying old texts available to them but lost to us probably engaged in implicit translation[74] in order to make those ancient texts comprehensible in their own times (we are dealing with a gap of up to and over a thousand years between e.g. Plato or Euclid and these scribes). From this very sound argument Fowler deduces that whatever Greek mathematics was in Plato's or Euclid's times, our evidence is filtered through the light of an arithmetic tradition that entered Greek mathematics only in the C2 B.C., and developed continually, leaving ratio theories aside. This methodological argument can stand alone, and is relevant for ancient science in general, for the same circumstances prevail.[75]

The gaps in Euclid's reasoning are of two kinds. First there are implicit assumptions, some of which qualify as axioms, such as the continuity of lines and circles: if two lines or circles meet, a missing

---

[74] This is not Fowler's term; he talks of numerical material being 'modernised and uniformised in what might then have been considered unimportant ways', 1992, p. 134, and goes on to give, in an illustrated Annex, wonderful examples of similar processes at work in modern editions.

[75] For example, although written (probably) in the mid-C4 A.D., Pelagonius' *Ars veterinaria* survives in one MS, a late C15 copy of a C7 or C8 MS.

postulate is required to say that they do so in a point (rather than in a gap between points). Secondly, some proofs implicitly depend on diagrams that do not depict all possible cases, and so some of the theorems, while true in general, have proofs for special cases only.

The achievement of Euclid's *Elements* is its amazing organization, and the rigour, depth, and scale of its analysis. Modern mathematical standards originate in the *Elements*. The work has a superb order of results, exemplary proofs, a brilliant choice of axioms, and hundreds of theorems. And Euclid has consequently had a profound influence on the development of mathematics and its application, not least through non-Euclidean geometry.

FURTHER READING

There are few modern work on Greek mathematics which do not assume or demand considerable mathematical competence on the part of the reader. A. Aaboe, *Episodes from the Early History of Mathematics* (Washington, 1964) is one of them. It makes comprehensible to non-mathematicians some important mathematical ideas, with examples from Euclid, Archimedes and Ptolemy. L. Bunt, P. Jones, and J. Bedient claim that 'many junior high school students' could follow a substantial part of the mathematics included in their *Historical Roots of Elementary Mathematics* (New Jersey, 1976, reprinted New York, 1988). They also give the ancient texts in both a literal translation and modern notation, with explicit discussion of the differences between them. T. B. L. Heath's *History of Greek Mathematics* (Oxford, 1921, reprinted New York, 1981) remains fundamental. J. Gow, *A Short History of Greek Mathematics* (New York, 1884) is comprehensive and brief. G. de Ste Croix, 'Greek and Roman Accounting' (London, 1956), W. Richardson, *Numbering and Measuring in the Classical World* (Bristol, 1985 and 1992) and O. A. W. Dilke, *Mathematics and Measurement* (London, 1987) are all excellent introductions to mathematics in use in Greek and Roman life. Two new books to look out for are R. Netz, *The Shaping of Deduction in Greek Mathematics* (Cambridge, 1999) and S. Cuomo, *Pappus of Alexandria and the Mathematics of Late Antiquity* (Cambridge, 2000).

Principal primary sources in English translation:

There is an excellent selection of Greek mathematical works in translation by
  I. Thomas, *Greek Mathematical Works*. Loeb 2 vols, 1939 and 1941 (vol. 1
  from Thales to Euclid, vol. 2 from Aristarchus to Pappus).
Apollonios of Perga, *On Conic Sections*. Trans. T. B. L. Heath (Cambridge,
  1896).

Diophantos, *Arithmetika*. Trans. T. B. L. Heath (Cambridge, 1885 and New York, 1964).

Euclid, *The Thirteen Books of Euclid's Elements*. Trans. T. B. L. Heath, 2nd ed., 3 vols. (Cambridge, 1926).

Proclus, *Commentary on the First Book of Euclid's Elements*. Trans. G. R. Morrow (Princeton, 1970).

IV. ASTRONOMY

4.1 *Introduction*

Astronomy is often considered the zenith of 'the exact sciences' in antiquity. Highly mathematical, it is quite distinct from cosmology, and was more concerned with modelling celestial phenomena than with speculation about why the heavens appeared as they did. In modelling the heavens astronomers sought to 'save the phenomena', that is, to 'explain' observations by means of a mathematical construction which located certain celestial bodies at certain places and certain times. Each construction aimed to be systematic – even axiomatic in the Euclidean style – and leave as few as possible 'anomalies', i.e., unexplained phenomena. After centuries of effort by mathematicians and astronomers, Claudius Ptolemy synthesized and developed their achievements to produce the *Almagest*. This is the Arabic name by which his *Mathematical Syntax*, the rules of the motion of the heavens, is better known. It became the bible of astronomy in the West and the Islamic world for the next 1500 years, until displaced in the Copernican Revolution.

Throughout antiquity astronomy was not clearly distinguished from astrology, which grew out of it. Indeed, the same Ptolemy went on to write the bible of astrology, the *Four Books*, or *Tetrabiblos*. Astrology aimed to explain events in a 'rational', 'natural' way, just like other sciences: celestial bodies, principally the sun, moon, and five visible planets, were thought to be the causes of natural phenomena, like the seasons and the tides, and to exert influence over all natural things: plants, minerals, regions of the earth, the people who live there, and parts of the body, for example.[1] It was thought possible to explain and predict astral influences, as eclipses could be explained and predicted.[2] And because of widespread belief in astral influences, astronomical

---

[1] Seneca attributes the majority of errors in astrological predictions to the fact that they were based on just the five planets and did not take adequate account of the fixed stars, *NQ* 2.32.7. The fragments and testimonia concerning Khairemon, one of the earliest surviving authors on ancient astrological ideas [C1 A.D., contemporary with Seneca], have been collected and translated into English recently by van der Horst 1984.

[2] Bowen 1999 argues that predicting eclipses in a precise way – when, where, duration of occultation – was not part of the astronomer's self-defined tasks until the C1 A.D. He sees it growing out of a literary *topos*. I would look also to the growth of astrology, for this is approximately the same period in which personal horoscopy developed.

knowledge had far wider application than it has today – in biology for example.[3] The most obvious application of astronomy is of course to time-keeping.

Before Sosigenes created a purely solar calendar for Julius Caesar's administrative convenience (and that of others wishing to run an empire), knowing exactly whereabouts in the seasonal cycle one was – as opposed to the official date on one or more of the local calendars – required an astronomer. The natural clock offered by the moon does not synchronize with the natural clock offered by the sun, and purely lunar calendars lose coherence with the seasons unless corrected. I am not suggesting that anyone other than astronomers wanted to know the time to within, say, a quarter of an hour.[4] Most ancient time-telling devices[5] were probably used as event markers rather than clocks as such: it is time to do X (meet, for example) when the shadow strikes Y.[6] But periodically all local calendars were corrected to correspond with the seasons, for the very good reason that religious sacrifices needed to be offered at the appropriate time of year.[7] Assuming that the Greeks involved in making these adjustments in democracies behaved like

---

[3] Thompson made what he called 'a somewhat startling' claim that 'very many of [ancient statements concerning animals] deserve not a zoological but an astronomical interpretation', 1895, p. xii.

[4] Hipparkhos observed that even for professional astronomers large errors could arise from the instruments used to measure it, *apud* Ptolemy *Almagest* 3.1: 'In the case of the solstices, I have to admit that both I and Archimedes may have committed errors *of up to a quarter of a day* in our observations and calculations [of the time]', Toomer trans., emphasis added. Ptolemy's attribution of such errors to the 'construction and positioning of the instruments' slightly precedes this quote.

[5] Principally gnomons and sundials, which could be flat or hemispherical, fixed horizontally or vertically, or portable.

[6] Similarly most water clocks were devices to apportion time, on the basis of the time it took for the water in the clepsydra to run out of the hole at the bottom, rather than devices to tell the time of day. Their use in the courts, for example, regulated the duration of speeches: the clock was started when the speaker started, plugged during the reading out of laws, and the speaker had to finish when all the water had run out. In like fashion, Herophilos' portable clepsydra 'measured' the patient's pulse rate.

[7] See Geminos, *Elements of Astronomy* 8. One of Aristophanes' complaints in the *Clouds* (production date 423) is that the *monthly* feasts and festivals are falling on days which do not correspond with the appearance of the moon. He is assuming that the gods of Olympos work with the lunar calendar, which we may suppose to be the traditional one. In the Athens of his day this has been interfered with by political adjustments or set aside in favour of a luni-solar or solar calendar, long enough for a very obvious asynchronization to have developed, and recently enough for Aristophanes to make an issue of it. Meton had offered to sort out the calendar in Athens nine years before Aristophanes produced the *Clouds* (see Diod. Sic. 12.36.2, recording public honours voted to Meton). He came up with his eponymous Metonic cycle of 19 years, and the first cycle started on 13 Skirophorion (the summer solstice) in 432 B.C. This is usually said to have been used only by the astronomers, and did not become the basis for a reformed civil calendar, but it does not follow from this that it was not used for occasional corrections to the civil calendar. Diodorus says that 'even down to our own day, the majority of the Greeks (οἱ πλεῖστοι τῶν Ἑλλήνων) use the

democratic Greeks deciding any other matter, then they would have resolved the matter by argument and evidence, i.e. by application of astronomical theories as understood by *ho boulomenos*.[8] The archon's calendar 'was controlled throughout by the politicians', as Pritchett says forcibly,[9] and in Athens, the politicians were the *politai*, the citizens.

One brilliant politician – Augustus – used astronomy as the basis for a piece of propaganda in an ideological campaign on those he sought to rule: the Horologium Augusti.[10] His association with the heavens, the gods, and time itself, was cemented when the eighth month was named after him, as the seventh had been named after Julius (Caesar). Coming down to earth again, anyone wishing to find their orientation with respect to the compass points, because they were lost, or laying out a new colony,[11] a farmhouse,[12] a temple, a body, or anything else that they wanted to align in a particular direction, could use a fragment of astronomical theory to settle the matter accurately, simply by pushing a stick in the ground and noting the position of its shadow on two moments either side of midday. And on the edges of the known world, explorers with a little astronomical knowledge could work out their latitude, so know at least how far north round the globe of the earth they were.

nineteen-year cycle' 12.36.3. Diodorus may not be the best historian from antiquity, but he did his research at the Library at Alexandria and had access to much material which has been lost to us. Corrections to the calendar in our own time may deal with seconds rather than months, but such correction is *still* necessary and is necessarily sporadic. Meton is actually a character in Aristophanes' *Birds* (produced 414), and does geometry at lines 1000 ff. On his water clock see Bowen and Goldstein (1989) p. 77.

[8] Such adjustments could involve dropping or adding months, not a mere 11 days (which caused so much upset for Pope Gregory's contemporaries). In Athens intercalations were made by the archon, and the calendar so adjusted was the one known as the archon's calendar. He made adjustments by moving the peg in the official *parapegma* (labelled board) the required number of slots forward or backward; on *parapegma* see Neugebauer 1975 vol.1 pp. 587–9. There were two other calendars in operation in Athens simultaneously: 1. the prytany calendar, of 10 months of 36 or 35 days each (*Ath. Pol.* 43.2), by which the ten tribes of Athens took turns to be presidents of the state; 2. the *kata theon* ('according to the god') calendar, the nature of which is disputed. See Pritchett 1963 esp. §4.

[9] Pritchett 1963 p. 339.

[10] Dedicated in 10/9 B.C. Some important remaining parts were found and published by its excavator, Buchner 1982. Besides being emperor, Augustus also had responsibility for keeping the civil calendar in step with the seasons (*qua* Pontifex Maximus), which at this date meant fine-tuning Caesar's system. This monumental sundial, next to the Ara Pacis, combined time-keeping and ideological (religious as well as political) functions. The ideological function was obvious to Cicero when Caesar first introduced this calendar: 'the heavens have to obey the dictator', Plutarch, *Caesar* 59.

[11] Astronomy was part of the formal education of the Roman *agrimensores*, on which see Dilke 1971 chapter 4.

[12] Besides optimizing solar gain in winter and cool shade in summer for the residents of the building, the importance of correct aspect for storage rooms of different products is stressed by most of the agricultural writers. See e.g. Columella on the olive-oil store.

Modern works in this area tend to be focused on *either* astronomy *or* astrology,[13] and there is very little modern literature on astronomy and other subjects, with the obvious exception of its application to calendar-making.[14] These studies, like works on astronomy generally, tend to be highly technical works demanding fluent numeracy on the part of their readers, and they sometimes lose sight of the everyday life aspects, even of time-keeping.

I shall divide up the subject into mapping the heavens and modelling the heavens, though there is some overlap between them. The latter includes a look at Aristarkhos' calculation of the distance of the sun from earth – all done with a handful of simple hypotheses and some squares – which shows well what can be done with a little geometry and a lot of imagination. Finally I turn to a different sort of text altogether, Plutarch's discussion of the face in the moon.

4.2 *Mapping the Heavens*

Theorizing about the nature and motion of the stars considerably preceded precise data-gathering, including developing a system of co-ordinates by which to locate accurately the position of celestial bodies. Eudoxos, for example, proposed his system of concentric spheres and the *hippopede* to explain planetary motion without having first observed carefully even where the centre of the heavens was.[15] Not surprisingly then, radically different explanations were offered by early astronomers for the same phenomena. Even when better data was available, it was sometimes impossible to choose between theories on the basis of observation, as the best of those who argued such cases recognized.

The accumulation of the basic data of astronomy, especially the movement of sun and moon and the location and brightness of the

[13] For example, Neugebauer 1975 or Barton 1994.
[14] E.g. Samuel 1972.
[15] See n. 18 below. Eudoxos had produced a (lost) description of the heavens, which Aratos versified, but its style and content must have been very similar to Aratos' surviving *Phainomena*. Hipparkhos considered them together in his *Commentary on the Phainomena of Aratus and Eudoxus*, and says explicitly 'Now Eudoxus gives the same collection of phenomena as Aratus, but has set them forth with greater knowledge . . . It is, perhaps, not fair to blame Aratos if in some points he is found to be in error; for in writing his *Phainomena* he has followed the arrangement of Eudoxos, without making any observations on his own account, and without professing to be speaking with the authority of a mathematician when giving details of celestial happenings which afterwards prove to be inaccurate . . . that Aratos followed Eudoxos' account of the phenomena may be gathered by comparing, at length, Eudoxos' text with that of the poem dealing with the same topic in each case . . . they practically agree in all but a very few details' [four examples follow], Heath trans. 1932 pp. 117–18.

fixed and the wandering stars, took many centuries. The wandering stars were the stars which seemed to move erratically, sometimes stopping and going backwards and then stopping and going forwards again; we call them the planets. Their movements (and the moon's) were ever a problem to explain, and the challenge of modelling their motions attracted the attention of some of the best mathematical minds, e.g. Eudoxos and Euclid.[16] But even the fixed stars were 'located' only in very vague terms (such as 'near X is Y') for a long time. Hesiod (*Works and Days*) and his contemporaries had talked of the risings and settings of the major constellations in the seventh century B.C., yet there was still no good system for identifying particular stars and where to find them in the sky five hundred years later. Then in the C2 B.C. Hipparkhos set about making a star catalogue,[17] and tried to give with reasonable accuracy *some* locational co-ordinates – inconsistently using several different reference systems, mostly declinations – for about half of the 850 stars he identified. Ptolemy added about 170 more stars about 200 years later, and used one system of proper co-ordinates (ecliptic longitudes and latitudes) for them all. His astronomy superseded all that had gone before and became the orthodox account of the heavens for the next 1500 years.

When the Greeks looked up at the night sky, what they saw was not what we see today. The most obvious difference is that the star Polaris was not the centre around which the heavens rotated. In Perikles' time Polaris was just another circumpolar star, travelling round in a circle about the celestial north pole, which at that time lay at a spot unmarked by a star in the sky, as Hipparkhos asserted against Eudoxos.[18] So there was no pole *star* as such. About 400 B.C., the celestial north pole was about twice as far from Kochab (β UMi), the star at the other end of Ursa Minor from Polaris, as is Pherkad (γ UMi), the other star at that end of Ursa Minor, and in the opposite direction from Pherkad.

---

[16] Eudoxos' work survives only in fragments, bits quoted or paraphrased by later authors. For discussion of his ideas and contribution to Greek astronomy, see Neugebauer, 1975, vol. 2 pp. 675–83. For Euclid's *Phainomena* see Health 1921 vol. 1 pp. 348–53 and 440–1. Both are excerpted and translated in Heath 1932 pp. 65–7 and 96–100 respectively.

[17] On which see Neugebauer 1975 1 pp. 277–88.

[18] *Comm. on the Phainomena of Aratos and Eudoxos* 1.4.1: 'In fact there is no star at the pole but an empty space close to which three stars lie, which together with the point of the pole make a rough quadrangle, as Pytheas of Massilia [better known as an explorer] tells us', trans. Heath 1932 p. 119, who thought the stars in question were probably Draco α and κ and UMin β; Roseman 1994 pp. 118–19 prefers nearer stars of lesser magnitude. Eudoxos' error had been repeated by Euclid, *Phainomena* Pref. 'But a certain star is seen between the Bears which does not change from place to place, but turns about the position where it is.'

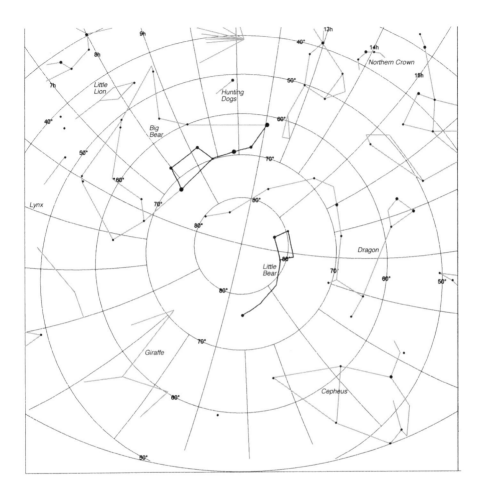

Fig. 4.1: The celestial north pole, as seen from Athens, *c.* 400 B.C. Produced by permission using Cybersky, www.cybersky.com.

So the two stars forming the back end of the little dipper could be used as a pointer to the celestial north pole, just as the back end of the big dipper is now used to point to Polaris. For this reason these end stars in Ursa Minor were known for centuries as 'the guardians of the pole',[19] they circled it fairly tightly (about two thumbspans). According to

[19] Jones 1995 p. 49. He does not say by whom they were thus known, but it would appear to be the Phoenicians (see the sources about to be cited in text). Nor is a date given for this label, but the stars would have lined up with the pole around the time of Christ, and would have orbited it tightly for centuries either side of that.

Diogenes Laertius (1.23), Thales first drew the Greeks' attention to the fact that while Greek sailors navigated by Ursa Major, the Phoenicians used Ursa Minor. Aratos confirms the distinction for his own times (C3 B.C.):

Encompassing it [the north celestial pole] and together circling round it are the two Bears, which are called Wagons[20] . . . Now the one men call by the name of Cynosura,[21] the other they call Helike.[22] It is by Helike that the Achaians on the sea judge where to direct the course of their ships, while the Phoenicians put their trust in the other as they cross the sea.[23] Now Helike is clear and easy to recognize, being large and visible from earliest nightfall; the other is smaller and yet better for sailors, for the whole of it turns in a lesser circuit, and by it the men of Sidon steer the straightest course.[24]

The anonymous *Aetna* suggests that the educated Roman layman of the C1 B.C. still used Ursa Major as a guide to the pole:

Not cattle-like to gaze on the world's marvels merely with the eye, not to lie outstretched upon the ground feeding a weight of flesh, but to grasp the proof of things and search into doubtful causes, to hallow genius, to raise the head to the sky, to know the number and character of natal elements in the mighty universe . . . to know the axle of Helice . . . [to know] under what constellation the sailor must furl or spread his sails, to know the paths of the sea and learn betimes the course of the heavens . . . (224–9, 242, 245–6, Duff trans.).

The apparent centre of the heavens has moved, and it was Hipparkhos who first realized that it was moving, ever so slowly, at about 1° every 100 years he thought. This phenomenon is called the precession of the equinoxes, and it is caused by the earth's polar axis (which tilts) rotating about a true vertical axis very slowly.[25] According to modern computations, a complete revolution takes about 25,800 years. Hipparkhos did not *observe* this movement: it could only be detected by comparison of then-current star positions with old records of star locations. The records

[20] This name is surely descriptive of their shape. An explanation for how the Greek name Bear could have derived from a Near Eastern word for wagon is given in Kidd 1997 p. 187, line 27.

[21] Literally, 'dog's tail': Ursa Minor.

[22] Literally, 'helix'; something with a spiral shape, which goes round, circles, coils. This is the first appearance of this name and surely reflects its circumpolar motion; Homer calls it the Bear. See Kidd 1997 p. 188, line 37.

[23] When mariners had the courage to cross open waters the positions of the sun or the stars were their navigational guides. Deep-water archaeology is re-writing the picture of ancient trade in the Mediterranean, which (as is now apparent) did not always tramp round the coasts in shallow waters but sometimes struck out for a direct crossing.

[24] *Phainomena* 26–44, Mair trans. slightly modified.

[25] Think of an earth globe and the tilt of the poles; they point 23.5° off the vertical. Rotate the globe's *stand* around 360° and you have this motion. As it moves round, the pole will point to different parts of the ceiling, describing a circle. So in reality earth's north pole points toward different parts of the sky, describing a cone from the centre of the earth 47° in diameter over the course of nearly 26,000 years.

used by Hipparkhos had been made by Timokharis of Alexandria about 170 years earlier, in 294 and 282 B.C. Precession determines that the circumpolar stars have changed, and some stars which were always visible from Greece are no longer so, but dip beneath the horizon for part of the year, while others which were never visible are so now.

A less obvious but equally important difference between ancient observations of the sky and those made in the present is that all the Greeks could see was what they could see with the naked, unassisted, eye: there were no optical lenses in antiquity, to enhance the sight of someone with 20/20 vision, or to correct defective eyesight. Lentoids, sometimes called lenses, are more convincingly explained as eyes for sculptures and other decorative pieces than as optical quality lenses.[26] Burning glasses, on the other hand, which are essentially the same shape, did exist, at least from Aristophanes' time (*Clouds* 771–3), to start fires by concentrating the rays of the sun. Images, including 'tiny and obscure writing' could be magnified by viewing them through a glass ball filled with water, and magnifying mirrors existed (Seneca *NQ* 1.6.5 and 15.7 respectively). The absence of light pollution may have compensated for unassisted observation in terms of the average person's perception of the fainter and transient lights in the sky, but atmospheric pollution, at least in some areas, could have been worse than in modern Britain.[27]

Measurements could be made by very rough and ready methods, such as using body parts for estimates, or by very sophisticated methods, such as constructing a celestial sphere following Ptolemy's text.[28] The adult's hand is an adequate tool for many purposes. Held up to the sky at arm's length, the tip of a finger (at the nail) covers about 1°; the fist about 10°. Observations of eclipses without damaging the eyes were made possible by viewing the events in a basin of pitch or thick oil (Seneca *NQ* 1.12.1). Ptolemy's instruments for accurate observations, on the other hand, need expert machining to work properly, even the 'simple' pieces of apparatus (see e.g. *Almagest* 1.12, 5.12), never mind the astrolabe (5.1) or globe (8.3).[29] The famous Antikythera mechanism was a C1 B.C.

---

[26] See Plantzos 1997.

[27] The range of meteoric phenomena distinguished (e.g. in Aristotle's *Meteorology* book 1; 'burning flames', 'shooting stars', 'torches', 'goats', 'chasms', 'trenches', 'comets', 'bearded stars' and 'haloes') illustrates the former point. For the latter, deposits in the polar ice-caps reveal that global atmospheric lead pollution was worse in Roman times than at *any* other time in history.

[28] Archimedes wrote a treatise (lost) *On Sphere-making*, and Cicero mentions both Archimedes' and Poseidonios' own spheres in *De Natura Deorum* 2.88, *Rep* 1.21 and 1.28, and *Tusc. Disp.* 1.63.

[29] On such instruments see de Solla Price 1957; also Maddison 1963.

'calendar-computer', with fantastically complicated interlocking bronze cog wheels designed to show on the display plate the positions of the sun and moon, and the risings and settings of major constellations, set to the Metonic cycle of 19 years.[30]

Numerous small errors in ancient observations of the night sky (not just those made by poets like Hesiod; also people like Euclid) must sometimes derive from the fact that observations were made with the naked eye and roughly 'measured' angles. The ancients themselves were aware of this: Hipparkhos, for example, commented on the unreliability of the data.[31] His discovery of precession was based on a shift of a mere 2° in the position of Spica relative to the autumnal equinox, and he was rightly cautious about the accuracy of the old records he depended upon. It would have been easy for him to dismiss Timokharis' figures as ever so slightly inaccurate.

4.3 *Modelling the Heavens*

Herakleides of Pontus[32] was the first person we know to take the amazing anti-intuitive leap and think the unthinkable: day and night are caused not by the rotation of sun and stars around a stationary us, but by *earth* rotating on its axis, to face alternately towards and away from the stationary sun. Most people thought he was crazy because they realized that the speed we would have to be travelling at, just from axial rotation, would be very high, and that didn't fit with anyone's experience of watching the world go by.[33] As Ptolemy states:

Although there is perhaps nothing in the celestial phenomena which would count against that hypothesis, at least from simpler considerations, nevertheless from what would occur here on earth and in the air, one can see that such a notion is quite ridiculous. Let us concede to them [for the sake of argument] that such an unnatural thing could happen as that the most rare and light of matter [stars etc.] should either not move at all or should move in a way no different from that of matter with the opposite

---

[30] On which see de Solla Price 1975.

[31] e.g. 'In *On the Length of the Year* [Hipparkhos] assumes only the motion which takes place about the poles of the ecliptic, although he is still dubious, as he himself declares, both because the observations of the school of Timokharis are not trustworthy, having been made very crudely, and because the difference in time between [Timokharis and himself] is not sufficient to provide a secure result', Ptolemy *Almagest* 7.3 Toomer trans. See also n. 4 above.

[32] On whom see Gottschalk 1980.

[33] The alternative is of course that the celestial sphere is rotating even faster, but this was acceptable. Indeed, it was even used by Nigidius 'the potter' as an argument in defence of astrology to explain why twins can be so different. Augustine *City of God* 5.3 reports Nigidius' demonstration of the point using a potter's wheel.

nature (although things in the air, which are less rare [than the heavens] obviously move with a more rapid motion than any earthly object);[34] [let us also concede that] the densest and heaviest objects have a proper motion of the quick and uniform kind which they suppose (although again, as all agree, earthly objects are sometimes not readily moved even by an external force). Nevertheless, they would have to admit that the revolving motion of the earth must be the most violent of all motions associated with it, seeing that it makes one revolution in such a short time; the result would be that all objects not actually standing on the earth would appear to have the same motion, opposite to that of the earth: neither clouds nor other flying or thrown objects would ever be seen moving towards the east, since the earth's motion towards the east would always outrun and overtake them, so that all other objects would seem to move in the direction of the west and the rear. But if they said that the air is carried round in the same direction and with the same speed as the earth, the compound objects in the air would none the less always seem to be left behind by the motion of both [the earth and the air]; or if those objects too were carried round, fused, as it were, to the air, then they would never appear to have any motion either in advance or rearwards: they would always appear still, neither wandering nor changing position, whether they were flying or thrown objects. Yet we quite plainly see that they do undergo all these kinds of motion, in such a way that they are not even slowed down or speeded up at all by any motion of the earth. (1.7, Toomer trans.)

But certain people,[35] propounding what they consider to be a more persuasive view, suppose that nothing is stationary and that there is no middle place in the universe. They suppose that the earth revolves around the sun, making one revolution in a year, and that the sun revolves around the Milky Way, taking 200 million years to complete one revolution, and that the Milky Way is flying though space towards the Centaurus constellation. But if this were the case, then the earth would be travelling around the sun at about 67,000 mph,[36] and the solar system would be travelling around the Milky Way at about 515,000 mph,[37] and the Milky Way would be moving across space at about 1,342,000 mph.[38] 'But such things are utterly ridiculous even to think of', Ptolemy would have said.

---

[34] This and the next clause in the argument are based on the notion of natural motion, according to which one would expect light things to move quickly and heavy things to move slowly. Axial rotation theory implies an 'unnatural' reversal of this situation, with rapidly moving earth and stationary stars.

[35] This paragraph is a paraphrase of Ptolemy's comments which lead into the section 1.7 quoted above, which I have rewritten to give the modern view of these matters. 'Certain people' here means all modern astronomers and astrophysicists. In the original version, Ptolemy presumably meant Herakleides of Pontus, Aristarkhos of Samos, and Seleukos of Seleukia at least, but he omits their names and anonymizes them.

[36] ≈ 30 km/s in Kaufmann 1994 p. 146.

[37] ≈ 230 km/s in Kaufmann 1994 p. 312; see p. 464 for the duration of this revolution.

[38] ≈ 600 km/s in Kaufmann 1994 p. 533.

Such things run counter to our intuitions, our common-sense, and our experience of the cosmos and our place in it. Look out of the window: are we *really* travelling at nearly 2,000,000 miles per hour? Look up into a clear night sky: Cassiopeia is there, a big W, as always, like clockwork, slowing circling the pole around which the heavens rotate each year, every year. If we are moving so far and so fast, why doesn't the night sky change, you might ask, quite reasonably expecting the appearance of something to change as we change our viewing position (a phenomenon called parallax). This is the same question that people asked of Aristarkhos' radical idea (heliocentric theory) that we go round the sun, and not the sun round us. And the answer then and now is essentially the same: the appearance of the heavens doesn't change because the stars are so far away that the earth has to them the same relation that a point has to the sphere in which the moon or stars move. In other words, the universe is so big that the movement of the earth is insignificant in observational terms.

Ptolemy, and almost everyone else[39] in antiquity and the Middle Ages, thought that this answer was clever but nonsensical.[40] Most of us, I think, would side with them *if* we relied on our senses and were not so well trained as to accept, without too much fuss, what the experts say. And so, if we consider the implications of what our experts tell us is the case, then we accept that we are on a small planet, one of nine, going round a star, which is one of millions of stars, in a galaxy, which is one of millions of galaxies, in a universe which is vastly bigger than the one that Aristarkhos had to suppose, Archimedes could count grains of sand in, and almost everybody else rejected as ridiculous. It is by thinking about parallax (which is observable, by the way, but not with the naked eye) or rather *its implications*[41] that we can perhaps best comprehend why astronomical theories sometimes impinge on people's beliefs, and attitudes to life in general, to such an extent that astronomers have been lampooned, as Aristophanes lampooned Sokrates in the *Clouds*, or prosecuted, as Kleanthes thought Aristarkhos should have been but evidently wasn't.

Who am I? Why am I here? Who cares? Is there a god? The answers

[39] Ekphantos, Hiketas, Aristarkhos and Seleukos sided with Herakleides. In addition, before and after Herakleides the Pythagoreans (who numbered many) believed that the earth did not occupy the middle of the universe, but orbited a central fire; therefore they must have had some answer to the sort of objections raised by Ptolemy.

[40] See the discussion of this point by Hanson 1973 pp. 18–21.

[41] Specifically, just *how* far away the stars must be and just *how* big the universe must be for our ever-changing position not to have any apparent observational effect.

to these sorts of questions tend to be very different depending on whether I think I am on the only inhabited place, sitting pretty in the centre of a bounded universe; whether I think I am too ignoble to occupy such a place (as the Pythagoreans did), so must be in orbit around the most noble thing in the cosmos (an invisible central hearth in Pythagoreanism); or whether I think I am on a fleck of stellar dust, somewhere (relatively speaking) in a boundless vastness, which will end in freezing darkness with the last visible star fading from sight as the universe flies apart. The first view puts humans at the centre of everything. The middle view puts humans in what the Pythagoreans considered to be an appropriate place in the cosmos. The last view renders humans insignificant.

Some ancients were persuaded by Herakleides' arguments. One amongst them was Aristarkhos, who is sometimes known as the Copernicus of antiquity because he suggested that the earth orbits the sun, and not vice versa. Unfortunately, we do not even know the name of the book in which he hypothesized this, never mind have a text surviving. What we do have is his treatise *On the Sizes and Distances of the Sun and the Moon*. This was not perhaps the first attempt at such a calculation, and it was certainly not the best in terms of agreement with modern figures – for the size and distance of the sun, that honour goes to Poseidonios; for the size and distance of the moon, to Ptolemy. But Aristarkhos's method is an ingenious early attempt to quantify celestial phenomena, and, if one changes Hypothesis 4 from 87° to 89° 50', then one gets (as near as matters) the right answer! It also has the advantage of being easily reproducible: one can contemplate the method by observing any full moon or half moon, both of which occur once a month – or indeed the moon in any state when it is visible during daylight, so that one can see both the moon and sun simultaneously, as happens not infrequently. As the Greeks themselves observed,[42] the atmosphere around the earth distorts light rays, so whilst one may thus contemplate the method, achieving accuracy is not quite as straightforward as it might appear.

The argument is not difficult to follow if you take your time and keep relating the text to the figure. Readers without trigonometry will find

---

[42] In the context of a lunar eclipse. Since a lunar eclipse is caused by the earth passing between sun and moon, it should not be possible to observe both sun and eclipsed moon simultaneously; the fact that on occasion both were visible simultaneously suggested to some that light rays were bent by earth's atmosphere. See Kleomedes, *De motu circulari* 2.6, conveniently in translation in Heath 1932 pp. 162–6, and discussed by Pederson and Pihl 1974 p. 135.

that it is easier to follow Aristarkhos than it is to follow some modern discussions of this computation.[43]

[Hypotheses]

1. That the moon receives its light from the sun.
2. That the earth is in the relation of a point and centre to the sphere in which the moon moves.
3. That, when the moon appears to us halved, the great circle which divides the dark and the bright portions of the moon is in the direction of our eye.
4. That, when the moon appears to us halved, its distance from the sun is then less than a quadrant by one thirtieth of a quadrant.[44]
5. That the breadth of the [earth's] shadow is [that] of two moons.
6. That the moon subtends one fifteenth part of a sign of the zodiac.[45]

We are now in a position to prove the following propositions:

1. The distance of the sun from the earth is greater than eighteen times, but less than twenty times, the distance of the moon [from the earth]; this follows from the hypothesis about the halved moon.
2. The diameter of the sun has the same ratio [as aforesaid] to the diameter of the moon.
3. The diameter of the sun has to the diameter of the earth a ratio greater than that which 19 has to 3, but less than that which 43 has to 6; this follows from the ratio thus discovered between the distances, the hypothesis about the shadow, and the hypothesis that the moon subtends one fifteenth part of a sign of the zodiac.

[Proposition] 7.

The distance of the sun from the earth is greater than eighteen times, but less than twenty times, the distance of the moon from the earth.

For let A be the centre of the sun, B that of the earth. Let AB be joined and produced. Let C be the centre of the moon when halved; let a plane be carried through AB and C, and let the section made by it in the sphere on which the centre of the sun moves[46] be the great circle ADE. Let AC,CB be joined, and let BC be produced to D. Then, because the point C is the centre of the moon when halved, the angle ACB will be right. Let BE be drawn from B at right angles to BA; then the circumference ED will be one thirtieth of the circumference EDA; for, by hypothesis [4], when the moon appears to us halved, its distance from the sun is less than a quadrant by one thirtieth of a quadrant. Thus the

---

[43] There was no trigonometry in Aristarkhos' time. With modern trigonometry (specifically the cosine function) it is quick and easy to prove Aristarkhos' Proposition 7 from his hypotheses. The origins of trigonometry can be found in the chord functions developed and used by Hipparkhos, Menelaos, and later Ptolemy, who drew up tables of their values to enable them to compute astronomical data.

[44] A quadrant is a quarter of a circle. If we divide it into 360°, a quadrant is then 90°, and one thirtieth of that is 3°. Therefore Aristarkhos hypothesizes that the angle is 87°. If you substitute 'less than a quadrant by one five hundred and fortieth of a quadrant' (89° 50') in the rest of the computation, then you'll get the modern figure, as near as matters.

[45] A sign of the zodiac is one twelfth of 360°, so 30°. One fifteenth of that is 2°.

[46] Although Aristarkhos proposed heliocentric theory, he here assumes a geocentric model; the sun A moves round a stationary earth B.

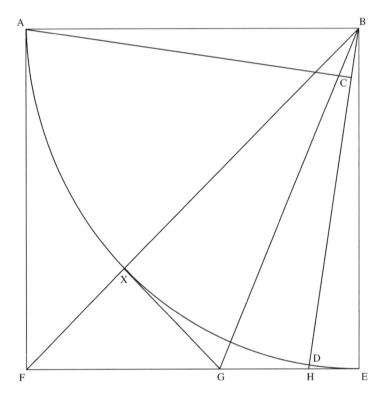

Fig. 4.2: Aristarchus on the distance of the sun.

angle EBC is also one thirtieth of a right angle. Let the parallelogram AE be completed, and let BF be joined. Then the angle FBE will be half a right angle. Let the angle FBE be bisected by the straight line BG; therefore the angle GBE is one fourth part of a right angle. But the angle DBE is also one thirtieth part of a right angle; therefore the ratio of the angle GBE to the angle DBE is that which 15 has to 2; for, if a right angle be regarded as divided into 60 equal parts, the angle GBE contains 15 of such parts, and the angle DBE contains 2. Now, since GE has to EH[47] a ratio greater than that which the angle GBE has to the angle DBE, therefore GE has to EH a ratio greater than that which 15 has to 2. Next, since BE is equal to EF, and the angle at E is right, therefore the square on FB is double of the square on BE.[48] But, as the square on FB is to the square on BE, so is the square on FG to the square on GE,[49] therefore the square on FG is

[47] Aristarkhos has neglected to tell us where to put H. From the demonstration as a whole it becomes clear that it is the point where an extension of BD cuts FE.

[48] By Pythagoras' Theorem, for which see chapter 3 (Mathematics).

[49] Aristarkhos assumes the reader knows this to be true. It can be demonstrated by adding one point, X, to the diagram, and one line, GX. Since G is found by bisecting FBE, GX and GE are equal. FG is the hypotenuse of the triangle FXG, and X is a right angle. Therefore FG is to XG as

double of the square on GE. Now 49 is less than double of 25, so that the square on FG has to the square on GE a ratio greater than that which 49 has to 25; therefore FG also has to GE a ratio greater than that which 7 has to 5.[50] Therefore [adding the 5 of GE to the 7 of FG to produce the total for FE][51] FE has to EG a ratio greater than that which 12 has to 5, that is, than that which 36 has to 15.[52] But it was also proved that GE has to EH a ratio greater than that which 15 has to 2; therefore, equally, FE has to EH a ratio greater than that which 36 has to 2, that is,[53] than that which 18 has to 1; therefore FE is greater than 18 times EH. And FE is equal to BE; therefore BE is also greater than 18 times EH; therefore BH is much greater than 18 times HE. But, as BH is to HE, so is AB to BC, because of the similarity of the triangles; therefore AB is also greater than 18 times BC. And AB is the distance of the sun from the earth, while CB is the distance of the moon from the earth; therefore the distance of the sun from the earth is greater than 18 times the distance of the moon from the earth.

Again, I say that it is also less than 20 times that distance. [Heath trans. The demonstration follows.]

It is worth noticing that the essential geometry for this *tour de force* – that the moon receives its light from the sun (hypothesis 1) and that when the moon appears halved the great circle which divides the dark and bright portions is in the direction of our eye (hypothesis 3) – is given in a more clumsy form in [Aristotle] *Problems* 15.7.

4.4 *Aperitifs and astrophysics*

Plutarch's long book *On the Face in the Orb of the Moon* is an extraordinary piece of literature. The scene is a dinner party, and the text pretends to be a discussion between the diners. The intended audience, one assumes, is the educated elite of the Roman empire. One of the speakers, appropriately called Aristotle, represents the Peripatetic view of things; another, Pharnakes, represents Stoicism; another, Lucius, brings in Pythagoreanism but generally takes a Platonic stance; two others, Apollonides and Menelaos, represent expert mathematical astronomers; another, Theon, represents literary critics;

FB is to FE. Since XG and GE are equal, so FG is to GE as FB is to FE. Note that Aristarkhos is working with squares on the lines, and only reduces to the roots, the lines, in the next step of the argument.

[50] The square roots of 49 and 25 respectively. He needed to choose numbers with integer square roots in the same proportions as his ratios, and he opted for 49 as not quite (less than) 50, which is double 25.

[51] Additional to Heath's translation, which has *componendo* here.

[52] Aristarkhos now multiplies both by 3, to compare with the 15 as a figure for the quarter of a right angle of 60 parts (done above).

[53] Dividing both by 2.

another, Sulla, stands for the mythographers; and finally Lamprias, the main speaker and the 'I' of the dialogue, is Plutarch's brother, and perhaps stands for the educated layman. What is extraordinary about this text from the point of view of Greek science is not merely what it states, which is surprising enough, but also what it doesn't say explicitly: what knowledge it assumes of its audience.

The text is mentioned most frequently in the modern literature for a paragraph in which one speaker comments that Kleanthes the Stoic philosopher thought that Aristarkhos should have been prosecuted for impiety for moving the earth from the centre of the heavens. Since references to Aristarkhos (by name) in ancient literature are few and far between, and references to clashes between science and religion are fewer still, it is understandable that these few sentences get highlighted, even if they are very unrepresentative of ancient concerns. But they are not even representative of this text, or of the participants' opinions on Aristarkhos's bold suggestion that the sun, not the earth, is the centre of the cosmos. What this discussion really shows, and should be emphasized, is that what then passed for astrophysics is a suitable subject of conversation at a dinner party, and that everyone present knows a fair amount about it, and other topics in natural history.

They discuss, for example, the theoretical implications and consequences of various theories on planetary motion and speed of travel, on optics, on possible inhabitants of the moon, on the nature of the stars (where Plutarch scores points off Aristotle with his notions of natural place and levity), and the nature and behaviour of matter more generally. In this dinner party piece – not a scientific treatise – we find the nearest thing in all surviving ancient literature to the concept of gravity. All the participants are also sufficiently familiar with literature to be able to quote from memory e.g. lines from the Attic tragedians or Pindar's odes, the sort of literature we more commonly associate with sympotic discussions. Although they each have special interests, they are all polymaths by today's standards. Let us allow them to speak for themselves, in an excerpt which gives some of the flavour of this long text:

Pharnakes spoke: 'Here we are faced again with that stock manoeuvre of the Academy: on each occasion that they engage in discourse with others they will not offer any accounting of their own assertions but must keep their interlocutors on the defensive lest they become prosecutors. Well, me you will not today entice into defending the Stoics against your charges until I have called you people to account for turning the world upside down.' Thereupon Lucius laughed and said: 'Oh, sir, just don't bring suit against us for impiety as Kleanthes thought that the Greeks ought to lay an action for impiety against Aristarkhos the Samian on the ground that he was disturbing the hearth of the universe because he sought to save [the] phenomena by assuming that the heaven is at rest while the earth is revolving along the ecliptic and at the same time is rotating about its own axis. We express no opinion of our own now; but those who suppose that the moon is earth, why do they, my dear sir, turn things upside down any more than you do who station the earth here suspended in the air? Yet the earth is a great deal larger than the moon according to the mathematicians[54] who during the occurrences of eclipses and the transits of the moon through the shadow calculate her magnitude by the length of time that she is obscured. For the shadow of the earth grows smaller the further it extends, because the body that casts the light is larger than the earth; and that the upper part of the shadow itself is tapered and narrow was recognized, as they say, even by Homer, who called night "nimble" because of the "sharpness" of the shadow. Yet captured by this part in eclipses the moon barely escapes from it in a space thrice her own magnitude. Consider then how many times as large as the moon the earth is, if the earth casts a shadow which at its narrowest is thrice as broad as the moon. All the same, you fear for the moon lest it fall; whereas concerning the earth perhaps Aiskhulos has persuaded you that Atlas

> Stands, staying on his back the prop of earth
> And sky, no tender burden to embrace.

Or, while under the moon there stretches air unsubstantial and incapable of supporting a solid mass, the earth, as Pindar says, is encompassed by "steel-shod pillars"; and therefore Pharnakes is himself without any fear that the earth may fall but is sorry for the Ethiopians or Taprobanians,[55] who are situated under the circuit of the moon, lest such a great weight fall upon them. Yet the moon is saved from falling by its very motion and the rapidity of its revolution, just as missiles placed in slings are kept from falling by being whirled around in a circle. For each thing is governed by its natural motion unless it be diverted by something else. That is why the moon is not governed by its weight: the weight has its influence frustrated by the rotary motion. Nay, there would be more reason perhaps to wonder if she were absolutely unmoved and stationary like the earth. As it is, while [the] moon has good cause for not moving in this direction, the influence of weight alone might reasonably move the earth, since it has no part in any other motion; and the earth is heavier than the moon not merely in proportion to its greater size but still more, inasmuch as the moon has, of course, become light through the action of heat and fire. In short, your own statements seem to make the moon, if it is fire, stand in greater need of earth, that is of matter to serve it as a foundation, as something to which to adhere, as something to lend it coherence, and as something that can be ignited by it, for it is impossible to imagine fire being maintained without fuel, but you people say that earth does abide without roof or foundation.' 'Certainly it does', said Pharnakes, 'in occupying the proper and natural place that belongs to it, the middle, for this is the place about which all weights in their natural inclination press against one another and

---

[54] *Mathematikoi* usually means more generally 'learned men'. Intellectual life was not such that learned men pursued one, and only one, subject. Some, however, had greater facility with mathematics than most, and these are clearly the sort of people Lucius has in mind here.

[55] Taprobane is Sri Lanka. Eratosthenes had located it on the same parallel as Ethiopia.

towards which they move and converge from every direction, whereas all the upper space, even if it receives something earthy which has been forcibly hurled up into it, straightway extrudes it into our region or rather lets it go where its proper inclination causes it naturally to descend.'

At this – for I wished Lucius to have time to collect his thoughts – I called to Theon. 'Which of the tragic poets was it, Theon', I asked, 'who said that physicians

With bitter drugs the bitter bile purge?'

Theon replied that it was Sophokles. 'Yes', I said, 'and we have of necessity to allow them this procedure; but to philosophers one should not listen if they desire to repulse paradoxes with paradoxes and in struggling against opinions that are amazing fabricate others that are more amazing and outlandish, as these people do in introducing their "motion to the centre". What paradox is not involved in this doctrine? . . . [many follow] . . . Nevertheless, though of tall tales of such a kind and number they have shouldered and lugged in – not a wallet-full, by Heaven, but some juggler's pack and hotchpotch – still they say that others are playing the buffoon by placing the moon, though it is earth, on high and not where the centre is. Yet if all heavy body converges to the same point and is compressed in all its parts upon its own centre, it is no more as centre of the sum of things than as a whole that the earth would appropriate to herself the heavy bodies that are parts of herself; and [the downward tendency] of falling bodies proves not that the [earth] is in the centre of the cosmos but that those bodies which when thrust away from the earth fall back to her again have some affinity and cohesion with her. For as the sun attracts to itself the parts of which it consists so the earth too accepts as [her] own the stone that has properly a downward tendency, and consequently every such thing ultimately unites and coheres with her. If there is a body, however, that was not originally allotted to the earth or detached from it but has somewhere independently a constitution and nature of its own, as those men would say of the moon, what is to hinder it from being permanently separate in its own place, compressed and bound together by its own parts? For it has not been proved that the earth is the centre of the sum of things, and the way in which things in our region press together and concentrate upon the earth suggests how in all probability things in that region converge upon the moon and remain there. The man who drives together into a single region all earthy and heavy things and makes them part of a single body – I do not see for what reason he does not apply the same compulsion to light objects in their turn but allows so many separate concentrations of fire and, since he does not collect all the stars together, clearly does not think that there must also be a body common to all things that are fiery and have an upward tendency.

Now', said I, 'my dear Apollonides, you mathematicians say that the sun is an immense distance from the upper circumference and that above the sun Venus and Mercury and the other planets revolve lower than the fixed stars and at great intervals from one another; but you think that in the cosmos there is no scope and extension for heavy and earthy objects. You see that it is ridiculous for us to deny that the moon is earth because she stands apart from the nether region and yet to call her a star, although we see her removed so many thousands of miles from the upper circumference as if plunged [into] a pit. So far beneath the stars is she that the distance cannot be expressed, but you mathematicians in trying to calculate it run short of numbers;[56] she practically grazes the earth and revolving close to it

> Whirls like a chariot's axle-box about,

Empedokles says,

> That skims [the post in passing].

Frequently she does not even surmount the earth's shadow, though it extends but a little way, because the illuminating body is very large; but she seems to revolve so close, almost within arm's reach of the earth, as to be screened by it from the sun unless she rises above this shadowy, terrestrial, and noctural place which is the earth's estate. Therefore we must boldly declare, I think, that the moon is within the confines of [the] earth inasmuch as she is occulted by its extremities.

Dismiss the fixed stars and the other planets and consider the demonstrations of Aristarkhos in his treatise *On Sizes and Distances* that "the distance of the sun is more than eighteen times and less than twenty times the distance of the moon", that is its distance from us . . .' (*Moralia* 922f–925d, Cherniss trans.)

This excerpt illustrates well not only the astronomical and physical debates of the time but also many of the points made elsewhere in this book on the nature and practice of Greek science. For example: the influence of past theories on present ones, and of present ones on each other; the distinction between the reasonably accurate observation or calculation of various phenomena and the much more speculative and widely divergent explanations for those phenomena; the penetration of scientific ideas into ordinary culture; and the use of rhetoric in argument.

FURTHER READING

O. Neugebauer's *History of Ancient Mathematical Astronomy*, 3 vols (Berlin, 1975) is the modern classic on ancient astronomy, but this is not easy reading. It is an excellent example of a modern mathematical commentary on the work of the ancients, going beyond implicit translation to create a modern reconstruction. For those undaunted by mathematical astronomy in principle, but who find Neugebauer more or less incomprehensible, it may be found helpful to have on the table at the same time a work like C. Barlow and G. Bryan, *Elementary Mathematical Astronomy* (5th ed. revised by H. Spenser Jones, London, 1944). M. Crowe's *Theories of the World from Antiquity to the Copernican Revolution* (New York, 1990) is very good for trying to see the

---

[56] It is precisely in the context of Aristarkhos' heliocentric model that Archimedes advances his 'Sand-Reckoner', as a system by which the huge numbers implied by Aristarkhos' immense cosmos might be expressed.

heavens from a pre-modern perspective. F. Hodson (ed.), *The Place of Astronomy in the Ancient World* (London, 1974) considers the usefulness of astronomy in ancient life, amongst other things. For astrology see T. Barton, *Ancient Astrology* (London, 1994).

Principal primary sources in English translation:

Aratos, *Phainomena*. Ed. and trans. by D. Kidd (Cambridge, 1997); also by Mair in the Loeb.

Archimedes, *The Sand-reckoner*. In T. B. L. Heath, *The Works of Archimedes* (Cambridge, 1897), reprinted by Dover, pp. 221–32.

Aristarkhos, *On the Sizes and Distances of the Sun and the Moon*. Trans. T. B. L. Heath (Oxford, 1913), reprinted Dover, 1981.

Chaeremon: Egyptian Priest and Stoic Philosopher. The fragments collected and translated with explanatory notes by P. W. van der Horst (Leiden, 1984).

Plutarch, *On the Face in the Orb of the Moon*. Ed. and trans. by H. Cherniss, *Moralia* vol. 12, Loeb.

Ptolemy, *Almagest*. Trans. G. Toomer (London, 1984).

Ptolemy, *Tetrabiblos*. Ed. and trans. F. E. Robbins, Loeb.

Ptolemy, *Optics*. Trans. and comm. by A. M. Smith (Philadelphia, 1996).

Ptolemy, *Planetary Hypotheses*. Trans. (from Arabic) and comm. by B. Goldstein (Philadelphia, 1967).

There is a good selection of astronomical works in translation in T. B. L. Heath, *Greek Astronomy*, 1932 (reprinted New York, 1969), many of which are also in his *Aristarchus of Samos*. The mathematical highpoints of Greek astronomy can also be found in I. Thomas, *Greek Mathematical Works*. Loeb, 2 vols, and Cohen and Drabkin, *Sourcebook in Greek Science* (Cambridge MA, 1948).

V. GEOGRAPHY

Geography is a broad and diverse area of study, a large tree with many branches. The different branches are *so* different that they tended even in antiquity – with less subject specialization and more polymaths – to be pursued by different people. The main types are (i) human geography, focusing on the landscape of human life,[1] (ii) physical geography, focusing on the land, sea, and sky,[2] and (iii) mathematical geography, focusing on mathematical modelling of aspects of physical and human geography.[3] Where geography and biology meet, we now have ecology and environmental science. This tends in ancient authors to be dealt with under biology and agriculture. The more sophisticated works, such as Theophrastos' works on botany, consider the effect of geology, soils and microclimates on plant physiology and growth.

Ptolemy practised mathematical geography, and his reconstructed maps often feature as frontispieces in modern books on the history of geography. He scorns human geography of the type written by his predecessor Strabo, much as Thoukudides scorns his predecessor Herodotos' type of history. We won't push the analogy while noting that Ptolemy's *Geography* is about as much fun to read as a telephone book, which it resembles, strongly. Strabo, for his part, complained that *his* predecessor Poseidonios' *On the Ocean* has too much mathematics and astronomy in it for geographers like himself (so too for would-be writers of geography like Cicero).[4] As with other fields in ancient science, practitioners were keen to carve out their own territories and make distinctions between what they thought and what their predecessors and contemporaries had written.

Those, like Ptolemy, who went in for mapping and mathematical modelling were often better known as astronomers, and were few and far between. Those, like Seneca, who concentrated their efforts on physical geography tended to pursue it as a part of natural history, especially physics/cosmology. Seneca includes some apparently gratuitous sex

---

[1] e.g. modern categories of urban and regional geography, historical geography, cultural geography.

[2] e.g. modern geomorphology, geology, oceanography, and meteorology.

[3] e.g. modern cartography, GIS (Geographic information systems), and spatial interaction.

[4] Strabo 2.2.1. See Heiberg 1922 p. 79. Strabo also criticizes Poseidonios for being too 'physical' (e.g. 1.3.12) and theoretical in the Aristotelian mould (e.g. 2.3.8).

and/or violence scenes,[5] perhaps added for the same sort of reasons as modern film-makers include them.[6] What we would call human geography was by far the most popular of the three types, combined with a strong interest in the flora and fauna of foreign places.

In keeping with its broad range and scope, geography connects to many other areas of Greek science. Physical geography theories were inseparable from general philosophical positions (a point made repeatedly and forcefully in all contexts by French in *Ancient Natural History*). Physical geography related strongly to one's view of the cosmos and man's place in it. In many societies nature and the forces of nature are expressed as gods: the Greeks had Gaia for earth, Ouranos for sky, Tartaros for the underworld, Zeus for lightning, Poseidon for storms, floods, and earthquakes[7] and so on. One's general philosophy in return determined one's response to the world. For example Seneca, a Roman Stoic (which means a pragmatic man in a pragmatic culture),[8] aimed to remove fear of the unnatural and the inexplicable, such as earthquake, flood, lightning, and other terrifying phenomena of nature, by rendering them natural and explicable. These natural explanations were all liberally peppered with Stoic philosophy in the form of reminders that we are all mortal, and that if one cannot prevent something bad happening, then there is no point fearing it.

As physical geography was useful to philosophers and moralists, so human geography was useful to empire builders and administrators. The Royal Road of Persia from Susa to Sardis was mapped out long before the Ionian revolt (Herodotos 5.52–3), though Strabo credits Anaximander with the first published map (1.1.11); Alexander's bematists' principal function was, as their name reveals, to measure distances between places to be conquered and places conquered (Pliny *NH* 6.61.4); and Agrippa's

---

[5] For example, following a discussion of optical illusions and atmospheric phenomena, he tells the story of Hostius Quadra's mirrored bedroom and what perverted things went on there, *NQ* 1.16; in 3.17–18 he describes the slow death of a fish (a red mullet) on a diner's plate; in 4A pref.17 Caligula's tortures and brutality; in 6.1–2 numerous ways to die from natural causes; and in 7.31 self-castration, among other things.

[6] Such scenes in ancient literature are usually assumed to have been included for their moralizing role (though that is not the usual explanation for such scenes in modern films), but that hardly explains the precise form that they take.

[7] The latter association probably arose because most epicentres were underwater, causing tsunami; for an ancient explanation of the association see Seneca *NQ* 6.23.4.

[8] Seneca has received quite a lot of attention in the last two decades, although much more of it is concerned with his literary works (tragedies, letters, and the like) or with the difference between the morals he professes and his actual behaviour, than with his *Natural Questions*. Rosenmeyer 1989 has attempted to link the two areas of Seneca's activity. For an introduction to Stoicism see Sandbach 1975 or Sharples 1996.

map (see Pliny *NH* 3.17) was connected with the demands of secure domination and taxation of the area thus mapped.[9] For Strabo, 'the greater part of geography subserves the needs of states' (1.1.16 C9). Specifically, he says, it enables governors to manage their affairs in a better way by telling them how large a country is, how it lies, and what peculiarities of sky or soil are there;[10] it enables hunters to fare better knowing the character and extent of the forest; it enables commanders sensibly to pitch a camp, set an ambush, or direct a march in unfamiliar territory; and most importantly, it can save military expeditions from disaster arising from geographical ignorance of the areas into which they moved (citing many examples of costly blunders).[11]

The group who were both consumers and producers of geographic knowledge, whom Strabo ignores in this section, were the private and state-sponsored seekers of exotic goods. These people are usually called traders, though that appellation overlooks two important things. Firstly the requirement for the early adventurous types, producers of geographic information, to be able to defend themselves, from whoever and whatever they might meet; and secondly the ancient habit of fighting for what they sought with whoever had it, rather than bargaining for it. Egyptian expeditions into the desert or other countries for metals, jewels, woods etc. were military campaigns.[12] Early Greek voyages of discovery and exploration were conducted by men who might otherwise be known as heroes or pirates.[13] When Nero sent an expedition (*c.* A.D. 60) south to Ethiopia, the reconnaissance of the upper Nile was conducted by a tribune and centurions of the Praetorian Guard (Pliny *NH* 6.181). Marcus Aurelius' embassy to China in A.D. 166, apparently sent to try to obtain some silk worms, offered to the Chinese Emperor Huan-ti ivory, rhinoceros horns, and tortoise-shell but no jewels, 'which fact throws doubt on the tradition', said the author of the Chinese annal recording this embassy.[14] Whether the Romans did offer anything, and if

---

[9] There is full discussion of this map in Dilke 1985 pp. 41–53.

[10] This obviously relates to governors who were not born into the area they govern, as appropriate for the Roman empire.

[11] Strabo's view on the unprofitability of invading Britain is interesting in this regard; 2.5.8 C115 end–C116. Meeting the needs of state is also illustrated by Arrian's *Periplous of the Euxine* (voyage round the Black Sea) which is written in the form of a letter to the emperor Hadrian; Arrian was legate of Cappadocia, probably when he researched if not wrote it. The same Arrian wrote the best ancient history of the expedition of Alexander the Great (the *Anabasis*), a description of India (the *Indika*) and a handbook on military tactics (the *Tekhne Taktika*), amongst other things.

[12] See Sheikh 'Ibada al-Nubi 1997.

[13] See Rihll 1993.

[14] Conveniently (and translated) in Schoff (ed.), Isidore of Charax, *Parthian Stations* p. 42.

so what, we know not, but we do know that the Chinese did not give up any of their precious moths, and finally the insect was smuggled out to the West under Justinian (Procopius, *Secret History* 8.17).

A relatively large part of ancient geographical knowledge survives, in whole or in part, largely because it has been found useful and worth keeping by many people in the intervening centuries. Many of the descriptive type geographies, which are the most readable and entertaining parts of the corpus, are compilations, based on information given by anonymous men over centuries; indeed, the authors of a fair number of these texts are not known, and so the works are assigned to 'Anon'. Many of the authors whose names survive did not discover or create the knowledge they relate, but organized, assessed, and integrated pre-existing and new knowledge. And they are self-conscious of this fact and their role. Eratosthenes, for example, commented upon the significant enlargement of geographic knowledge during and following Alexander's conquests (Strabo 1.3.3). Strabo emphasizes that the expansion of the Roman and Parthian empires has extended geographical knowledge, and that integration of this new information requires some modification of old ideas – even a few ideas advanced by those of his predecessors for whom he has the greatest respect (1.2.1).

The range and scope of ancient geography has not been to its advantage as a subject of study by moderns. Thomson's lament from 1948 is still, perhaps *more*, applicable today: 'this subject is seldom well understood. It deserves to be treated in its full scope, as here conceived, and only so can it be given its due, no more but no less, in the story of geographical discovery and science as a whole. There is no doubt that a comprehensive and critical survey is needed. With the difficulties of the evidence and the mass of detail to be controlled, it is a hard enterprise. If the present effort seems ambitious, it has cost the writer more years than he foresaw or than he sometimes cares to look back upon . . . By its very nature it leads in every direction to the borders of the unknown, and few subjects are therefore better worth research. The task here undertaken involves the whole range of ancient history and literature, and needs doing in *their* interest . . . the original sources are of every kind and value and still variously interpreted in many important matters.'[15]

Similarly, the problems he noted in his 'Note on books' (pp. 392–4) still apply: 'various writers do not always agree, of course, and the difficulty is to get an intelligent survey of what matters in this vast mass

---

[15] *History of Ancient Geography*, Preface p. xi, emphasis added.

of scattered detail . . . some writers have been much edited like
Herodotus, but others, including the most important, Strabo and
Ptolemy, are not nearly so familiar or so fully explained . . . the usual
histories of philosophy are partly relevant, though most pay too little
attention to the matter in question, for instance the earth-globe, how it
was first conceived and presently applied to geography. Such things are
handled more for their own sake elsewhere [refs. to astronomical
studies] . . . Ancient geography is sometimes handled as part of general
histories of geography . . . or it may be treated, without the theory, as
part of histories of exploration . . . in general histories of all science the
subject is often too slightly and sometimes uncritically handled . . . all
good histories of the ancient world are relevant, of course . . . but . . . it is
strange how seldom they [ancient historians] think of giving a contemporary map or description (if they did, they would sometimes be less
ready to assume distant trade and trade-routes) . . . There is much
bearing on trade and travel in economic histories.' This is a fair
summary of the situation today, particularly with regard to the neglect
of the subject by classicists, ancient historians, and ancient philosophers.

However, the problems have been compounded by the growth in the
number and variety of publications produced by a much larger number
of academics working in a much larger and more diverse world of higher
education. Since Thomson wrote, Islamic, Indian, Chinese, and other
regional-based disciplines have revealed new sources and evidence from
their parts of the world which are relevant to Greco-Roman interaction
with them. These, needless to say, present a rather different picture to
that painted by the *still* unfamiliar Greek sources. Then there are new
relevant topic-based disciplines, such as oral history, folklore studies,
and communication studies. Even anthropology, which has much to
offer in terms of cross-cultural perception and communication, was a
rather new and uncertain subject when Thomson wrote. Meanwhile
physical geography and mathematical geography have changed almost
beyond recognition since he wrote; plate tectonics, catastrophic event
horizons, and volcanology, for example, all have something to offer the
modern student of ancient geographical studies.[16] It becomes ever more
difficult to analyse and synthesize the subject.

Which perhaps explains why the whole field has been rather neglected
of late. Over the last 30 years there has been little published except

[16] For example, it is only since the eruption of Mount St Helens (1980) that we have finally
understood the type of eruption which corresponds with and explains the ancient descriptions of
Vesuvius' catastrophic eruption and the archaeological evidence of Pompeii and Herculaneum.

O. Dilke's books on *The Roman Land Surveyors* (the *Agrimensores*) in 1971 and *Greek and Roman Maps* in 1985. H. M. Hine published *An Edition with Commentary of Seneca Natural Questions Book 2* in 1981. For the 1990s, D. Lindberg's *Beginnings of Western Science* has next to nothing to say on geography until p. 145, dealing with 'the last Roman compiler', Martianus Capella, C5 A.D.[17] French, however, has a chapter on it (and much else) and scattered remarks throughout the other recent wide-ranging survey, *Ancient Natural History*. In the area of cultural geography and ecology R. Sallares wrote *Ecology of Ancient Greece* in 1991; D. Cosgrove 1993 has a sensitive interpretation of Greek myth and landscape, with many interesting points on the φύσις/νόμος (nature/culture) polarity in ancient thought; and N. Purcell argues for a complex and sensitive approach to the subject of the ancients and the spatial dimension.[18] The thrust of these studies, however, is in a rather different direction to that of ancient geographical studies. They are much more concerned with *our* understanding of the land/-scape of *Greece* (or Italy) as it was perceived by the ancients who lived on and worked that land, as opposed to *the ancients'* understanding of *other people and other places*, which is what most ancient geographic literature is about. For many purposes, Bunbury's two volumes, though antiques (published 1879), are as indispensable today as they were for Thomson.

We will take geography in the broad branches set out in the introduction.

5.2 *Human geography*

The Greeks' interest in other peoples and other places is apparent from the first. Homer's listing of contingents on both sides of the Trojan War continues with, for example, Delphi's role as geographic centre and database in the days of colonization, Kolaios' discovery of Tartessos, Herodotos' very wide-ranging interests and travels, Pytheas' circumnavigation of Britain and exploration of the Baltic, Alexander's recruitment of the Indian philosopher Calanus to his court, and Plutarch's speculations on possible inhabitants of the moon.

[17] Except, of course, for a brief mention of Eratosthenes' calculation of the circumference of the earth, raised, of course, in the context of astronomy, p. 98, mentioned again on p. 144. Lindberg does say that Capella failed to understand Eratosthenes' method, but he does not indicate that Capella is not even consistent: his character Geometry gives a figure of 252,000 stades (596), whilst later Astronomy says (858) that Geometry had said 406,010 stades! For an assessment of Capella see Stahl 1971.

[18] Purcell 1996; this volume of papers by diverse hands is devoted to environment and culture.

A significant number of texts are entitled *periplous* or *periegesis*, meaning a sailing round or a walk across.[19] These texts are designed to be used by travellers. Their principle of organization is a journey around or across a part of the world, discussing places in the order in which one would come across them as one travelled the coast or the road, like a very simple and summary Blue Guide. Some of these explorers, notably Pytheas, recognized the importance of astronomical observations in terrestrial location-finding, and went out of their way to record e.g. daylight hours at the solstice or equinox, or the height of the sun above the horizon at the same.[20] Phenomena like the sun moving in the 'wrong' direction (Herodotos 4.42, on the voyage sent out by Pharaoh Necho to circumnavigate Africa) were unmissable, even by the most unobservant and uninterested crewman, and needed no special effort to note or remember.[21]

Conquerors and traders found the sort of information gathered by travellers extremely useful, and what we would call human geography early had very obvious practical applications. We noted above the more obvious military and imperial applications. As for the traders, an awareness of far-flung regional specialities in, and the supply of exotic products (natural and man-made) to, Theophrastos' Athens (C4) is exemplified in his stereotype of 'the obsequious man' (*Characters* 5.9): 'He is apt to keep a pet monkey, and buys a pheasant, and some Sicilian doves, and dice made from gazelle horns, and oil flasks from Thurii of the rounded sort, and walking sticks from Sparta of the twisted sort, and a tapestry embroidered with pictures of Persian soldiers, and his own little *palaistra* with sand and handball court'.[22] The 'man of petty ambition' has an Ethiopian slave (21.4) and a Melitian dog, to which, when it dies, he raises a monument with name plaque (§9).

To give some idea of the range and scope of texts in human geography, I will discuss briefly four works. Two are early, two are from the C1 A.D., and only one of them was written by someone now thought of as a geographer.

---

[19] There is a good discussion of these, with extracts in English translation, in Dilke 1985 chapter 9.

[20] The text and testimonia concerning Pytheas have been edited and translated by Roseman 1994.

[21] Indeed, this observation needed more effort to believe: Herodotos didn't.

[22] As Rusten notes in the new Loeb edition (1992), this section (along with sections 6–10) seems to have been misplaced during transmission of the text, and to belong not to the obsequious character but to some other such as the man of petty ambition, on which see continuation of the main text.

The earliest surviving geographical text, though it survives only in fragments, is about one of the farthest-flung places from Greece. It is the *Indika* written by Skulax of Karia in the C6 B.C. It is mentioned by Herodotos (4.44). This was motivated by a conqueror's interests. Skylax was a Greek mercenary in Darius' service. This Persian king conquered part of the Indus river region *c.* 515 B.C. – about two hundred years before Alexander repeated the achievement – and twenty-five years before he turned his attention to the West and invaded Greece, to face Aiskhulos and his compatriots at the battle of Marathon. This treatise apparently was the report of an expedition which set out to follow the Indus from its headwaters to its mouth. Skylax commanded the fleet.

Hekataios of Miletos, one of the prime movers in the Ionian Revolt, wrote a *Periodos* which survives only in fragments. This was a first in two senses: it was the first attempt at a systematic description of world, and it was one of the first pieces of literature to be written in prose rather than poetry.[23] Book 1 (Europe) covered the Mediterranean coast and islands, and set the paradigm for the *periplous* as a genre; book 2 (Asia, which included Africa) gave an outline of the rest of the world as known to Hekataios and his sources in the early C5 B.C. The first volume focused on the coastal area but made some reference to inland tribes; the second seems to have included reference to all the provinces of the Persian empire.[24]

Strabo[25] of Amasia (Pontus) was born around 65 B.C., and died sometime after A.D. 21. His *Geography* is generally reckoned to be the best ancient geographical treatise to survive – best with respect to the structure of the work, its comprehensiveness and its interest. It was written just after Augustus' death, and is an excellent source on Augustan organization of the empire. The first 2 books concern the views of his predecessors, especially their theories on physical geography, and are immensely valuable for modern reconstructions of those earlier contributors to the subject. Fifteen books follow, working systematically around the *oikoumene*, the inhabited world as known at the time.

---

[23] See Strabo 1.2.6, naming Kadmos and Pherekydes with Hekataios as early prose writers. Pliny *NH* 7.205 and Suda s.v. Φερεκύδης name only the first two, but the latter contradicts himself and names Hekataios with Pherekydes s.v. Ἑκαταῖος Ἡγησάνδρου.

[24] On Hekataios see Bunbury 1879 vol. 1 chapter 5. Hekataios was a resident of a Greek city under Persian rule; given his role in the Ionian Revolt (499–3), the gathering of this information might be considered 'intelligence'.

[25] The name means 'cross-eyed', but does not necessarily mean that his eyesight was impaired. Pliny reports the case of another called Strabo who reputedly could see ships passing out of the harbour of Carthage while standing in Lilybaeum in Sicily (123 Roman miles away), *NH* 7.85.

There are many historical digressions within the text, which reflect Strabo's previous interest and (now lost) work, *Historical memoirs*, which filled 43 books. This history covered the period from the destruction of Carthage and Corinth (where Polubios stopped) to the death of Caesar or the battle of Actium. Had this work survived, Strabo might now be known as a historian rather than a geographer.

The anonymous *Periplous of the Erythraian Sea*[26] is a manual for traders operating around the Red Sea, East African coast, and across the water to India; it is not a geographical treatise as such. It is fascinating particularly for the lists of trade goods imported and exported at each port mentioned, and it was evidently written by a practising merchant, probably in the C1 A.D. For example, in the Indian town of Barygaza[27] the reader is advised (§49) that there is a good market for: wine – Italian wine is preferred here, failing that, Laodicean and Arabian; copper, tin, and lead; coral and topaz; thin and inferior clothing of all kinds; bright-coloured cubit-wide girdles; storax and sweet clover; flint glass, realgar (an inorganic red pigment), antimony, gold and silver coins – which can be exchanged for the money of the country at a profit; and cheap ointment in small quantities. The reader is advised to bring for the local ruler expensive silver vessels; boys who can sing; beautiful women to add to the harem; fine wines; quality thin woven clothing; and the best ointments. Such gifts are presumably meant to earn the ruler's goodwill or pay the local sales tax. In return, the trader will find here for sale spikenard (aromatic herb from the Himalayas), costus (spice from Kashmir), bdellium (aromatic tree gum), ivory, agate, carnelian, lycium (variety of Himalayan berberis used for pigment and medica-ments), cotton cloth of all kinds, silk cloth, mallow cloth (rough local cloth), yarn, long pepper, and other local produce. Besides trade goods, we hear of an official pilot service for ships wishing to navigate the mouth and river Nammadus (modern Narmada) up to Barygaza (§42–4). The area appears to have been subject to tidal bores, making it extremely difficult and dangerous, especially for non-local crews and vessels (§46). According to Schoff,[28] in the Gulf of Cambay ordinary tides rise and fall by 25 feet, and move at 4.5 to 6 knots. High spring tides can rise and fall 33 feet, and run at 6 to 7 knots. For sailors more familiar with the almost non-tidal Mediterranean or Red Seas, this phenomenon would have been particularly shocking.

---

[26] Another work of the same title is attributed to Agatharkides.
[27] Modern Bahruch, 21°42′N, 72°59′E.
[28] *Periplous* p. 183 n. 45.

5.3 *Physical geography*

Discovering the size and shape of the earth tended to be in the province of mathematician/astronomers like Ptolemy or polymaths like Eratosthenes.[29] The rest of what we call physical geography received attention usually under the heading of *Meteorology*. This concerned not just the weather and comets but also (despite its title) down-to – or even *in* – earth subjects like earthquakes, volcanoes, the tides, the formation of minerals and metals, and physical/chemical change generally. But as the bedrock on which all natural history exists, the earth itself is the subject of numerous comments and sections in many general 'natural philosophy' texts (e.g. Seneca's *Natural Questions*), general geography texts, history texts, and even theological writings. For example, our knowledge of Xenophanes' association of fossilized fish, other marine animals and marine plants found in rocks with changes in sea-level and the deposition of dead bodies in mud which in due course turned into stone, is thanks to Hippolutos mentioning it in his *Refutation of All Heresies*.[30]

Specific texts addressed specific issues, like Theophrastos' *On Stones* (surviving complete), *On Weather Signs* (surviving),[31] *On Metals* (few fragments only), *On Water* (lost) or *Meteorology* (surviving in Syriac-Arabic translation).[32] As ancient 'scientists' were polymaths and knew their own 'arts' literature, so 'lay' people were reasonably *au fait* with at least some scientific theories. Consider Philostratos, an art historian, and even more significantly the artist whose picture he is discussing:

The two islands next to these [islands] were formerly both joined as one, but having been broken apart in the middle by the sea its two parts have become separated by the width of a river. This you might know from the painting, my boy; for you doubtless see the two severed portions of the island are similar, and correspond to each other, and are so shaped that concave parts fit those that project. [Mainland] Europe once suffered the same experience in the region of Thessalian Tempe, for when earthquakes laid open that

---

[29] Eratosthenes' computation of the circumference of the earth is discussed in many places. See Cohen and Drabkin 1966 pp. 149–53 for the primary sources.

[30] 1.14.5–6, conveniently in Barnes 1987 p. 99. Herodotos made a similar observation in Egypt, 2.12; Strabo tells us of more observations by others, e.g. of cockle and scallop shells in Armenia and Phrygia observed by Xanthos of Lydia (C5 B.C.), and vast numbers of shells seen thousands of stadia from the coast of Egypt observed by Eratosthenes and Strato, 1.3.4. Theophrastos' lost work *On Things Turned to Stone* perhaps concerned fossils.

[31] Although attributed to Theophrastos, and Theophrastos certainly wrote a work with this name, the authenticity of the treatise which has survived to us is now doubted; see Cronin 1992.

[32] Recently published with the Syriac fragments, the Syriac and Arabic translations, and an English translation and commentary, by Daiber 1992.

land, they indicated on the fractures the correspondence of the mountains one to another, and even today there are visible cavities where rocks once were, which correspond to the rocks torn from them, and moreover, traces have not yet disappeared of the heavy forest that must have followed the mountain sides when they split apart, for the beds of the trees are still left. So we may consider that some such thing happened to this island (*Imagines* 2.17, Fairbanks trans.).[33]

Ancient ideas on physical geography generally have received little attention in modern times, but there is much here of interest. For example, Aristotle weighed equal volumes of salt and fresh water and knew that salt water is heavier. He theorized that the 'earthy stuff' (salt and other unknowns) in sea water 'thickened' its 'consistency', increasing its buoyancy. He described a simple experiment to do at home to demonstrate this: make a strong brine and an egg will float in it.[34] 'Again if, as is fabled, there is a lake in Palestine, such that if you bind a man or beast and throw it in it floats and does not sink, this would bear out what we have said', he adds correctly.[35] Turning from water to wind, his idea that hot and cold winds existed and sometimes blew underground – and were responsible for the formation of metals and minerals, for earthquakes[36] and other subterranean phenomena – may be re-examined in the light of the recent discoveries of (i) an unexplained hot wind which vents from the mouth of the Lechugilla cave in New Mexico and (ii) the hot water vents of the world's oceans. Many volcanic regions have fumeroles and other vents through which hot gases and steam escape from below, depositing sulphur and other minerals around the hole, and it is not surprising that someone like Aristotle noted their existence and speculated on the existence of 'underground winds' of which these were surface manifestations.

The anonymous author of *Aetna*,[37] written some time before Vesuvius

[33] See Aristotle *Meteorology* 2.7–8, Strabo 1.3.16–20, and Seneca *NQ* 6.4–31 for reviews of earlier philosophies, and places and things said to have been ripped apart in the same way, though usually lacking the geological detail of the Philostratos passage. The earliest reference to Tempe being torn apart by an earthquake is Herodotos 7.129. Another example of the interpenetration of 'arts' and 'science' is Ovid's *Metamorphoses*, where Pythagoras can be found giving a lecture on geology, 15.66–71, 262–356.

[34] As any cook (and Pliny, *NH* 10.75) knows, but Aristotle does not mention, bad eggs float – so make sure it is a fresh egg. Test by immersion in fresh water: if it sinks, it's fresh. Then try it in a strong brine. The same experiment is repeated in [Aristotle] *Plants* 2.2, 824a15–26, which also goes on to talk about the Dead Sea, calling it such.

[35] *Meteorology* 2.3. What was for him 'fabled' is probably the Dead Sea.

[36] See e.g. *Meteorology* 2.8: 'it has been known to happen that an earthquake has continued until the wind that caused it burst through the earth into the air.' Aristotle's underground winds sometimes burst out not just violently but also on fire. Hence for him earthquakes and volcanoes were very closely related.

[37] Which came down in the MS tradition under the name of Virgil, but is now thought by most

erupted (for that volcano is described as inactive) has very graphic and very detailed descriptions (in Latin verse) of eruptions of Etna.[38] This includes pre-eruption seismic activity, 'thick fluid' and bitumen flows, violent ejection of rocks large and small, liquefication of soils, mudflows, lava flows, ash clouds, and of course the explosive violence of fire and flame. The author is as concerned to explain these phenomena in a scientific way as he is to describe them.[39] Aristotle's theory of underground winds forms the basis of the explanation, but it is well developed here[40] and constantly related to observation. This is natural history in the style of modern coffee-table books and natural history television programmes, but with an explicit theoretical and argumentative edge. It is also from an age without photographs, when images had to be described, and scenes had to be pictured in the mind on the basis of that description. Picture the scene:

a thousand fires in a moment of time will set before you the true cause [of Aetna's eruptions]. Facts and your eyes instruct you . . . a cloud of burnt sand is driven in a whirl; swiftly rush the flaming masses; from the depth foundations are upheaved. Now bursts a crash from Aetna everywhere: now the flames show ghastly pale as they mingle with the dark downpour. Afar off even Jupiter marvels at the mighty fires and trembles speechless in his secret haunt, lest a fresh brood of giants be rising to renew long-buried war, or lest Pluto be growing ashamed of his kingdom and be changing Tartarus for heaven; while outside all is covered with heap upon heap of rock and crumbling sand. They come not so of their own accord: unsupported by the strength of any powerful body they fall. It is the winds which arouse all these forces of havoc: the rocks which they have massed thickly together they whirl in eddying storm and roll from the abyss. For this reason the rush of fire from the mountain is no surprise. Winds when swollen are called 'spirit' (*spiritus*), but 'air' (*aer*) when sunk to rest. The violence of flame unaided is almost ineffectual; true, fire has always a natural velocity and perpetual motion, but some ally is needed for the propulsion of bodies. In itself it has no motive energy (*impetus*): where spirit is commander, it obeys. Spirit is emperor: fire serves in the army of this great captain (190–218) . . . As soon as it stirs its forces, and threatens havoc, it flies in different

not to have been written by him; the author was *perhaps* Seneca's correspondent Lucilius Junior, Procurator of Sicily. Goodyear 1965 pp. 56–9 discusses all ascriptions that have been offered in his *Aetna* edition with introduction and commentary (but no translation). The text with translation is in the Loeb 'Minor Latin Poets' volume trans. J. W. and A. M. Duff. It should be noted that the MSS of this text are pretty corrupt and the apparatus extensive, so the text should be checked before any great weight is placed on a particular word or line.

[38] It is interesting to compare this with Strabo's earlier account of Etna in *Geography* 6.2.

[39] He makes disparaging remarks about other sciences, such as astronomy or botany, as being less relevant to man or trivial respectively (e.g. 252–73; 265–70 seems to refer to Theophrastos' concern with soils), but saves his most satirical comments for mythographers (e.g. 17–23, 74–93) and superficial sightseers who ogle at natural phenomena but do not seek to understand them (569–600).

[40] Paisley and Oldroyd 1979 have a useful table (p. 12) showing the many and varied scientific ideas which have influenced the author of the *Aetna*.

directions, dragging at once the soil with it: [there follows a short section of corrupt text with lacunae] while the eruption is announced by a deep rumbling underground accompanied by fire. Then shall you think fit to flee in panic and yield place to the divine event. From the safety of a hill you will be able to observe all. For of a sudden the conflagration blazes out, loaded with its spoils; masses of burning matter advance; mutilated lumps of falling rock roll forth and whirl dark shoals of sand. They present vague shapes in human likeness . . . then any stone that a surface fire has liquefied becomes, when the fire is quenched, more rugged – a sort of dirty slag like what you see drop from iron when smelted . . . the lava liquid begins to boil hotter and at last to advance more in the fashion of a gentle stream, as it lets its waves course down the slopes of the hill. By stages the waves advance some twice six miles.[41] Nay, nothing can recall them: nothing checks these determined fires: no mass can hold them – 'tis vain: all is war together. Now woodland and crag, here again earth and soil are in flood. The lava-river itself aids their supplies and adjusts the compliant material to its own course . . . the lava-streams come to a standstill inside their margins and harden as they cool; slowly the fires shrink and the appearance of a waving harvest of flame is lost. Each mass in turn, as it stiffens, emits fumes, and, dragged by its very weight, rolls on with enormous din; whenever it has crashed pell-mell into some solid substance which resounds with the impact, it spreads abroad the fires of the concussion and shines with white-glowing core wherever it has been opened out. A host of sparks flash forth at every blow: the glowing rocks (look, you see the flashes in the distance – look, raining down in the distance!) fall with undiminished heat (462–507) . . . But in vain I try to marshal each effect with its determined cause if a lying fable remains unshaken in your mind, leading you to believe that it is a different substance which liquefies in fire, that the lava-streams harden in virtue of their cindery property, or that what burns is a mixture of sulphur and glutinous bitumen. For clay also, they assert, can fuse when its inner material is burnt out, and potters are a testimony to this: then by the process of cooling it recovers its hardness and tightens its pores. But this analogous indication is unimportant – an ineffectual reason given on hasty grounds. An unfailing token makes the truth evident to you. For as the essence of gleaming copper, both when fused with fire and when its solidity is unimpaired, remains constant and ever the same, so that in either state you may distinguish the copper portion, in no other way the lava-stone, whether dissolved into liquid flames or kept safe from them, retains and preserves its characteristics, and fire has not ruined its look (511–526) . . . The lava-stone is rigid; its surface barrier resists all fire, if you seek to burn it with small fires and in the open air. Well then, confine it in a narrow white-hot furnace – it cannot endure or stand firm against that fierce foe. It is vanquished: it relaxes its strength; in its captor's grip it melts. Now, what greater engines, think you, can skill apply with the hand, or what fires can it support with our human resources to compare with the mighty furnaces with which Aetna burns, ever the mother of secret fire? Yet her fire is not of the limited heat within our own experience, but more akin to

---

[41] Etna normally erupts basaltic lavas, which have relatively low viscosity, so flow and spread more easily than some other types. Since 1535 Etna has erupted less than 4 cubic kilometres of lava, and the largest single flow within that time was half a cubic kilometre; Cas and Wright 1987 p. 62. At times, however, it has been capable of pushing lava out more than 18 km from the summit, as in 44 B.C. On that eruption, and its effects on atmospheric visibility in Rome and the Caesar comet, with all relevant primary sources in English translation as well as in the original, and a very useful up-to-date bibliography, see Ramsey (classicist) and Licht (physicist) 1997.

that of heaven or the kind of flame with which Jupiter himself is armed.[42] With these mighty forces is allied the gigantic volcanic spirit forced out of straightened jaws, as when mechanics hasten to pit their strength against masses of natural iron, they stir the fires and, expelling the wind from panting bellows, rouse the current in close array. Such is the manner of its working: so goes far-famed Aetna's burning. The earth draws in forces through her perforations; volcanic spirit compresses these into narrow space, and the path of conflagration lies through the mightiest rocks. (550–568. Duff trans.)

Some ancient descriptions of volcanic eruptions[43] are accurate for the kind of eruption witnessed and televised, with top-quality videos made by volcanologists, at Mount St Helens in 1980.[44] On the basis of the archaeological evidence it is now clear that when Vesuvius destroyed Pompeii, Herculaenum, and Pliny the Elder, whose eagerness to observe this event cost him his life (as Mount St Helens cost one volcanologist[45] and about 60 other people their lives), it erupted in much the same way as Mount St Helens did.[46] Until 1980, just how far and how fast a pyroclastic volcanic ash cloud could move was not well understood, nor what was a 'safe' distance.[47]

[42] The temperature of Etna magma was measured at between 1050 and 1125° C over the period 1970–75, Cas and Wright 1987 p. 19 table 2.2.

[43] Which were so at variance with received wisdom when Cohen and Drabkin wrote that they omitted them from their sourcebook. Pliny the Younger's letter to Tacitus, *Letters* 6.16 is the main source for the Vesuvian eruption and the Elder Pliny's death. Pliny is now the eponym for a type of eruption the cloud form of which he described as 'like an umbrella pine' (plinian, with refinement types sub-plinian, ultra-plinian and phreatoplinian). He would be pleased: 'I know that immortal fame awaits him if his death is recorded by you' he said to Tacitus, though it is Pliny the Younger's record rather than Tacitus' which assured him of that fame.

[44] On which see e.g. Foxworthy and Hill 1982 for an excellent non-technical and illustrated account.

[45] David Johnston, who was observing the volcano nearly 6 miles from the summit.

[46] For a long time Vesuvius and Pompeii have been an archaeogeological mystery. Bodies found on dense layers of ash indicate that the volcano had been actively pouring pumice and ash into the atmosphere for some time but also that the inhabitants had felt secure enough not to flee. When the end came however, it came so quickly that people were caught wherever they were. Hundreds of people in Herculaneum who had time to run and tried to find refuge in doored arched storage caverns were nevertheless exposed to such surface temperatures that a hand raised to protect the face was burnt to the bone, while the other hand, unexposed to the blast, was not. This was clearly not the kind of eruption where lava flowed sedately downhill or ash rained gently from the skies for months. With the eruption of Mount St Helens the nature of pyroclastic flows and the forces of lateral blast have become much better known to modern volcanology. The St Helens' blast cloud travelled at speeds of about 220–250 miles per hour, and had a temperature of about 360° C (680° F). The contortions of the bodies were explained by the similar type of eruptions on Monserrat in 1997, in which 19 people died: pyroclastic flows can be so intensely hot and can arrive so quickly that the muscles and ligaments are seared, contracting and making the limbs bend. This is consistent with the archaeological record of Pompeii and Herculaneum.

[47] A pyroclastic flow is a flow of hot, dry, fragmented volcanic debris, largely pumice and rock fragments, carried in a fluid medium of heated air and other gases; Major and Scott 1988 p. 5. For a good discussion of ancient volcanic activity, with full reference to the primary sources which tell of the historical effects (e.g. on the 'gloomy year' 44 B.C. when the sun seemed dimmed and crops failed, as a result of Etna's volcanic aerosols in the upper atmosphere), see Stothers and Rampino 1983.

Poseidonios of Apameia in Syria was a distinguished and influential philosopher of *phusis*,[48] chief exponent of what we call the Middle Stoa, who included a lot of geographical material in his writing.[49] He may have been a major influence on the author of the *Aetna*. He is cited more frequently by Strabo than any other author, and was the main source[50] for Pliny in book 2 of the *NH*. He knew men in the highest circles of Republican Rome,[51] being personally acquainted with Cicero and Pompey, though he lived in Rhodes and only visited Rome periodically (the first time he went was as ambassador for his adopted country, Rhodes).

He travelled widely – which does not mean frequently. One journey was to southern Spain, the outward leg apparently via the coast of France, and the return leg, which took three months, wandered between Sardinia and the North African coast. It may not be coincidence that his friend Pompey started his pirate campaign at Gibraltar and swept eastwards, driving pirates onto whatever shore they fled to, or further along the Mediterranean.[52] The naval forces at his command were those of Rome's allies, including Rhodes and Marseilles. The zigzagging of this voyage – whether caused by unfavourable winds or the pursuit of pirates – apparently did nothing to undermine the idea that the Mediterranean ran in a more or less straight line, north of a more or less straight north African coastline. The most important cartographic meridian in ancient mapping [36°] ran through the straits of Gibraltar to

[48] Only one specifically geographical work is known, *On the Ocean* (lost). The fragments are collected in Edelstein and Kidd 1972. His student Geminos wrote a Commentary on Poseidonios' work on astronomy, and an Epitome of that commentary which survives in the modified form of a textbook. A long excerpt of this Epitome, translated literally, can be found in Farrington 1944 vol. 2 pp. 139–42.

[49] Another Stoic, Khairemon, wrote a lost work *On Comets*, which seems to have been concerned at least partly with their astrological significance; see Origen, *Contra Celsum* 1.59.

[50] Via Varro; Pliny frequently used Latin translations and epitomes of Greek works, or Latin compilations of data drawn from Greek and Italian sources, e.g. Celsus.

[51] On Stoicism and Rome, see Colish 1990.

[52] In 67 B.C. Kidd 1988 vol. 1 pp. 16–17 follows Laffranque in preferring the 90s B.C. for Poseidonios' trip to Spain, but suggests that perhaps he did not publish *On the Ocean* until the 70s (p. 220). This implies what seems to me to be an implausibly long gap between research and publication for a man who studied, wrote and published on a wide variety of subjects. Strabo 11.1.6 says that Pompey visited Poseidonios during his command against the pirates, and before he campaigned against Mithridates. However, Kidd describes Strabo's criticisms of Poseidonios here as 'weird, confused and petty' (vol. 2 p. 741), and Strabo's account makes difficulties for the standard chronology of Poseidonios' life and works. The core of the story is that Poseidonios and Pompey were in personal contact at about the time of the pirate campaign. Perhaps Poseidonios was on the pirate campaign, with the Rhodian contingent in Pompey's forces. As he is thought to have been born *c*. 135, and visited Rome for the last time in 51 (aged at least 84), the chronology is possible. See also Cicero *Tusc. Disp.* 2.61, Pliny *NH* 7.112, and Plutarch *Pompey* 42.5, Edelstein and Kidd T35, 36–9.

the Gulf of Issus, and these two are as near as matters on the same latitude. But in between these Mediterranean extremes the ancient line ran north of the North African coast, whereas it should cut it; it cut Sardinia, whereas it should run well south of that island; and it cut Cape Tainaron on the Peloponnese, whereas the Cape lies over 100 miles north of the 36th parallel. Errors like these had the effect of straightening out the Inner Sea.

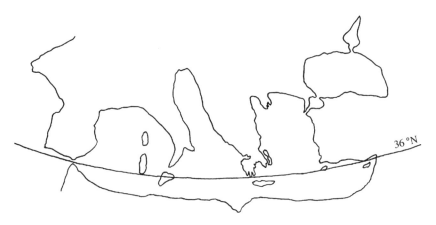

Fig. 5.1: The Mediterranean according to ancient mapmakers.

Poseidonios adopted from Seleukos (one of the astronomers who agreed with Aristarkhos) and further developed a theory on the tides which involved the movement of the moon and the sun,[53] whether it was Seleukos or Poseidonios who explained the temporal correlation in terms of astral forces is not clear, but Poseidonios seems more likely. The idea that the tides were somehow tied to the moon perhaps prompted, or was prompted by, his belief in astrology, to which he 'seems to have been addicted' in Clagett's words.[54] The link is expressed clearly in Ptolemy's bible of astrology, the *Tetrabiblos* 1.2.1–3, from which I excerpt: 'The moon, as the heavenly body nearest the earth, bestows her effluence most abundantly upon mundane things, for most of them, animate or inanimate, are sympathetic to her and change in company with her; the rivers increase and diminish their streams with

---

[53] See Strabo 3.5.8–9. See also Kidd's commentary and diagrams, vol. 2 on frg. 217b.

[54] 1955, p. 121, who adds that five separate books on astrology are attributed to Poseidonios, and that St Augustine studied them. These books are normally known by an alias which is more respectable in the modern world, namely *On Divination*. Kidd takes a more defensive line on Poseidonios' astrological interests, *Comm.* vol. 1 pp. 59–60.

her light, the seas turn their own tides with her rising and setting, and plants and animals in whole or in some part wax and wane with her' (Robbins trans.). Pliny reports an explanation of why the tides sometimes lag behind the sun and moon's movements, to wit that optical images travel across space faster than the tidal influence (*NH* 2.99.216). By Vegetius' time the theory was taken for granted, but the difficulty of relating the moon's position to tidal behaviour in any particular place prompted him to give very practical advice: 'he who is going to fight a naval battle ought to find out the characteristics of the sea and locality before any encounter' (4.42). Today, much the same situation prevails because of the highly complex relationship between the moon, the earth, and the oceans. It is a commonplace that the moon's gravitational pull 'causes' the tides, but anyone putting to sea consults tide tables or listens to radio broadcasts on tide times – they do not attempt to compute tidal positions and flows by watching the moon.

Poseidonios was also interested in the substance of the earth. He studied the Roman mines in Spain (Strabo 3.2.9, 13.1.67), possibly also the copper mines on Cyprus (3.4.15), the asphalt 'mines' at Nymphaeum near Apollonia, at Pierian Seleucia (on the border of Cilicia and Syria), and on Rhodes (7.5.8), and a naphtha spring in Babylonia (16.1.15).[55] For those interested in the nature of the ground beneath our feet, mines offered a sort of peephole into the innards of the earth. Seneca (*NQ* 5.15.1) reports from Asklepiodotos (a student of Poseidonios) that men sent into old mines by Philip II of Macedon saw deep underground 'huge rivers and vast reservoirs of still water, equal to ours above ground and . . . with a vast free space overhead'. Just how much they could see with their flame torches is anyone's guess. Seneca adds (5.15.4) that others 'dared to descend to a place where they found a strange order of things, layers of earth hanging overhead, dead winds in the darkness, dreadful springs of water flowing for no man, and a night other than our own, and perpetual. Then, after doing these things, they fear the Underworld!' he adds mockingly.

Strabo (6.2.11 C277) preserves Poseidonios' record of a new island formed by volcanic activity in the Lipari Isles (between Italy and Sicily), in 126 B.C. Seneca summarizes Poseidonios' account of the formation of a new volcanic island in the Aegean (*NQ* 2.26.4–6), and refers to another which rose in his own time.[56] Justin (*Epitome of Trogus' Philippic*

---

[55] This passage contains reference to vinegar being used as fire extinguisher, alternatively mud, alum, or bird-lime, in circumstances where water will not work unless used in huge quantities.

[56] 6.21.1. Hine ad loc. 2.26 remarks that Seneca's account of this contemporary event, brief in

History 30.4.1–4) tells of the sudden formation of a new island between Thera and Therasia around 200 B.C., and Pliny lists newly formed volcanic islands in *NH* 2.202. As land could be raised out of the sea, and could sink into the sea, Poseidonios thought it possible that the Atlantis story could have a basis in fact (Strabo 2.3.6, 297–303). There are a number of references in Strabo concerning the idea that the sea-beds might rise and fall.[57]

That data were not entirely qualitative by this time is indicated by another fragment of Poseidonios' writings which are preserved by Strabo (1.3.9), that the greatest depth of sea *that had been measured* was over 1000 fathoms (in the Sardinian Sea). Oppian (*Hal.* 1.9–12) refers to anonymous fishermen who 'by their *techne* have mapped out the measures (*metra*) of the sea'. The technology in question was probably a sounding line, weighted and knotted at regular intervals. When another new Aegean island was formed by volcanic activity in A.D. 46, Asklepiodotos said that the sea at that point had been 200 feet deep (Seneca *NQ* 2.26.6). No man has reached or measured the greatest depths of the sea, says Oppian, but 'down to three hundred fathoms (*orguiai*) men have explored and more or less know the deep' (1.82.5). The three here is symbolic (meaning 'lots') or Oppian is exaggerating wildly: 300 *orguiai* is about 1,800 feet. Three hundred feet would have been an achievement for ancient divers.[58]

Aristophanes' *Clouds* takes meteorological phenomena as its spring-board and symbol of philosophical studies. The water cycle was well worked out, and early.[59] Ancient weather-lore consisted largely of correlations between types of weather and other phenomena. In the case of astronomical phenomena, the weather could be compared with centuries-long folk-lore or written records of observations (*parapegmata*), the latter originating in Babylonian omen literature and made by the Greeks from Meton's time.[60] The Hippocratics believed weather was a factor in disease, and so they enquired into and frequently noted what the

contrast to those fuller reports by earlier authors of earlier events, should be seen in context: Seneca was in exile on Corsica at the time (A.D. 46) and may have found information-gathering difficult.

[57] e.g. 1.3.4–5. The general point is in Aristotle *Meteorology* 1.14, who also noted that this process 'takes place so gradually and in periods of time which are so immense compared with the length of our life, that these changes are not observed', for which we now have the phrase 'geological time'.

[58] On which see p. 113 n. 37 below.

[59] See e.g. Aristotle *Meteorology* 1.9 346b–349b10.

[60] See e.g. Aristotle *Meteorology* 2.5 361b32–5 on Orion for a 'folk-lore'-type correlation and Hipparkhos Frag. L (with commentary) in Dicks, 1960, pp. 54–5 and 111–12, for correlations (and predictions) based on a body of historical records and observations made by Hipparkhos himself.

weather had been like just before the onset of ill-health in the patient.[61] In the case of corresponding animal behaviour, such as ants moving their 'eggs' (pupae in fact),[62] or tiny spiders spinning single threads by which they float in the air,[63] we seem to be still in the realm of folklore or common beliefs, comparable with modern weather-forecasting lore such as if cows sit down it's going to rain. Aristotle and others attempted to explain correlations between the weather and astronomical phenomena (with or without astrological elements), but this remains an inexact science, modern theories and technology notwithstanding.

5.4 *Mathematical geography*

Astronomical observations from near and far enabled the mathematic-ally able to compute the size and shape of the earth, make maps with different projections, and locate on them significant cities or rivers. Our word climate derives from Greek *klima* (pl. *klimata*), which literally means inclination, and originally meant a line on the globe of the earth, parallel to the equator, on which the length of the longest day was the same, e.g. 14 hours 30 minutes at Rhodes and at everywhere on the same *klima*. These lines were drawn at regular arithmetical intervals, usually half-hourly, from 13 hours at Meroë in Ethiopia to 16 hours at Borysthenes on the north coast of the Euxine. In application to geography, *klima* came to signify also a band or zone around the earth, and it is from this secondary development that our word climate derives.

After mapping the heavens and writing the *Almagest* Ptolemy took it upon himself to make a more accurate map of the earth than had hitherto existed. Apart from new knowledge gained by the expansion of empire and trade links, there was now available more astronomical data than hitherto, and it was only on the basis of such data that accurate maps could be drawn. This is not to say that there was much such data, but there was some. His finished work gives a spurious air of accuracy, however, because he decided to present *all* the material to hand – and not just the carefully observed data – in a digital fashion. For example, when told that the journey from X to Y took '10 or 12 days' to cover, Ptolemy translated this into degrees of latitude or longitude via a thumb-

---

[61] See e.g. *Epidemics* 1.1, a summary of the year's weather preceding an epidemic of mumps on Thasos.
[62] See e.g. Theophrastos *On Weather-signs* 22.
[63] See e.g. [Aristotle] *Problems* 26.61.

rule of average number of *stadia* covered per day, and made other adjustments which in general seem to arise primarily from a desire to simplify the computations. So the tables of locations set out in his *Geography* look precise and scientific, but the vast majority of the numbers therein are essentially guesstimates. Ptolemy does not hide this fact: though he is not as explicit on his methodology as we might like him to be, he cautions the reader in book 1.1–6 on the quality of the data he has had to work with. It should also be noted that lists of numbers are peculiarly liable to error in the transmission of the manuscript down through history: try copying out a page of telephone numbers. So some of the errors we find in Ptolemy's *Geography* probably entered the text in the course of copying, but it is usually impossible to know which. The digital presentation was not merely for show. The aim of the work is to provide the reader with everything he needs to know to be able to make his own maps, emphasizing his own part of the world, at his own preferred scale and projection. The digital reference system for locations was, in this context, vastly superior to the descriptive type which preceded it. By contrast, if ten different people tried to draw a map from, say, Strabo's *Geography*, there would probably be ten quite different maps as a result.

5.5 *Maps and politics*

Maps are political. For entirely natural reasons they are often distorted by being generous with the area whence the mapmaker comes, which is shown in detail, exaggerated in size, and usually placed centrally on the image, whilst as one moves out from that area, they are distorted in the opposite way, with sizes and distances being increasingly underestimated and more and more detail omitted. This is true even of modern maps. For example, wall maps of the world sold in Britain have Europe in the middle, Americas in the west, and the Far East in the far east – note the label, attached by people who evidently lived around the other side of the world, in what they took to be the centre of it when they named the region. The ancient Chinese, of course, made maps which called China the 'Middle Kingdom'.[64] Other things are more subtle; for example, we prioritize 'north', and the compass points may be marked simply by the N, leaving the viewer to work out which way are S, E and W. The Chinese, who invented the magnetic compass, prioritized south,

---

[64] Berthon and Robinson 1991 p. 27.

e.g. the south-pointing spoon.[65] Sometimes the politicization is more obvious. Strabo says, for example, 'For, so far as science (ἐπιστήμη) is concerned, it is sufficient to assume that, just as it was appropriate to fix a limit of the habitable world by proceeding three thousand *stadia* south of Meroë, so in this case too (northern extreme) we must reckon not more than three thousand *stadia* north of Britain, or only a little more, say, four thousand *stadia*. And for governmental purposes there would be no advantage in knowing such countries and their inhabitants, and particularly if the people live in islands which are of such a nature that they can neither injure nor benefit us in any way because of their isolation' (2.5.8 C115, Jones trans.). Agrippa's map was almost certainly bounded by the limits not of the known world but of the Roman Empire: the Rhine, Danube, and Euphrates rivers to the north and east; deserts to the south; oceans to the west.[66]

Maps were available early and, apparently, were not rarities. Aristagoras (regrettably for him) brought a map of the Persian empire to Kleomenes (Herodotos 5.49–50); the founder of a new colony drew up a map of the area marking the allotments to polis, gods, and individual settlers;[67] the map in Aristophanes' thinking-shop showed Sparta uncomfortably close to Athens (*Clouds* 200 ff.); visitors to the Lyceum after the death of Theophrastos could study maps of the world painted on wooden panels (DL 5.51); Strabo (1.1.21 C13) expects his audience to have seen a model globe showing the celestial sphere with great circles, ecliptic, and so on;[68] even the Roman man-in-the-street was exposed to a map of the world in the portico of Octavia on the Via Lata. The Romans also produced Peutinger-style 'road maps', which gave distances in Roman miles between places en route.[69] Terrestrial and celestial spheres were depicted on coins from C1 B.C. on.[70] As Field points out, given the small size and few details on numismatic images, 'viewers are presumably expected to recognize the object from rather slender clues' (ibid.). I would point out that this indicates their familiarity. Terrestrial spheres perhaps were less popular and less

[65] See Needham 1962 §26 pp. 249, 261–79, 314–34. The 'spoon' is the Chinese name for the constellation we call Ursa Major, the Great Bear or Big Dipper, which circles the north celestial pole.

[66] Augustus' lost *Epitome* of the empire and description of Italy suggests that this is where Agrippa's patron's interests, if not his own, really lay.

[67] See e.g. Metraux 1978 pp. 59–75 on Herakleia in south Italy.

[68] Archimedes' own sphere was taken to the Temple of Virtue in Rome, Cicero *Rep.* 1.21–2. Strabo 1.3.3 refers to a sphere-lathe, a machining tool for producing perfect spheres.

[69] On which see Dilke 1985 chapter 8.

[70] See Field 1996 p. 111.

common than celestial spheres because they revealed unequivocally how little of the earth's surface was known and still less inhabited.[71] This did however help Seneca make his point about the inconsequentiality of human life and material possessions, when conducting his thought-experiment of the view of earth from space: 'As the mind wanders among the stars it delights in laughing at the mosaic floors of the rich and at the whole earth with all its gold . . . the mind cannot despise colonnades, panelled ceilings gleaming with ivory, trimmed shrubbery, and streams made to approach mansions, until it goes around the entire universe and looking down to earth from above (an earth limited and covered mostly by sea – while even the part out of the sea is squalid or parched or frozen) says to itself "Is this that pinpoint which is divided by sword and fire among so many nations? How ridiculous are the boundaries of mortals!" . . . that is a mere pinpoint on which you navigate, on which you wage war, on which you arrange tiny kingdoms – tiny, even though ocean does run to meet it on both sides' and so on (*NQ* 1 Pref. 7–11).

Besides these cultural aspects there are practical ones. Mapping onto a globe is straightforward. But any map which tries to project a three-dimensional object, the earth, onto a two-dimensional surface, a sheet of papyrus, block of stone, or computer screen, distorts it: stretching, squeezing, cutting, or twisting parts of it. It is not possible to show accurately on the same map more than one thing – distances, or areas, or directions, or shapes. So the mapmaker has to choose which property to prioritize, and around which point or line, and distort the rest as necessary, or choose to project an image which is inaccurate in all respects but which minimizes the distortion in all.

What is remarkable about the best ancient mapmakers is not their errors, which follow the usual pattern of ethnocentricity, exaggeration close to home, and progressive omission and underestimation as they move further from their known world into the unknown, but their self-consciousness of such 'human error', and their desire to overcome it by using astronomical data to locate places and size regions accurately and without prejudice. Their problem then was the rarity of such data (the latitudes of only Alexandria, Marseilles, Rhodes, Rome, Syene and a few other places were astronomically determined). Ptolemy, moreover, appreciated the distortion created by a projection.

---

[71] See e.g. Strabo 2.5.10–11, C116–7, assuming that people will make a 2D map of at least seven-foot width rather than a more accurate 3D globe of at least ten-foot diameter, of which only 'a small fraction' will be the inhabited world.

The awareness of human error in geography extended beyond the difficulties of accurate mapping to the difficulties of obtaining accurate information of any sort. As Plutarch noted in his introduction to his *Life of Theseus* (Perrin trans.), 'Just as geographers, O Socius Senecio, crowd on to the outer edges of their maps the parts of the earth which elude their knowledge, with explanatory notes that "What lies beyond is sandy desert without water and full of wild beasts", or "blind marsh", or "Scythian cold", or "frozen sea", so in the writing of my Parallel Lives, now that I have traversed those periods of time which are accessible to probable reasoning and which afford basis for a history dealing with facts, I might well say of the earlier periods: "What lies beyond is full of marvels and unreality, the land of poets and fabulists, of doubt and obscurity".'

FURTHER READING

E. H. Bunbury's *History of Ancient Geography*, 2 vols (London, 1879), reprinted Amsterdam, 1979) is still a good place to start for a comprehensive survey of the subject. J. O. Thomson's *History of Ancient Geography* (Cambridge, 1948) also provides an overview. O. A. W. Dilke's *The Roman Land Surveyors: an Introduction to the Agrimensores* (Newton Abbot, 1971), and *Greek and Roman Maps* (London, 1985) contain much more than their titles suggest. A new introduction to ancient geography by K. Brodersen and a study on ancient meteorology by L. Taub are soon to be published, both by Routledge.

Principal primary sources in English translation:

Anon., *Periplus of the Erythraean Sea*. Trans. W. H. Schoff (New York, 1912, also by Huntingford, Hakluyt Soc., 1980).

Anon., *Aetna* is in the *Minor Latin Poets* volume, ed. and trans. J. W. and A. M. Duff, Loeb, 1935.

Aristotle, *Meteorology*. Ed. and trans. H. D. P. Lee, Loeb, 1952.

Posidonius, Vol. 3: *The Translation of the Fragments*, by I. G. Kidd (Cambridge, 1999).

Ptolemy, *Geography*. Trans. E. Stevenson (Mineola, 1991); another by Berggren and Jones is promised.[72]

Pytheas, *On the Ocean*. Ed. and trans. C. Roseman (Chicago, 1994).

Strabo, *Geography*. Trans. H. Jones, 8 vols., Loeb, London, 1917–32; vol. 1 reprinted in 1989.

Theophrastos, *On Weather-signs* in Loeb *Enquiry into Plants*, vol. 2; *On Stones*

[72] Riley 1995 p. 231 n. 16.

text, trans. and comm. by E. Caley and J. Richards (Columbus, 1956), also by D. Eichholz (Oxford, 1965).

The *Corpus Agrimensorum Romanorum* is being done by Campbell (trans. and comm.) as a JRS monograph to appear soon.

A selection was translated into English by M. Cary and E. Warmington in *The Ancient Explorers* in 1929, and by E. Warmington, *Greek Geography* in 1934. A different sort of text altogether was provided by Rhys Carpenter in *Beyond the Pillars of Hercules* (1966), a reconstruction of some ancient voyages, with many fragmentary sources in translation, and a few in full.

VI. BIOLOGY AND MEDICINE

6.1 *Introduction*

Biology and medicine form a huge area. I am treating them together because there is a very close link between all the life sciences in the ancient sources.[1] The Greeks were never in any doubt that humans are a type of animal, and not some special separate kingdom of life on earth. Aristotle's famous dictum 'man is an animal meant to live in a polis',[2] Arion's dolphin,[3] Herodotos' werewolves (4.105), people turned by gods into animals and plants,[4] Aesop's fables, Medusa, the centaur, minotaur, siren, and other half-human and half-animal creatures, all reveal the depth of the perceived affinity between humans and other species of life on earth. In the field of medicine, ideas about human anatomy were based to a significant extent on animal anatomy.[5] People and animals could be observed to suffer from the same epidemic disease,[6] and the same cure for X could be offered as treatment for people or animals.[7] [Aristotle] *Physiognomics* is a politically very in-correct comparison of physical features of people with those of different animals, and likens such appearances to corresponding personal char-acteristics. Poseidonios debated ethics and the emotions with his fellow-Stoic Khrusippos using children and animals as examples,[8] and Plutarch

[1] Even linguistically: what we translate 'body fluids' or 'humours', χυμοί, can also mean fruit juice or plant sap.

[2] Better known in a less literal translation as 'man is a political animal'. Throughout this chapter the word 'man' is used consciously. The ancients regarded the adult male as the highest human form; woman was deficient in some degree; children were deficient in larger degree. Therefore on many occasions to substitute 'human' or 'person' would be to misrepresent them; they said man and they meant man. In the case of Aristotle's dictum, for example, 'human' would make nonsense of his point, for only adult males could be citizens, *politai*, full members of the polis.

[3] Oppian records a special friendship between a boy and a dolphin in his own time, *Hal.* 5.458–518. He goes on (line 520) to say that dolphins 'have a heart so much at one with men' (Mair trans.; the key terms are θυμός and ὁμοφρονέω).

[4] E.g. Circe's pigs or Narcissus. The gods themselves were portrayed in e.g. literature and sculpture as larger-than-life people, and there are also half-human half-animal figures such as Pan.

[5] Most of Galen's errors derive from his superimposition of ape soft tissues on a human skeleton.

[6] E.g. Thoukudides 2.50 on the Athenian plague of 430 killing dogs and carrion birds as well as people.

[7] E.g. preparations made from blister-beetles for skin complaints and birth problems; for full discussion see Beavis, 1988, pp. 168–73.

[8] See frags. 33, 159, 169 in Edelstein and Kidd 1972. Since Greek philosophers typically reserved possession of the highest human and rational faculties to adult men, it could be argued that they drew a stronger line between adult men and all other animals than between humans and all other animals.

and others argued for the rationality of animals.[9] Aristotle said that 'nature passes from lifeless objects to animals in such unbroken sequence, interposing between them beings which live and yet are not animals, that scarcely any difference seems to exist between two neighbouring groups owing to their close proximity'.[10] The Peripatetic *On Plants* opens with a discussion about whether or not plants have souls and senses.[11] But while man was seen as an animal, the anthropocentric element in ancient biological work is paramount. The ancient scientists used man as the measure of all things. Even when they were not explicitly concerned with the utility of particular animals and plants to people, the vast majority of their basic data about animals and plants had been obtained from people who utilized those animals or plants.

The difficulties of undertaking any study of ancient biological works should not be underestimated.[12] How much ancient material exists on zoology is indicated by, for example, two recent studies of what is generally an unpopular category, insects[13] (about which Aristotle, the main exponent of ancient zoology, was *relatively* little interested).[14] These studies were researched independently but published almost simultaneously, and they deal, for the most part, with different material and take quite different approaches.[15] Insects also feature in studies of

[9] E.g. *The Cleverness of Animals, Mor.* 959b–985c, *Animals are Rational, Mor.* 985d–992e. In general on these ancient arguments about animals and human use of them see Sorabji 1993.

[10] *Parts of Animals* 681a10–15 (Ogle trans.), in the context of various types of sea creature, such as sea-anemones. There is an extended discussion of borderline life-forms and their relevance to Aristotle's methodology in Lloyd 1996a chapter 3.

[11] Aristotle's view in *On the Soul* is that plants, like all living things, have soul, but soul varies from the 'nutritive' or 'vegetative' soul of plants to the rational soul of man.

[12] As Meiggs commented in his preface, 'there was much more evidence to find than was generally assumed' for his book on *Trees and Timber in the Ancient Mediterranean World* 1982, which he brought to a close somewhat reluctantly after 10 years' research. This work is not a study of ancient scientific ideas on trees; Meiggs was an ancient historian utilizing scientific sources to better understand history, drawing his information especially from Theophrastos' botanical works and Pliny's encyclopaedia. A major problem besetting all modern works on ancient biology is identification; some scholars may appear to others as being too ready, or too slow, to identify an ancient X with a modern Y. There is a good brief discussion of the problems in Riddle 1985 pp. xxii–vi.

[13] Davies (classicist) and Kithramby (zoologist) 1986; Beavis (classicist and entomologist) 1988.

[14] This is not to say that Aristotle was not interested in insects; the emphasis is on the 'relatively'. See Davies and Kithramby pp. 16–29 for general discussion.

[15] Beavis considers all primary sources up to A.D. 600, and some later Greek works; he includes all insects except the honey bee (which has been well treated elsewhere in studies of apiculture), and all invertebrates except snails (which were done in Thompson 1947) and internal parasites (apparently not yet done by anyone). He assesses previous identifications, and gives excellent summaries of ancient beliefs and uses – including medicinal uses – associated with each of the invertebrates and insects covered. Davies and Kithramby are less comprehensive in the literary sources utilized and taxa covered, but they include the honey bee, discuss etymology, folklore, and other social contexts in which insects feature (including art), and comparative anthropological material on the same.

ancient toxicology[16] which examine the surviving scientific texts associated with the art of the poisoner, and those who sought to thwart him
or her. Aristotle's biological works have received a lot of attention over
the last generation, though this attention has a stronger philosophical
bent than a zoological focus as such, and they have not apparently been
studied for what light they can shed on social and economic history.
There are other ancient works related to zoology, besides Aristotle's,
which may not be as good *qua* science, but which do not deserve to be
completely ignored in Aristotle's favour. Moreover, as representatives of
other ancient times and places, they are fascinating sources for the
theories, and the histories, of their times. Plants have been studied more
for their relation to medicine (pharmacology) than in their own right,
and so here I will highlight some of the work of the father of botany,
Theophrastos.[17] Medical history is thriving,[18] as many texts survive and
many scholars are interested in their contents, and one is spoilt for
choice of topic. Veterinary medicine, by contrast, is only just beginning
to receive any attention at all.

Given the range of ancient work in the biological area and the
consequent danger of drowning in a sea of disconnected details, I am
going to focus on one theme for the zoological material. That theme is
marine life, and most of my examples of ancient views about animals
(and to a lesser extent plants) will concern those to be found in the sea. I
have chosen this area for examples because it is clearly defined, and
because it shows ancient scientists going out of their way to gather data –
sea life cannot be observed from casual observation out of one's
portico.[19] As Aristotle observed 'ample data may be collected concern-

---

[16] See esp. Scarborough's articles on Nicander.

[17] There is also a 2-volume work *On Plants* attributed to Aristotle, which survives as a Greek
translation of a medieval Latin translation of an Arabic translation of the original Greek; needless to
say, it is not a very satisfactory text, littered with textual difficulties. A considerable part of book 1 is
concerned with the sheer variety of plant life; a considerable part of book 2 is concerned with
physical (four-elements) theories.

[18] The Wellcome Institute for the History of Medicine produces a quarterly international
bibliography on *Current Work in the History of Medicine*, which started in 1954. A compilation of
these up to 1977 fills 18 volumes: *Subject Catalogue of the History of Medicine*, Munich 1980. Much
of this concerns other periods of course, but ancient medicine is well represented.

[19] This applies to Roman times too, when all manner of exotic animals were shipped to Rome for
the private enjoyment of the emperor and public entertainment of the plebs (and were sometimes
made available for people like Galen to dissect after their 'performance' in the arena). Amongst
these, the range and number of sea-creatures reported are very few: a replica (model) of a beached
whale was brought into the arena in Septimius Severus' time (A.D. 193–211), Dio *Epitome of
Roman History* 76.16.5; a polar bear, Calpurnius *Eclogue* 7.64–8 (the association with seals is the
crucial element – the white bear in the Pompe of Ptolemy and presumably kept in the Alexandrian
zoo was perhaps an albino rather than a polar bear; see Jennison 1937 p. 34); and unspecified sea-
beasts in Pliny *NH* 9.5.15.

ing all the various kinds [of plants and animals], if only we are willing to take sufficient pains'.[20] Besides, Greek society was a maritime society as well as an agricultural society, and these sources shed fascinating light on the Greeks' history, as well as their science. Medicine will be treated more broadly, to give an overview of this field.

6.2 *Man and other animals*

Aristotle spent a great deal of his time and effort on zoology. He wrote five works with animals in the title, of which *History of Animals* (*HA*), *Parts of Animals* and *Generation of Animals* are major works, and *Movement of Animals* and *Progression of Animals* are minor. He also wrote a number of other major and minor works relevant to zoology, of which nine survive: on the *Soul*; *Senses*; *Memory*; *Sleep*; *Dreams*; *Prophecy in Sleep*; *Length of Life*, *Youth*; *Old Age, Life and Death* (one work); and *Respiration*. The *HA* is the largest and most studied of these works. Earlier generations of scholars assumed either that the *HA* was a not-very-well-organized set of notes, or that Aristotle was attempting to produce a taxonomy, a hierarchical classification, of the animal king-dom, not very successfully. Balme got to work on the problem in the 1960s, and laid the foundations of the dominant current opinion, that Aristotle was rather attempting something more preliminary: to identify things in the bodies of animals – specifically, things which some animals have and others do not, such as a womb – which he could then use as an analytical tool to group and ultimately to understand animals.[21] His aim was then to explain those differences (and similarities), to be able to say why those animals – and only those – had that feature, to give the cause of that feature. *Parts of Animals* pursues this question. Thus his observations on any particular animal might be scattered across one or more books within and between different works.

Later generations continued to collect and record data on animals, but did not as a rule subject the data to analysis. Amongst Aristotle's corpus have come down works now thought not to have been written by him, but by others of his school, e.g. *On Breath*. These texts tend to be more empirical and less theoretical than is Aristotle's usual style. Works written later still tend to organize the information in a more encyclo-paedic fashion. They describe one animal more or less fully, or retail

---

[20] *Parts of Animals* 644b30 Ogle trans.
[21] The same animal thus might appear in several different sets, each defined by the difference in question. See Balme 1987, Lennox 1991 and 1994, Gotthelf 1985 and 1988, and Lloyd 1996a.

anecdotes about that animal (particularly if the animal or behaviour was unusual) and then move on to describe another, with little if any interest in, or reference to, questions of pattern, or explanation for why things were the way they were. On the whole, the standards deteriorate as we move forward in time.[22] Plutarch stands apart in this respect, for he continued to engage with biological theory and posed – if rarely answered – questions about the data.[23] The post-Aristotelian works on animals reflect the 'science' of their day, as the agricultural works of the Roman world succeed – in time if not in scientific content or approach – Theophrastos' botanical studies. They have been largely neglected by historians of science, but they are rich as well as unexploited sources, especially for the social historian.

There are numerous fishy references and allusions in literary authors,[24] e.g. Peisistratos' casting his net over the Athenians (Herodotos 1.62) and Agamemnon entangled in a net-like robe (Aiskhulos, *Libation Bearers* 492–4). Fish are dealt with at length and in tremendous observational detail in Aristotle's biological works. Two such observations were made again only in the C18 and C19 A.D.[25] At the same time, eels are one of those animals that Aristotle thought were generated spontaneously from the earth (mud in this case; *HA* 570a). This scientific error was not an observational error – on the contrary, it was based on acute observations.[26] Aristotle's observations were, on the whole, excellent (e.g. no eel *had* ever been seen with an egg, *HA* 538a8), but he could not observe everything, and sometimes the problem was not the absence of a microscope. In this case, the additional observations

---

[22] By the time we get to Tzetzes (C12 A.D.) we find confident assertions of such nonsense as 'Some uncritical people say that vultures bring forth live young, and that they produce milk and have breasts and other things. But I have discovered that, just as all tigers are males, so also all vultures are female. During five days flying with the rump against the winds, they conceive offspring begotten by the wind' *Khiliades* (ed. Leone 1968) 12.723–8. The general idea of impregnation by the wind goes back to Homer (*Iliad* 16.150), and even Aristotle believed in 'wind-eggs' (e.g. *GA* 750b24), but for him these were unfertilized eggs.

[23] See especially *Whether Land or Sea Animals are Cleverer* (*Mor.* 959–85) and *The Causes of Natural Phenomena* (*Mor.* 911–19). Curiosity is not entirely absent in Aelian; for example, he records an experiment (burning) to try to establish the nature of an old and badly preserved pickled specimen which some claimed was a Triton, 13.21.

[24] Davidson 1997 is full of them, including translations of many fragmentary and obscure sources, most of which are given in Greek in Thompson 1947. See also Richmond 1973.

[25] That two particular fish are hermaphrodite, and that one type of dog-fish embryo is attached to the uterus by a placenta, respectively; for the latter there is a diagram in Thompson 1947 p. 41.

[26] For another Aristotelian case of spontaneous generation based on acute observation, to wit the emergence of itch mites from subcutaneous tunnels in human flesh, see Keaveney and Madden 1982.

needed to sort out the life cycle of the eel could not be made until crossing the Atlantic was common (after A.D. 1500), and the actual observation of eel spawning was not made until the 1920s. Now we know that eels spawn (and then die) off the Bermudas; that their young swim across the ocean for about 3 years to appear in European rivers as elvers;[27] and that elvers can travel overland for some distance. Aristotle tried to make sense of what he *could* see.

The interest in sealife continues with works by Theophrastos,[28] minor authors, excerptors, and compilers, culminates in Pliny's *NH* books 9 and 23, and effectively ends with Oppian's poem *Halieutica*, of which parts are copied and more or less wholesale by Aelian in his *De natura animalium*.[29] The differences of approach between these authors are illustrated by, for example, their discussion of the use of poisoned bait in fishing: Aristotle mentions fishing by using a 'barley-cake' which was poisoned as bait (*HA* 591a18–25 with 602b31). Pliny (*NH* 25.116) adds an accurate description of what happens to the fish when it takes the bait, and names the toxin (cyclamen 'root'[30]); and Oppian gives a confident but confused account (*Hal.* 4.647–84).

Oppian has other strengths however. He gives a fascinating account of whaling:[31]

For these monsters the line is fashioned of many strands of well-woven cord, as thick as the forestay of a ship . . . the well-wrought hook is rough and sharp with barbs projecting alternately on either side, strong enough to take a rock and pierce a cliff . . . a coiled chain is cast about the butt of the dark hook – a stout chain of beaten bronze . . . in the midst of the chain are set round wheels close together, to stay his wild struggles and prevent him from straightway breaking the iron in his bloody agony, as he tosses in deadly pain, but let him roll and wheel in his fitful course . . . roused by the wound, first, indignant, he

---

[27] This great Atlantic migration, like others of its type, probably developed over a geological time-scale with and because of the continental drift of the Americas away from Europe.

[28] His *On Fish* has recently been published with text, translation, and commentary by Sharples 1992. Theophrastos also included sealife in treatises such as *On Animals which Change Colour* (notably the octopus).

[29] Or the sources for parts, in which case the close agreement between the relevant passages results from both Oppian and Aelian copying from the same earlier source. They were contemporaries, living in the late C2 early C3 A.D.

[30] The use of the term 'root' for corms, bulbs, tubers and so on is normal in ancient texts. Even Theophrastos failed to distinguish these structures from roots.

[31] Whales swim in the Mediterranean. Sperm whales were the most common large species in Thompson's day (1947, p. 280). Aristotle refers to whales several times, especially regarding respiration and reproduction, and seems quite familiar with them. Aelian 17.6 refers to large whales off the Laconian coast and Kythera, and his 'Ram-fishes' of the Sardinia/Corsica area (15.2) are perhaps killer whales, Thompson s.v. κριοί. I include Oppian's account not only for its intrinsic interest but also because it seems to have been overlooked in histories of whaling, which typically state that whaling (by peoples other than Inuits) began many centuries later.

shakes his deadly jaw against [the barbs] and strives to break the brazen cord; but his labour is in vain. Then, next, in the anguish of fiery pain he dives swiftly into the nether gulfs of the sea.[32] And speedily the fishers allow him all the length of line; for there is not in men strength enough to pull him up and to overcome the heavy monster against his will. For easily he could drag them to the bottom, benched ship and all together, when he set himself to such. Straightway as he dives they let go with him into the water large skins[33] filled with human breath and fastened to the line. And he, in the agony of his pain, heeds not the hides but lightly drags them down, all unwilling and fain for the surface of the foamy sea. But when he comes to the bottom with labouring heart, he halts . . . but the skins allow him not, even if he would, to remain below, but swiftly speed upward and leap forth from the sea, buoyed by the breath within them; and a new contest arises for the whale . . . and he indignant rushes again to the innermost deep of the brine, and many a twist and turn he makes, now perforce, now of his own will, pulling and being pulled in turn . . . [comparison with woodcutters using large two-man saw] . . . even such is the contest between the hides and the whale – he being dragged up, while they are urged the other way . . . now when the deadly beast is tired with his struggles and drunk with pain and his fierce heart is bent with weariness and the balance of hateful doom inclines, then first of all a skin comes to the surface, announcing the issue of victory . . . and immediately other skins rise up and emerge from the sea, dragging in their train the huge monster, and the deadly beast is hauled up all unwillingly (*Hal.* 5.131–51, Mair trans.).

As the largest predator on the planet, with a mouth and teeth[34] designed to catch and eat giant squid (but also adequate for dealing with sharks), a sperm whale would certainly strike fear into ancient mariners. Nearkhos[35] saw on his voyage a shoal of large whales which clearly terrified the crews on his ships.[36] Apparently on the same voyage the crews saw corals: 'in deep water there existed certain shrubs the colour of cow-horn where they branched out, and red at the top. These were brittle when handled, like glass, but turned red-hot in fire, just like iron, their original colour returning when they had cooled down' (Pliny *NH* 13.140, Rackham trans.). These unusual 'shrubs' were not merely observed, but were subjected to the common test for trying to establish the nature of anything suspicious or unknown: trial by fire.

No man has reached or measured the greatest depths of the sea, but

---

[32] Sperm whales can dive to great depths (2,500 metres recorded, and over 3,000 metres on the evidence of stomach contents) and can stay underwater for well over an hour; Cherfas 1988 pp. 34–5.

[33] εὐρέας ἀσκούς. These seem to be sewn cattle-hides like Cato's *culleus*, *De agricultura* 154, which there is used for transporting overland large quantities of wine.

[34] On lower jaw only; they fit into sockets in the upper jaw.

[35] Alexander the Great's admiral for the voyage down the Indus, along the Indian Ocean coast, and up the Persian Gulf.

[36] Arrian, *Indika* 30; he says they were seen 'along the coast from Cyiza'. Aelian refers to huge whales off the coast of Gedrosia, 17.6.

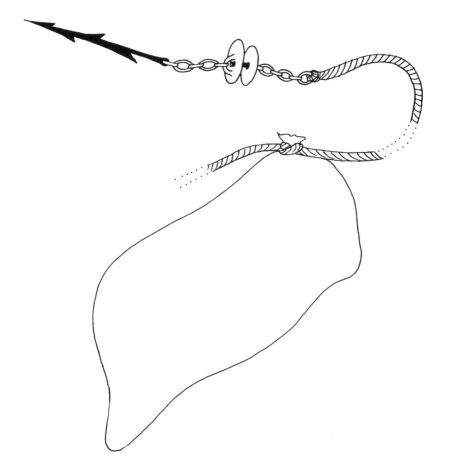

Fig. 6.1: Ancient whaling gear as described by Oppian.

'down to three hundred fathoms (*orguiai*) men have explored and more or less known the deep', says Oppian, exaggerating.[37] Diving for 'lifeless' things is mentioned in Plato *Sophist* 220a, in a long discussion using fishing as a topic on which to practise constructing definitions, with consequent details about types of nets, hooks, and techniques.[38] Aristotle refers to divers using some kind of breathing tube in *Parts of*

[37] Oppian *Hal.* 1.82–5. At about 6 feet to the *orguia*, this translates to *c.* 1800 feet or 600 metres. A recreational diver informs me that, using weights to descend fast (as the ancients did), 180 feet is quite possible without breathing apparatus (100 feet holding the breath is apparently routine), and that *c.* 300 feet is achieveable 'but scary'. The current world champion free diver can swim down to 150 m, where the pressure is so great that his lungs are compressed to 1/7th of their normal volume, and back to the surface, on one lungful of air, in about 5 minutes. Don't try this at home.

[38] 219d–221c. There are more details of gear and techniques in Aelian 12.43.

Animals 659a8–15 (Ogle trans.): 'Just as divers are sometimes provided with instruments for respiration, through which they can draw air from above the water, and thus may remain a long time under the sea, so also have elephants been furnished by nature with their lengthened nostril; and, whenever they have to traverse water, they lift this up above the surface and breathe through it'. [Aristotle] *Problems* 32 has a number of references to divers. In §2 we are told that their ear-drums burst; in §3 that they insert sponges into their ears to try to prevent this happening, in §11 that they pour olive oil into them instead for the same purpose.[39] In §5 we are told that they split their ears and nostrils to facilitate rapid exhalation,[40] and (amazingly) that they used an inverted cauldron as a diving bell. In considering common notions about (and presumably questioning) divers, the scientists were trying to find out, to understand, and to explain what happens to the human body in the alien environment of water. Divers' lore was being considered particularly in relation to respiration – which at that time was thought by the philosophers to be chiefly for the purpose of heat exchange, between the internal fire of the body and the external cold of the air.[41]

Who went diving? Pearl fishers may be the first to spring to mind[42] but sponge-divers went deeper than anyone else, because the quality of the sponge improves the deeper the water in which it grows. By Aristotle's time (if not before) three distinct qualities of sponge were recognized;[43] the thick, hard, and rough 'goats'; an unnamed thinner

[39] For this curious practice I know no parallel. However, sperm whales have quantities of a liquid wax (once thought to be the whale's semen, hence the name sperma-ceti) in their heads, which we now know aids buoyancy, because its density varies with temperature and they seem to be able to control that temperature (how is not known). They also (like other whales) sometimes have a waxy plug in their ears. It seems to me possible that the ancient sponge divers were imitating nature's greatest diver, on the basis of their understanding of the anatomy and physiology of that great 'sea-monster'.

[40] Again this practice may possibly have started in imitation of the whale, which can empty and refill its lungs in half the time humans take, shifting thousands of times more air in the process. A whale's almost explosive exhalation is its most distinctive feature as seen from the surface. Aristotle certainly thought that the divers' chief concern on reaching the surface was exhalation.

[41] See e.g. Aristotle *PA* 669a. Theophrastos was not so sure; in *On Fish* 3 he says 'perhaps more remarkable than [that a creature should be able with the same organs to take in air at one time and moisture at another] is that at one time air should be suitable for the cooling, *or whatever it is that is the effect of respiration*, but at another moisture' (Sharples trans., emphasis added). Habitat, diet, and anatomy were other concerns which arose particularly with regard to animals which have a double way of life (*amphibios*, Demockitos' term, whence our term amphibian) or dualize (*epamphoterizein*, Aristotle's term), and Theophrastos went on to consider [Marine] *Creatures that Remain* [for a while] *on Dry Land* (lost).

[42] See e.g. Pliny *NH* 9.111. Octopuses also seem to have been caught by divers – at least, that is the obvious way to make sense of *NH* 9.86: 'their lairs can be pin-pointed by the broken shells lying in front of them . . . the octopus is stupid, for instance it swims towards a man's hand'.

[43] *HA* 548a32–549a13. Named sponge-diving places are off the coast of Torone, Lycia, the Hellespont, and Cape Malea. Theophrastos *HP* cites the north coast of Crete for the same, 4.6.5. In

and softer type of sponge; and the uncommon thin and close-textured but strong 'Achilles' type of sponge, which Aristotle tells us was used to line helmets and greaves[44] – in Pliny's time this type was used to apply paint (*NH* 9.148). The latter two types would have come from the deep waters plumbed by the ancient divers, for as Aristotle recognized, 'as a general rule, sponges that are found in deep calm waters are the softest'. Oppian gives a vivid account of the sponge-diver's work:

Than the task of the sponge-cutters I declare that there is none worse nor any work more woeful for men . . . they zealously take watchful care that their breath may abide unscathed when they go down into the depths and that they may recover from past toil . . . A man is girt with a long rope above his waist and, using both hands, in one he grasps a heavy mass of lead and in his right hand he holds a sharp bill, while in the jaws of his mouth he keeps white oil. Standing upon the prow he scans the waves of the sea, pondering his heavy task and the infinite water. His comrades incite and stir him to his work with encouraging words, even as a man skilled in foot-racing when he stands upon his mark. But when he takes heart of courage, he leaps into the eddying waves and as he springs the force of the heavy grey lead drags him down. Now when he arrives at the bottom, he spits out the oil, and it shines brightly and the gleam mingles with the water, even as a beacon showing its eye in the darkness of the night.[45] Approaching the rocks he sees the sponges which grow on the ledges of the bottom, fixed fast to the rocks . . . straightway rushing upon them with the bill in his stout hand, like a mower, he cuts the body of the sponges, and he loiters not, but quickly shakes the rope, signalling his comrades to pull him up swiftly . . . swift as thought he is pulled to the surface; and beholding him escape from the sea one would rejoice at once and grieve from pity: so much are his weak members relaxed and his limbs unstrung with fear and distressful

Aristotle's time sponges were said *by some* to have a certain sensibility (they contract when they sense a sponge-diver), but the people of Torone dispute this, he cautions (*HA* 487b10–15). The difference between Aristotle and some of his successors can be illustrated well here: the assertion about a sponge's sensibility is repeated essentially unchanged but without the caution by Pliny 9.148, is embroidered by Aelian 8.16, and is elaborated with blood by Oppian 5.651 (omitted from excerpt). Thompson (1947 p. 250) says that this behaviour may be true of the limpet, but is not true of the sponge, thus the people of Torone were right and Aristotle was right to be cautious. Lloyd, 1996a, chapter 3 argues that this case and others like it (is it an animal? is it a plant?) testify to Aristotle's undogmatic approach to biological classification.

[44] Note that Aristotle does not refrain from commenting on the utilitarian aspects of the 'scientific' material under consideration, as we saw also with the diver's respiration tube.

[45] This practice and its purported effect is also reported by Pliny *NH* 2.234 and Plutarch *Causes of Natural Phenomena* 12 (*Mor.* 915a) and *On the Principle of Cold* 13 (*Mor.* 950b–c). In both cases Plutarch mentions it as a physical problem requiring explanation; in the former he offers the idea that the greater density of oil pushes the sea apart and offers channels of transparency, in the latter that air in the oil provides the transparency. Ptolemy seems to promote a theory in which light is related to brightness and colour, and which is derived from Aristotle (e.g. *On the Soul* 418b1–19a25); see e.g. *Optics* 2.5 'colours are never seen in darkness, except for [the colour of] an object that shines from inherent whiteness or that is exceedingly polished, for each of these is a case of brightness, and brightness is a kind of luminosity' (Smith trans.). This is consistent with the notion of white oil of itself being able to provide illumination, irrespective of the truth of either the empirical or theoretical claims. The light levels below the surface vary with the condition of the water, but all waters are pitch black by 900 ft/300 m.

labour.[46] Often when the sponge-cutter has leapt into the deep waters of the sea and won his loathly and unkindly spoil, he comes up no more, unhappy man, having encountered some huge and hideous beast. Shaking repeatedly the rope he bids his comrades pull him up. And the mighty sea-monster and the companions of the fisher pull at his body rent in twain, a pitiful sight to see, still yearning for ship and shipmates. (*Hal.* 5.612–74, Mair trans.)

6.3 *Man and plants*

Theophrastos set out to do for botany what Aristotle had done for zoology, namely to collect, analyse, and synthesize information collected from as many quarters as possible, in order to find patterns in the flux of life.[47] *History of Plants* and *Causes of Plants* are the result. The Greek word *historia* as used here is meant very much in its original sense of enquiry; hence the same work is sometimes known in English as the 'History of Plants' (*HP*) and sometimes as the 'Enquiry into Plants' (*EP*). So-called *Causes* is more a discussion of plant generation and physiology than of causes as such (and corresponds more closely to Aristotle's *Generation of Animals*). Although these are Theophrastos' most famous scientific works, and he is known amongst botanists as the father of their discipline, he was a true polymath who studied and wrote on many other subjects.[48] In his botanical works Theophrastos struggled with the variety of plant life, which in many ways is more difficult to organize than animal life, for the same plant can look quite different at different times of year, and at different years in its life. When he established the Lyceum as a registered religious association, with a bounded sacred area in which private buildings were erected, he also developed a garden. We assume that at least some of his detailed physiological work was done on plants grown in this garden. When he died he asked to be buried in the garden, and gave two slaves their freedom on condition that they gave four years' future work in it and

[46] The current record for holding the breath underwater is over 7 minutes, though this was set in an environment involving no exertion. Anyone attempting to stay underwater for more than a couple of minutes risks blacking out, 'relaxing' in Oppian's words.

[47] See Gofthelf 1988.

[48] The Theophrastos Project, under the direction of W. W. Fortenbaugh, began in 1979, and produced a fundamental two-volume work *Theophrastus: Sources for his Life, Writings, Thought and Influence*, Leiden, 1992. This work gives all texts in Greek, Latin, or Arabic with English translation of references to Theophrastos' works from earliest times to C15 A.D. Annual conferences on Theophrastean Studies are published by Rutgers University in the Studies in Classical Humanities Series (RUSCH), Transactions Publishers, London and New Brunswick. For further information, contact Prof. W. Fortenbaugh, Project Theophrastus, Alexander Library, Rutgers University, New Brunswick, New Jersey 08903, USA.

that their behaviour during this time was blameless. The tendence of the whole precinct was supervised by a manumitted slave called Pompulos, who went on to achieve fame as a philosopher in his own right.[49]

However, Theophrastos cast his net much wider than his garden, including – to continue our theme of sealife – even the flora of the sea. The various types of seaweed are described in sufficient detail for some at least to be identified with modern botanical precision.[50] In addition to a detailed description, there is regular mention of the utilization of such plants, for example two plants used for dyes (4.6.5,[51] 4.6.8), a sea 'olive' which produces a gum used in drugs to staunch bleeding (4.7.2), and a type of seaweed which he says was collected by divers and sponge-divers but he does not specify for what purpose (4.6.4).[52]

Cultivated and harvested plants form the mainstay of Theophrastos' database, and he spends considerable effort and space on, for example, methods of cultivation (*HP, passim*), insect pests and what to do about them (e.g. companion planting in 7.5.4), and the collection of 'juice' from medicinal plants (e.g. 6.3.2 with mention of quotas for taking roots of silphium, or 9.8.2, with mention of the opium poppy).[53] This corpus of botanical knowledge was taken up by Romans who wrote on agricultural matters, such as Cato, Varro, and Columella, none of whom were professional philosophers or educators.[54] They turned the

[49] The details of Theophrastos' Last Will and Testament are given by Diogenes Laertius 5.52–5. On Pompulos, see Aulus Gellius, *Attic Nights* 2.18.8.

[50] The first comprehensive attempt to identify the plants mentioned by Theophrastos was undertaken by Sprengel in 1822. His views were taken up by Wimmer, Teubner edition. Thiselton-Dyer provided the identifications for Hort's English translation in the Loeb, and where identifications were impossible or were to plants unfamiliar to British readers, Hort cautiously transliterated the Greek or rendered it literally on etymological principles. Meiggs notes that some of these need reconsideration (1982, p. 481 n. 6).

[51] This plant is actually a coastal margin plant, litmus, rather than a sea-plant as such.

[52] In modern times seaweeds are used to make food for humans and animals, fertilizers, and (as a Greek student informs me is done today in some parts of Greece) an alcoholic drink. According to Lobban and Harrison 1994 p. 283 collection of seaweed for food started in Europe *c.* 500 A.D., but Theophrastos was writing *c.* 800 years earlier than this. Nicander mentions a seaweed for snakebite (*Theriaca* 845) and Pliny mentions a seaweed used to treat gout ('the sovereign remedy' for this ailment in his view), other problems of the joints, and as a dye, *NH* 26.66.

[53] The human tendency now and in the past to focus attention on cultivated or harvested plants is discussed by Preus 1988.

[54] Cato is better known as the Censor, which office was the highpoint of his distinguished political career, and for his dictum 'Carthage must be destroyed'. Varro was born ten years before Cicero in 116 B.C.; his political and military career included serving under Pompey in Spain in 76–1 and in the campaign against the pirates in 67, being elected tribune of the plebs (in ?70), and praetor (in ?68). After being on the losing side in the Civil War, his learning was recognized by Caesar, who promoted him sideways (and out of politics) to the headship of the public library in Rome (Suetonius, *Caesar* 44.4). He wrote prolifically on numerous subjects, especially history and language. He died in 27, aged 89. Columella was a native of Cadiz in Spain, living in the C1 A.D.,

data into something more like manuals for plantsmen and women, dropped most of the theorizing about causes and consequences, and added more practical advice on how to grow and tend particular plants which were important to the Roman farmer. There was plenty in Theophrastos for them to quarry. So Columella's practical advice on dung (2.14) for example, echoes Theophrastos' observation[55] that 'manure does not suit all [trees] alike, nor is the same manure equally good for all [trees]. Some need it pungent, some less so, some need it quite light. The most pungent is human dung: thus Khartodras says that this is the best, pig-manure being second to it, goat-manure third, fourth that of sheep, fifth that of oxen, and sixth that of bushy-tailed animals [i.e. horses and mules]. Litter manure is of different kinds and is applied in various ways: some kinds are weaker, some stronger.' For the practising farmer this is all far too vague, and later writers are much more specific about which plants like which type of manure, and when it is best applied. They also record significant variations from Theophrastos, either indicating their use of other works, now lost, or promoting their own beliefs over the 'ancient wisdom' being handed down through Theophrastos.[56] For example, Columella thought pig-dung was in general the poorest type of manure, not the second-best after human.

Given the current interest in organic methods, Theophrastos' botanical works might be usefully compared with modern methods and theories. For there were no synthetic chemicals in antiquity of course, and all farmers worked with what are now considered organic techniques, some of which will be familiar to 'green' readers. For example, besides the instance of companion planting above mentioned, interplanting (celery with other crops) is mentioned in *HP* 7.1.3, the soil warming effect of manure in 8.7.7, and green manuring (with beans) in 8.9.1.

6.4 *Medicine*

Medicine can be entertaining in a way that other areas are not, partly because empathy with ancient patients and their would-be healers

---

and a contemporary of Seneca and Pliny. He served as military tribune in Syria, probably during Tiberius' reign.

[55] *HP* 2.7.4 (Hort trans.); other comments on manure are scattered throughout the work.

[56] A good discussion of this process, with reference to his minor rather than his botanical works, is given by Sharples 1988.

comes easily to any reader, and partly because some of the ancient ideas and treatments strike the modern reader as funny, either in a humorous[57] or a peculiar sense.[58] Perhaps because of this some of the modern scholars in this area have a lightness of touch and sense of humour which tends to be absent in other areas.[59] In response to earlier generations' concentration on the so-called 'best' (i.e. most like modern) aspects of ancient medicine, it has been stressed recently that there was a *variety* of medical beliefs and approaches during antiquity (simultaneously and over time).[60] What we recognize as the forerunner of 'modern' 'medicine' was not the only approach to health and disease, still less was it the main method of curing sick people. The wider context of medical theory and practice has also come to the fore in modern studies of ancient medicine, and a number of specific but interrelated issues have been highlighted.

There were no recognized medical qualifications in antiquity, and anyone could set themselves up as a healer. Some professed a specialism, e.g. umbilical-cord-cutter, root-cutter, or bone-setter; others were general practitioners. When the Roman authorities became interested in defining medical status, their motivation did not concern the standard or

---

[57] E.g. succussion, wherein the patient (suffering from a variety of ailments, but particularly prolapse or other wanderings of the womb) is tied to a ladder or plank longer than herself. The ladder is then banged vigorously on the floor, patient head up or head down, depending on which direction the doctor seeks to move the offending organ or part. It is somewhat reminiscent of the modern tendency to fix electrical things by thumping them.

[58] E.g. the various medicaments involving urine or dung of one sort or another, ingested or applied externally. There is a notable overlap here between medicaments and cosmetics: crocodile-dung, for example, was used in Roman times as a foundation (to whiten the face) and as a treatment for skin problems like eczema. It was probably a lot more healthy (for consumers as well as collectors/producers) than the material normally used as a foundation at least since the C6 B.C. – white lead. However, the term 'crocodile-dung' may be an Egyptian code-name for 'Ethiopian soil' (presumably a particular earth found beyond Upper Egypt; Lemnian and Samian earths were highly prized for skin preparations); thus it appears in the substitution list in Betz 1966 pp. 167–9. Other substances used are liable to make the modern reader cringe (e.g. a woman's menses or equine amniotic fluid), but the sanitization of modern life keeps most of us in a state of blissful ignorance about similar things used as ingredients in our cosmetics and drugs (e.g. human placentas, which I am told are sold by some hospitals to pharmaceutical and cosmetic companies, who want them for their hormone content). Do not be too hasty to judge the ancients, especially on subjects which are modern taboos.

[59] Notably Majno 1975, Nutton (many articles and books, mostly on Galen), and Scarborough (esp. articles on pharmacology). Even Heiberg can be funny when he talks about ancient medicine e.g. on Galen being saved from 'drowning in his own ink-pot', 1922 p. 99. Although Heiberg is best known for his editions of the Greek mathematicians, he also motivated the production of the *Corpus Medicorum Graecorum* (and his name appears on part 1, volume 1 of it), edited Paul of Aigina (medical compiler of C7 A.D., *CMG* 9.1–2) and Simplicius' *Commentary on Aristotle's De Caelo*; he completed the edition of Hero's *Opera* (vols. 4 and 5), and contributed to the *Catalogue des manuscrits alchimiques Grecs*; see Keyser 1990b.

[60] Lloyd and others, e.g. the Wellcome team in *The Western Medical Tradition* 1995 (henceforth *WMT*).

correctness of medical care, but tax liabilities and civic duties (registered healers were exempt from some of each).[61] The various alternative approaches were not independent of one another nor mutually exclusive: people might go to one type of healer (e.g. a Hippocratic) when suffering from one health problem, and to another type of healer (e.g. the god Asklepios, approached via one of his healing shrines) when suffering from another.[62] There was considerable overlap in theory and in practice between what different individuals and groups said or did. For example Herophilos, probably the most famous scientific anatomist of antiquity, called drugs 'the hands of the gods',[63] and Galen was motivated (or encouraged) to enter medicine by Asklepios appearing in a dream to his father when sick;[64] Galen was 16 at the time. But his belief in Asklepios did not end there, for much time and many papyri later he called himself 'a worshipper of Asklepios'.[65] Even within the relatively small subset of healers who wrote about their medical ideas, pluralism abounds. As Vivian Nutton put it, 'The medical market-place had many stalls and many stall-holders, and patients, as well as their physicians, could choose what to buy'.[66]

'Medical market-place' reminds us that all medicine was private, as well as that people could choose between different remedies, therapies, and opinions on what they should do to relieve their problem. If they lived in a place big enough to have a market-place, that is. Nutton has pointed out[67] that rural communities could not and did not sustain specialist drug-sellers, full-time healers, or academic theories of health and disease. The fancy parts of ancient medicine, both exotic substances or instruments and intellectual theories, are products of the cities and urbanity.[68] Most people in antiquity did not live in big cities, and utilized more traditional, down-to-earth and locally available remedies. For example, [Aristotle] *On Things Heard* (801a28–32) explains the mechanics of three devices used by the hard-of-hearing: a clay pitcher

---

[61] See Nutton *WMT* p. 45; see also his 1985a, esp. pp. 29–30. The same set of regulations disqualified *calculatores* from such tax immunities, as we saw in chapter 3 above.

[62] See Nutton *WMT* p. 16.

[63] See T238a–c and T249 in von Staden 1989.

[64] *The Order of My Own Books*, 19.59K.

[65] *My Own Books* 2.19.19; more generally, see Kudlien 1981.

[66] *WMT*, p. 4. Porter 1983 p. 15 was the first, as far as I know, to stress this aspect, saying that 'medicine has always been, to a large degree, a buyers' market'.

[67] *WMT*, p. 39f.

[68] Galen makes the contrast explicit when he comments e.g. on remedies used by 'rural doctors', such as cooked centipedes or millipedes for ear-ache, *On Simples* 11.49 (12.366–7 K), or on the honesty of small-town doctors compared with the charlatans and professed healers in Rome, *Prognosis* ['to Epigenes' has no MS authority] 1.4 (14.603–5, 620–23 K).

(*keramos*), a pipe (*aulos*) and a sort of trumpet (*salpinga*). The first would have been to hand in any house; the second would have been widely available wherever music was taught and practised; the third would have been much more scarce. Several scholars have pointed out that most ancients, living on and from the land, knew well the plants which grew around them, unlike most moderns.[69] This point is relevant not only to herbals and pharmacopeias[70] but also to e.g. recipes given in manufacturing (such as dyeing), recommendations for particular woods in carpentry, and treatises like Theophrastos' work on plants. Most people would know their local flora well, and the lore associated with different plants. But lay knowledge of the healer's art reached well beyond this, as Nutton emphasized in the context of Seneca's descriptions of his own health problems and a modern commentator's consequent assumption that he must have been a professional doctor.[71] Nutton also stresses that the difference between a layman (even one writing on medical matters, such as Celsus)[72] and the practising doctor lay more in their respective self-image and self-definition than in anything else.[73]

The medical groups are perhaps the most common 'schools' in antiquity, so I give now an outline of them.

In the classical period the Asklepiads of Kos, of Knidos and of Rhodes were schools of medicine whose teachers took apprentices and trained them up in Hippocratic methods and theory, forming extended pseudo-families of practitioners.[74] These groups are relatively prominent in the literary sources, but the number of such practitioners may have been few. The *Hippocratic Oath* barely gets mentioned in ancient medical texts, and there is plenty of evidence that many doctors did not follow its

[69] E.g. Scarborough, 1986, p. 60 (don't let the cheap typescript production put you off reading this book). We might compare the one apparently widespread bit of folk-knowledge today, that dock leaves take the sting out of nettles.

[70] And not just works entitled *Readily Accessible Remedies* or suchlike.

[71] Nutton, 1985a, p. 31 n. 24.

[72] Celsus' *De medicina* is essentially a Latin translation of a Greek text by Aufidius, a Sicilian; Farrington, 1949, p. 127. The range of Celsus' original encyclopaedic work is indicated by the fact that Vegetius' *Epitome of Military Science* book 1 (on the recruitment and training of troops) was once thought to be based largely on Celsus; Milner, 1996, pp. xvii–xxi. The lost part of Celsus' work also included some material on veterinary medicine.

[73] Nutton, 1985a, pp. 33–8. Lloyd 1995 stresses the links between this and the epistemological concerns of some writers on Greek medicine.

[74] The pseudo-familial element comes out best in the Hippocratic *Oath*, which those who joined such groups had to swear. The initiate swears to respect his master *as his parents*, to regard the master's sons *as his brothers*, and to pass on the knowledge to his own sons, his master's sons, and to those pupils duly apprenticed and sworn in to the sect.

injunction not to give abortives,[75] assist a suicide,[76] or use the knife.[77] Healers trained in one of these schools were sometimes sought out by would-be patrons,[78] in much the same way that members of the Lyceum might be recruited to tutor young princes, as Strato went to Alexandria to tutor Ptolemy II.

In the Hellenistic period medical groups tend to take the names of people rather than places, and followers of 'great' healers label themselves as such: Herophileans, Erasistrateans, Hippocratics. This is an era which perceived heroes in its midst, in medicine and mechanics as in politics and war; an age which promoted greatness in individuals and lost that spirit, sometimes called envy, which in previous generations flashed periodically to take the overbearing individual down a peg or two and spread the credit for achievements more widely. After Alexander blazed across the known world and went beyond it, and citizens did not hold back from promoting – or at least acquiescing in the self-promotion of – their mortal rulers to heroic or even divine status, so scholars and scientists did not hold back from promoting the man behind their brand of medicine or the inventor of a machine, by naming it after him. But as Alexander could not have done it alone,[79] so neither did the great medics or mechanics, and after this temporary spell of deference to authority, from C2 B.C. more labels arise, now based on the practitioner's preferred philosophy of medicine.

Thus self-styled Empiricists arise, who lumped together and labelled all previously-existing groups as Rationalists or Dogmatists, allegedly for emphasizing theoretical reason or dogma rather than empirical evidence (or so said the Empiricists). Thus 'Rationalists' or 'Dogmatists' is a label which does not reflect one sect or school but a mixed bag of them, and could be applied to any healer who promoted or developed theories

---

[75] On which see Riddle 1992.

[76] It is not clear what sort of assistance, if any, people needed in this matter. Pliny, for example, states in a discussion of suicide that every man 'has the power to produce (a timely death) for himself' *NH* 28.9. Stoic philosophy recommended suicide in some circumstances, and there are numerous famous or glorious, real or fictional, suicides in Greek and Roman culture, e.g. Alkestis, Demosthenes, Midas, the 300 Spartans at Thermopylai, Dido, Cato, Cleopatra, Mithridates. Hippokrates, *Places in Man* 39, offers remedies to help improve the mood of those who wanted to hang themselves. Amundsen 1996 chapter 4 discusses the impact early Christianity made on ancient attitudes to suicide.

[77] On which see Jackson 1990 with illustrations of all known types of Roman medical instrument, and select bibliography of works on Roman medicine published in the 1980s.

[78] For example, Sherwin-White 1978 pp. 266–74 lists honours awarded by different communities around the Aegean to 10 different healers trained in the Hippocratic school on Kos who had moved to those communities and served their citizens particularly well. See especially no. 5, which describes how states applied to the Coans for a doctor to be sent out to them.

[79] And could not continue when the army mutinied at the River Huphasis.

which went beyond mere observation and passive experience. Consequently it includes healers and anatomists of widely diverging and sometimes contradictory opinions. The emergence of the Empiricists is part and parcel of the general intellectual trend away from speculative theory and towards practical utility and experience which reflects the triumph of Roman values as well as Roman arms.

The first Greek doctor to work in Rome, one Arkhagathos, was known as 'the butcher' because of his fondness for surgery and cautery (Pliny *NH* 29.13). The activities of him and his kind prompted Cato to think that sending healers to Rome was one way in which the Greeks sought revenge on their captors (Plutarch *Cato* 23). But things changed in the C1 B.C. when a Bithynian healer called Asklepiades arrived in the imperial capital and attracted many followers to his way of healing. His philosophy was based on atomist physics, not on the four elements and humours, and his arrival coincided with Lucretius' poetic exposition of Epikouros' version of atomist physics in *De rerum natura*. They both moved in the circle of Cicero, Crassus, and other members of the elite. Lucretius made widely known the general atomist theory which provided the philosophical underpinnings of Asklepiades' beliefs and methods.[80] But much more important to Asklepiades' patients was the fact that he avoided using drugs and surgery if regimen – diet and lifestyle – could cure the problem. He aimed 'to cure safely, swiftly, and pleasantly'.[81] This was very popular with the Romans, who were more or less disgusted by some of the ingredients to be found in Greek medicines, and liked bathing and wine, both of which were heartily endorsed by Asklepiades. In the medical market-place of that time Asklepiades did well. Shortly after, the Methodists appear, whose point of distinction from other healers was the pursuit of simple-to-follow[82] rules of regimen, and a holistic approach to keeping or making the body not too wet and not too dry, these extremes being seen as the root of all health problems.

Galen was born in A.D. 129 and died in 204 or later. His eclecticism, his opposition to all his rivals,[83] his rhetorical as well as his medical skills,

---

[80] The interrelationships between physical theories and medical theories were explored in antiquity in a number of treatises, and a number of philosophers dealt with both, Theophrastos for example; see the list of his book titles in Diog. Laert. 5.44–6. Longrigg 1998 concentrates on what may be called the more theoretical parts of ancient medicine, where physical theories and medical theories meet explicitly. The same interest is apparent in Longrigg 1993.

[81] Fragment quoted by Stannard in the *DSB* vol. 1 p. 315.

[82] And simple to learn: 6-month training allegedly. See Kudlien 1970 pp. 3–27, esp. p. 17.

[83] He gave his own view of the major sects of his time in *On the Sects for Beginners*.

and perhaps above all the sheer volume of his work (which must have practically swamped any serious medical library)[84] resulted – as early as the C4 A.D. – in Galen being left almost the only exponent of the medical art to later ages. But Galen is like Plato in the sense that both are highly atypical: as Plato is, on the whole, excellent evidence of what the average Greek did *not* think, so Galen is, on the whole, excellent evidence of what the average healer did not think, or do. The tendency to take Galen's rhetoric at face value and confuse his high ideals with the actual practice of most people at the time – including himself – has aptly been called by Nutton (*WMT*, p. 60) 'the creeping tyranny of Galen'.

Turning from practitioners to treatments, we will follow the order of the Hippocratic *Aphorisms* 7.87, as most healers – and presumably even more of their patients – preferred to (Jones trans.): 'those diseases which drugs cannot cure, the knife cures; those which the knife cannot cure, fire cures; those which fire does not cure must be considered incurable.'

Drug-lore, which we aggrandize by calling it pharmacological information, was a popular topic in ancient times. In the same way and for the same reason that the majority of the populace needed to be self-sufficient in foodstuffs, so they needed to be self-sufficient in healthcare, although there were specialist 'root-cutters' from early times.[85] There was, consequently, a wide and interested readership for this sort of information. Theophrastos' *HP* book 9 is full of medicinal recipes. A large amount of Pliny's *NH*[86] concerns herbal and other remedies – over 900 substances across 13 books.[87] Pliny was aiming to inform the Roman *paterfamilias* so that he could treat his household as in Cato's

---

[84] He wrote over 350 works, which vary in length from 30 to 500 pages, and the modern printed edition of the corpus (ed. Kuhn), which has only 133 works (not all of which are genuine, e.g. *On Urine* in vol. 19) runs to 8,000 pages, Nutton *WMT*, p. 60. Eighty or so works carry his name but were not written by him. Falsey attributed works started appearing in his own lifetime, and prompted him to write *On My Own Books*. Wilamowitz called him a windbag (Seichbeutel), Heiberg described him as 'unattractive' and 'offensive', and those scholars who have devoted the much time required to get to know the man through his writings seem to go off him in the process. E.g. Kudlien in the *DSB* makes his point by saying that Galen may 'have inherited something from his mother', whom Galen himself likened to Sokrates' wife Xanthippe, who had a reputation as a battleaxe. Nutton, who has probably read more of Galen's works than anyone else has, somewhere calls him 'obnoxious'. Galen seems not to have won any popularity contests in antiquity either, having no known students, and establishing no school (Galenism is a phenomenon which arises after he was dead, on which see Temkin 1973).

[85] Sophokles wrote a tragedy called 'Rootcutters', which is lost unfortunately. It featured Medea, perhaps the most famous witch of antiquity. The fragments of this and other lost plays by Sophokles have recently (1996) appeared in the Loeb Library.

[86] Which work is described amusingly by Heiberg 1922 p. 82 as 'an old curiosity shop' with 'precious information' lying side by side 'with all the rubbish which lay so readily to the hand of the tireless excerpter'. Beagon 1992 is more kind.

[87] Scarborough 1986 p. 59. The books in question are 20–32.

idealized portrait, and thus avoid the perils of using Greek doctors and becoming medical fashion-victims.[88]

Pharmacology has strong links with cosmetics: many of the same substances were used as ingredients both for cosmetics and medicines. Some conditions, e.g. dandruff or spots, could be considered as cosmetic or as medical problems, and some medical treatments might have been more acceptable if accompanied by appropriate cosmetic adjuncts. One of Apollonios Mus' remedies for dandruff, for example, is to wipe the scalp with bull's urine for a few consecutive days.[89] During this time perfume would be a nice adjunct for other people's noses, if not for one's own. Colonic irrigation, on the other hand, was only used as a medical treatment, and then one of last resort.[90] Mus wrote on both pharmacology and cosmetics: *On Easily Available Remedies* and *On Perfumes and Unguents* were two of his more famous works, the former much cited by Galen and other medical writers, and the latter extensively quoted by Athenaeus (e.g. 15.38.688e–9b). The popularity of the former work no doubt derived partly from the fact that the vast majority of the ingredients were easy to obtain – growing commonly in the wild, in fields, or in gardens, from where they could be gathered at no cost, or available at little expense from ordinary town and country markets and fairs. Some doctors had gardens in which they grew their own simples (e.g. Antonius Castor mentioned by Pliny *NH* 25.9). The remedies must have had a good reputation for efficacy too, of course!

The earliest sophisticated work on drugs seems to have started in the search for poisons and antidotes against them (*pharmakon* means drug, and can mean poison, beneficial drug, or even magical spell; when used in a negative sense the word 'deleterious' is often added). The royal courts which patronized intellectuals unintentionally fostered the development of poisons, for the monarchical power and prestige which permitted such patronage was sought by others, who needed to dispose of the current incumbent in order to further their own ambitions. Political assassinations are rare in ancient democracies, but potentially ever-present in absolutist monarchies of the ancient kind. Philip, Alexander, and those who went before and after them rose to and kept their seats on the Macedonian throne partly by disposing of rivals – a tradition carried on in the Successor states, and later by many Roman

---

[88] See Nutton's amusing caricature, 1985a, pp. 43–4.
[89] *apud* Galen, *Compound Drugs by Location* 1.8, 12.475–82K.
[90] See e.g. Celsus 3.21.9. This for extreme and painful flatulence. Other treatments he gives for the same condition include cautery of the abdominal wall.

emperors. Powerful people needed to protect themselves from those who would take their power. Thus poisons to kill men spawned antidotes to save them,[91] and both became recognized as useful drugs when mixed with other substances.[92] In the late Roman law on sale[93] there is a discussion dealing with the problem of differentiating between poisons and medicines: 'Some are of the opinion that a contract to buy poisonous drugs will not stand [as a legal contract] any more than a partnership or a mandate for an improper purpose: this opinion may be considered sound with respect to those [poisonous drugs] which do not admit of being compounded with another substance into something useful to man; but the contrary is true of those which lose their hurtful qualities by mixture with other substances, so that antidotes and other health-giving medicines are prepared from them.' Things had been simpler in Theophrastos' day: with regard to wolf's bane (aconite) he reported 'it is said that it is not lawful even to have it in one's possession, under pain of death' (HP 9.16.7, Hort trans.). Judicial executions were not unusual in ancient Athens, but the number of offences which carried the death penalty automatically on conviction were not many,[94] so if Theophrastos was well informed on this point, this is quite significant. This was not the same poison as was used for judicial executions, by the way: Sokrates' execution, as tradition records, was by hemlock.

Thus it is to the absolutist kingdoms of the Hellenistic period that we must turn to find the earliest Greek treatises on poisons.[95] An Alexandrian doctor called Andreas (fl. 240–200 B.C.) was a renowned pharmacologist. He was court physician to Ptolemy IV, and benefited from royal patronage, as did Krateuas (court physician to Mithridates), Diokles (court physician to Attalus III), and Galen (physician to Marcus Aurelius, Commodus, and Severus). Andreas' works are lost, but he was one of only two predecessors of Dioskorides to win that great pharma-

---

[91] This point is made by Justin in his *Epitome of the Philippic History of Trogus*, 37.2.4–6. See also Tacitus *Annals* 14.3 on Agrippina.

[92] Modern medicines can be very toxic (esp. chemotherapy) – the aim is to kill the bad things in the patient without killing the patient, hence the effort in modern times to make targetable drugs.

[93] *Digest* 18.1.35.2; see also *Digest* 48.8, which gives full discussion of the law on sale of poisons.

[94] The death penalty was automatic on conviction for: treason, certain kinds of theft including any theft by night or temple-robbing, for illegal return if exiled (and for harbouring an exile), for failing to observe some conditions of disenfranchisement, for self-prostitution for reward (applied only to citizens), and for citing a non-existent law in a court. Execution without trial was a possibility in certain cases, e.g. for 'do-badders' (*kakourgoi*) caught in the act of committing certain offences and confessing to the Eleven, or for a convicted murderer found in the Agora or sacred precincts; see Hansen 1976 and Harrison 1971.

[95] Earlier recipes for antidotes existed in the Near East, where power was also concentrated in few hands. Some of these may go back to Assyrian times, according to Scarborough 1977 p. 19 n. 7.

cologist's grudging praise for accuracy. Not so Nicander, who was probably contemporary with Andreas. He was not a scientist but a litterateur. He took earlier generations of scientists' accurate observations, organization, and terminology of toxicological material,[96] and scrambled them to produce the *Theriaka* and the *Alexipharmaka*. He subtracted accuracy, structure, and sense in order to add literary allusions, colour, or interest, and he squashed, stretched, or substituted information until it fitted his chosen metre. Poetic licence and scientific treatise do not normally mix well, and certainly do not do so here. Scarborough worked hard to recover some pharmacological sense from Nicander's poems.[97]

Dioskorides' *De materia medica*, written around A.D. 60, is the most important ancient pharmacological text surviving from antiquity. It mentions some 4,740 drugs. Riddle 1985 has shown that the organizing principle of this work – for long a mystery, rather like Aristotle's *History of Animals* – is the physiological effects of the drugs he describes. And this system was based on very careful and acute observation, an empirical method, informed by then current theories of physical properties such as 'drying' or 'heating'. This method was not appreciated by his successors, who preferred to arrange the material by a system of organization more like an A–Z by drug name, or by location of the problem, which made the resulting book easier and quicker to consult and use.

Galen brings together the work of many distinguished predecessors and contemporaries, some well known such as Dioskorides, others less so such as Andromakhos or Statilius Crito. He wrote three large treatises on drugs: *Mixtures and Properties of Simples*, which lists about 440 plants and 250 other substances in alphabetical order; *Compound Drugs Arranged by Location of Ailment*, which starts with the head and works down to the feet,[98] and *Compound Drugs Arranged by Kind*, which orders them by the type of drug – purgatives, ointments, caustics, and so on.

---

[96] Especially the lost *On Poisonous Animals* and *On Poisons* by Apollodoros, *c.* C3 B.C.

[97] See Scarborough 1977 and 1979. Hipparkhos made similar complaints about another very popular poem in antiquity: Aratos' *Phainomena*, a versification of Eudoxos' astronomy, both of which Hipparkhos then attempted to correct in a commentary. Being neither good astronomy nor good poetry, as Nicander's is neither good pharmacology nor good verse, Aratos' popularity is a vivid illustration of the foreignness of the ancient world. Needless to say, Aratos was translated into Latin (by Cicero, Varro of Atax [not the author of *De re rustica*] and Germanicus Caesar, amongst others) and many MSS survive, whilst Eudoxos' original and Hipparkhos' commentary were not, and exist only in fragments. The same happened with Nicander and his predecessors.

[98] This arrangement of the material, and the arrangement by kind, was begun by Mantias (*fl.* 170 B.C.) in Alexandria; see von Staden Part 2 chapter 18.

His personal store of precious drugs (e.g. cinnamon bark), along with other treasures and a large part of his library, was lost in the fire of A.D. 192 when the Temple of Peace and surrounding buildings were burnt to the ground (14.64–66 K). Earlier in his life he had made considerable efforts to locate and secure supplies of especially important substances, such as Lemnian earth, Cypriot copper ores, and aloe.[99]

Before moving on to surgery a word or two about anaesthetics is in order. There were none to speak of. Painkillers and sleeping potions were available, but they were not given before surgery, and their efficacy has in most cases yet to be tested (assuming that the drugs used can be identified in the first place). Celsus once mentions opium as a painkiller for a headache. He tells the reader to soak a piece of bread in 'poppy head decoction', and then wear it ('put the bread on the head', *De medicina* 3.10.2).

Much of human anatomy was based on animal anatomy, because there was a taboo against desecrating human bodies,[100] even in Egypt – embalming is not dissection, still less vivisection. The esteem in which surgeons are held these days is really very modern; until recently, surgeons were approached by patients and other healers as a last resort. This may have had something to do with the lack of anaesthetics, or the fact that some of the surgeon's instruments are essentially carpenter's tools made of better materials, for example the bow saw for drilling holes or bone chisel for tidying up fractures.[101] Surgery has not been a popular topic in the history of medicine, perhaps because one needs a strong stomach to work even as a historian in this area. As Celsus said of the ideal surgeon:

Now a surgeon should be youthful, or at any rate nearer youth than old age,[102] with a strong and steady hand that never trembles, and ready to use the left hand as well as the right; with vision sharp and clear, and spirit undaunted; filled with pity, so that he wishes to cure his patient, yet is not moved by his cries to go too fast or cut less than is necessary, but he does everything just as if the cries of pain cause him no emotion.[103]

In these circumstances one might ask: who needed the greater courage – the patient, or the surgeon? From my own experience[104] I would think

---

[99] In general on Galen's early years see Nutton 1973.

[100] See e.g. Pliny *NH* 28.5: to inspect human entrails is considered sinful.

[101] Diagrams of these and other surgical and cautery instruments in Jackson 1990.

[102] A Roman period epitaph for a surgeon who died aged 17 (*L'Année épigraphique*, 1924, p. 106) seems excessively young by modern standards.

[103] Spencer trans., Loeb 7.Proo.4. Compare Hippokrates, *Physician* 5.

[104] In a modern European hospital I had fractured and dislocated bones reduced, and severed nerves, vessels, and flesh repaired, all without anaesthetics. Anaesthesia is not risk-free, even today, and it is not given to casualties with head wounds.

that the surgeon needed the more courage. For the patient would go through the experience rarely or just once, in circumstances not of his own choosing, and in desperation; by contrast, the surgeon would go through it in the course of his daily work, his chosen occupation, trying to help people but having to hurt them in the process. Further, despite being conscious throughout, the patient may remember nothing of it afterwards, the mind apparently being able to short-circuit traumatic memories; by contrast, the surgeon would need active effort of will to keep the screams which he caused out of his mind and his nightmares. A certain insensitivity must have been required of any surgeon, and the development of sensitivities over time and through experience perhaps tended to make surgery the province of the young. Galen avoided surgery after his three years' or so youthful experience patching up gladiators. He recommended to his readers using pigs, not apes, when vivisecting around the head, on the grounds that 'the unpleasing expression of the ape'[105] distracted students from following the lesson, and we may assume that the expressions – as well as the noises – made by people under the knife were a good deal more upsetting for the surgeon, as well as any apprentices he might have with him.

This leads on to consideration of the practice of human vivisection, performed by Herophilos and Erasistratos in quite exceptional political and economic circumstances. Those circumstances were the private patronage of one or possibly two kings,[106] whose rule was absolute, and whose power over the life and death of their subjects included the power to choose the method of execution for condemned criminals. One or both kings chose – for whatever reason – to spend time and money on supporting intellectuals of various types, and they were prepared – for whatever reason – to sanction and support the vivisection of some people in the interests of anatomical research by two other men. Viewed in the light of normal surgical practices, and in particular the absence of anaesthetics, human vivisection was at that time not so far from the norm as it would appear to be today. The essential difference was that surgeons aimed to improve the life of their subjects, or at least not to make things worse, whilst vivisectionists aimed to understand the workings of the subjects' bodies, and were expected to kill them in the process. That is

---

[105] *On Anatomical Procedures bks 9–15* trans. Duckworth *et al.*, 1962, p. 15.

[106] Ptolemy II, possibly also Seleukos I. Herophilos worked at Alexandria under Ptolemy's patronage; his contemporary Erasistratos may have worked at Alexandria, or at Antioch under Seleukos. Euclid and Ktesibios were amongst Herophilos' other contemporaries in Alexandria. On Herophilos see von Staden. On Erasistratos see Fraser 1969.

a big difference, and I do not underestimate it. But we live in an age when even laboratory rats are rendered unconscious before vivisection, and the idea of humans being cut open whilst conscious is, I suspect, more shocking to us than it should be in this context. In antiquity, *all* cutting was done on sentient people and animals. Surgical texts and aphorisms spell out for the reader the symptoms and prognosis for clinical shock, caused by such an assault on the senses: death. There simply was not a nice clean line between surgery which saved and vivisection which killed; cutting was done without anaesthetics whoever wielded the knife, for whatever purpose, on whichever person, and was potentially lethal in any case. If one survived the surgery one could be killed by a post-operative infection, since there was no knowledge of microscopic organisms or understanding of sterilization.[107] This leads us nicely to nature's universal cleanser: fire. Cautery does have something to recommend it.

I know of no modern study of cautery, antiquity's version of laser treatment. It was used principally for cutting and sealing minor wounds and haemorrhages,[108] cleaning up putrid wounds and gangrenous tissue,[109] and burning off some kinds of growths and other protrusions.[110] Theophrastos (*On Fire* 37) mentions cautery for warts, for example. Branding is very similar, except that it creates a skin 'blemish' rather than removes it.[111] The iron is used widely in Columella for medical treatment of animals, and even for a sort of castration of cocks,[112] so there seems little reason to think that specialist cauterers were required to apply the iron. Celsus provides a general account of how to look after post-cautery burns.[113]

---

[107] Some ancient wound dressings had antiseptic, antibiotic, or caustic properties, e.g. wine, vinegar, or quicklime, but there was no protection against e.g. tetanus. In this context it is worth noting that Karasszon says (1988, p. 55) that the practice of pouring libations onto the ashes of blood sacrifices would have produced hot potash-water, which would have disinfected the altar. If so, this was surely a happy accident for the recipients of altar-meat.

[108] See e.g. Hippokrates, *Places in Man* 40.

[109] See e.g. Celsus 5.26.33–4.

[110] Other uses include fixing repetitive shoulder dislocations, Hippokrates, *On Joints* 11; treating bite wounds caused by rabid dogs, Celsus 5.27.2; burning off dead flesh e.g. Celsus 5.28.1.b; treating erosive cancers, Celsus 5.28.3.e; whitlows, Celsus 6.19.3; eye problems, e.g. Celsus 7.7.15.f–k; and gum disease, Celsus 7.12.1.

[111] Public slaves in Athens had the letters *ΔH* (abbreviation for *demos*) branded on their foreheads, and recaptured runaways in Rome were branded on the forehead too; see e.g. Petronius, *Satyricon* 103. Tattooing was another form of marking slaves or prisoners of war, on which see DuBois, 1991 chapter 7. Martial 6.64.24–6 refers to a barber called Cinnamus who specialized in removing such marks.

[112] Burning off their spurs, 8.2.3. There is no reference to branding animals in Columella, and when the occasion arises that it is felt necessary to mark animals (7.9.12; sows and their piglets in this case), the use of liquid pitch is recommended.

[113] 5.27.13. That this section on the treatment of burns applies to cautery in general, see 7.7.15 k.

The Hippocratic treatise on *Haemorrhoids* gives some idea of treatment by cautery (§2, Potter trans.):

First, undertake to find out where the haemorrhoids are; for to incise the anus, to amputate from it, to lift it by sewing, to cauterize it, or to remove something from it by putrefaction – these seem to be dangerous, but in fact will do no harm. I bid you to prepare seven or eight irons, a span in length, and the width of a wide probe; bend these at the end, and also make them flat at the end like a small obol. Clean the site you are attempting to cauterize beforehand with a medication, have the person lie on his back, and place a pillow beneath the loins. Force the anus out as far as possible with your fingers; heat the irons red-hot, and burn until you so dry the haemorrhoids out that you do not need to anoit: burn them off completely, leaving nothing uncauterized. You will recognize haemorrhoids without difficulty, for they rise above the surface in the interior of the anus like livid grapes, and when the anus is forced outwards, they spurt out blood. Let assistants hold the patient down by his head and arms while he is being cauterized so that he does not move – but let him shout during the cautery, for that makes the anus stick out more.[114] After you have applied the cautery, boil lentils and chickpeas in water, pound them smooth, and apply this as a plaster for five or six days. On the seventh day, cut a soft sponge as thin as possible – it should be six fingers broad in every direction – place a piece of thin fine linen cloth equal in size to the sponge on top of it, and smear with honey.

It continues by telling the reader what to do with his sponge.

Finally, an interesting but difficult study of ancient psychiatry by G. Roccatagliata 1986 is worth mentioning because there is very little modern work in this area, although ancient sensitivity to the mind at work was not confined to logic and epistemology, but extended well into psychology and mental health.[115] For example, there is a surprisingly large number of words for mental disorders in the Hippocratic corpus and other medical texts – indeed, there are more Greek words than English words for such disorders. The Peripatetic author of *Physiognomics* argues explicitly about the relationship of mind and body, with reference to psychiatric treatment (e.g. 808b11–30). Roccatagliata treats magic and religious aspects as well as general philosophical positions and clinical approaches.[116]

---

[114] In the context of cauterizing carbuncles, Celsus points out that the cauterization of dead flesh does not hurt, precisely because the flesh is dead, and that in such cases one stops cauterizing when the patient *can* feel it, 5.28.1 b.

[115] See also Simon (a psychoanalyst with Greek and Latin) 1978.

[116] However, he assumes throughout familiarity with modern Italian psychiatric technical terms, and the reader needs to recognize the context in order to turn some anglicized Italian words into common English forms, e.g. p. 112 Tholomeus = Ptolemy. One is also given the impression that Hippokrates and other Greek authors wrote in Latin. In short, this is not a book for beginners, but I know of no other which treats the same subject with similar range and scope.

6.5 *Animal medicine*

There is little modern work on this subject, and most of what has been and is being done is in German.[117]

Some diseases strike both humans and other species, e.g. foot and mouth. The bones of men and animals break in much the same way and need much the same treatment to mend. Thus, as in more recent periods, healers may treat both humans and animals, and we find for example Orion *the groom's* panacea mentioned by Galen, and treatments for mange in Dioskorides. The Roman *paterfamilias* (ideally) looked after the health of his family, his slaves, *and* his animals. It is not then surprising that there are parallels to be found for health problems and treatments in surviving works on human and animal medicine.[118] Outside military service, most veterinarians, like most doctors, were probably non-professional, but in the late empire a body of hereditary public slaves, the *mulomedici*, existed to tend the animals used in the Roman imperial postal service, and were based at the service stations along the routes.[119]

The word *hippiatros*, horse-doctor, is attested from the C3 B.C. (Fisher, 1988, pp. 191–2). *Veterinarius* is an older word than *mulomedicus*, horse/mule doctor, which is first attested in Diocletian's Edict of A.D. 301. The word *veterinarius* has been given different origins in recent literature. According to Dixon and Southern,[120] it is derived from *veho*, to draw or pull, emphasizing the link with draught animals; they offer no explanation of the rest (the bulk) of the word. According to

---

[117] There is a large project underway in Munich to translate into German the *Mulomedicina Chironis*, the *Hippiatrika* and parts of the *Geoponica*. For discussion of this project and a good survey of recent work in veterinary history see Fischer 1988, though this understandably misses Karasszon, which was published in the same year.

[118] For example, Columella states explicitly that broken legs of sheep are treated no differently from broken legs of men, 7.5.18; see also 7.10.5 (treatment for upset tummy), 7.13.2 (treatment for scab). Fischer quotes (p. 196) an author in the *Hippiatrika*: 'it is necessary to suture the peritoneum with the same technique that doctors use on a human', and cites other cases. On the other hand, post-cauterization dressings for animals (see e.g. Columella 6.11) typically feature urine (animal or human), liquid pitch or old axle-grease, which are not normally included in recipes for application on humans. Cautery was also used more freely on animals: 'Almost all bodily pains, if there is no wound, can in their early stages be better dissipated by fomentation; in the advanced stage they are treated by cauterizations and the dropping of burnt butter or goat's fat upon the place,' Columella 6.12.5. At a more structural level, the common arrangement of treatments from head to foot (*a capite ad calcem*) reflects the usual order of human drug texts which are arranged by location of ailment.

[119] See Codex Theodosianus 8.5.31 (dated 15 August 370).

[120] Dixon and Southern 1992 p. 224, following Lewis and Short. Thanks to the editor for noting that the OLD offers yet another idea, that it comes from *vetus*. The *Thesaurus Linguae Latinae* has not yet got to V.

Karasszon (p. 86) it is derived from *sus-ovis-taurus*, pig-sheep-bull, and he cites in support of this derivation the *suovetaurinarii*, who look after these animals prior to sacrifice.[121] Besides the more complete account offered by Karasszon, I note that one of the earliest uses of the phrase 'veterinary medicine' occurs in the context of the delivery of lambs,[122] and sheep were never, as far as I know, used as draught animals.

There is a reasonable amount on animal diseases and cures in Aristotle's *History of Animals* (book 8), the information coming largely from farmers and herders, it would seem. At about the same date a large treatise was written by the Carthaginian Mago, which his lost, but its influence was felt for over 1300 years. On the orders of the Senate it was translated into Latin in 146 B.C.; Cassius Dionysius translated it into Greek early in the first century B.C.; and Diophanes of Bithynia then epitomized it into 6 books. All these are lost. However, Mago continues to be cited through these translations and abridgements in those writers which have survived to us, e.g. Columella and Pliny, the latest being the C10 A.D. *Geoponica*.

Virgil's *Georgics* describes sick animals in some detail, and offers remedies, but this information has for the most part come from Varro's *Rerum Rusticarum*.[123] Columella and Pliny also discuss animal welfare in more or less detail.[124] Varro (2.1.21) distinguishes between those ailments of cattle which need treatment by a veterinarian, and those which the skilled herdsman ought to be able to treat successfully himself.[125] Pliny (*NH* 8.63) offers preventive treatments for dogs against rabies, which includes putting chicken-dung in the dog's food for the 30 days when Sirius is shining. Columella thought that dogs could be rendered immune to rabies if their tails were docked in a certain way (7.12.14). Columella also describes the construction of a *machina* to hold large animals firmly, to enable the less pleasant treatments, such as castration (6.26), to be administered safely (6.19). It is a confining pen with optional head holds. Something similar was built to make life easier for donkey stallions attempting to cover mares (Columella 6.37.10).

---

[121] Invocation of the three together in, for example, the prayer offered up by Cato in *De agricultura* 141.

[122] Columella 7.3.16: *quare veterinariae medicinae prudens esse debet pecoris magister.*

[123] See the 'Note on the Obligation of Virgil to Varro' in Harrison 1913 for detailed comparisons between the two works.

[124] Columella has much more to say on this subject (especially in books 6 and 7) than the other Latin agricultural authors. He also talks about fish-farming (at the end of book 8), though the only health advice seems to be to keep the water clean.

[125] As with sheep (2.2.20) and goats (2.3.8), he assumes that the herdsman 'keeps his prescriptions written down in a book and carries with him what he needs in the way of remedies'.

Most surviving ancient veterinary treatises concentrate on horses.[126] There was a certain amount of hippomania in the Ancient world. To cite only the most famous cases, the plot of Aristophanes' *Clouds* is motivated by a young man's expensive obsession with horses; Alexander named a city after his horse Bucephalus; Augustus erected a funeral mound for a horse; Caligula tried to make his horse Incitatus consul; Nero gave his favourite horses official (and paid) positions; Hadrian built a magnificent tomb for his favourite Borysthenes; and Commodus had Pertinax's hooves gilded. Turning from idiosyncratic emperors to the rest of the population, the role of the circus in pleb-management during the late Republic and early empire is well known and enshrined in the idiom 'bread and circuses'. That developed in the late empire into a situation where supporters of racing teams were more dedicated/fanatical than some modern football fans – one riot between the Blues and the Greens turned into a full-scale revolt, which left many thousands dead (the lowest ancient figure is 30,000), parts of the city of Constantinople in ashes, and 'all but cost Justinian (emperor A.D. 527–65) his throne'.[127] The heavy bias in ancient veterinary works towards horses is not, in this context, surprising.

Vegetius' *Mulomedicina*[128] (the only Latin veterinary work surviving entire) was based, according to the author, on all previous Latin authors on horse medicine. Two of those, whose works survive in an incomplete state, were his younger contemporaries Pelagonius, who wrote the *Ars veterinaria* (C4 A.D.),[129] and the author of the *Mulomedicina Chironis*,[130] which, despite its title, was written not by (the centaur) Chiron but by Hierokles. Vegetius adds that he consulted *medici* (human doctors) as well as *mulomedici* (horse doctors).

The *Geoponica* is a compilation of farmers' lore collected by the Byzantine scholar Bassus in the C10 A.D.,[131] which includes a fair amount of material on the medical treatment of draught and farm

---

[126] For an overview see Hyland 1990 chapter 3.

[127] For this interpretation of the riots as hooliganism, see Cameron 1976. The quote is from this work p. 278, and this episode is known as the Nika riot or revolt.

[128] Text ed. E. Lommatzsch, Leipzig, 1903. Most are now agreed that this is the same Vegetius who wrote the *Epitome of Military Science*; see e.g. Fischer 1988 p. 197, Milner 1996 pp. xxxi–ii.

[129] Text ed. K-D. Fischer, Leipzig, 1980.

[130] Text ed. E. Oder, Leipzig, 1901. Fischer described this as 'undoubtedly one of the most obscure texts in the Latin language' (1988, p. 203); he is working on a new edition of the text (see p. 205).

[131] Text ed. H. Beckh, Leipzig, 1895. Books 16–19 concern animal husbandry and welfare.

animals. The *Hippiatrika*[132] is another compilation, contemporary with the *Geoponica*, which drew on the works of about 400 authors and is concerned (as its name suggests) with horse medicine above all; but mules, asses, and oxen are mentioned occasionally.

FURTHER READING

For biology, see G. E. R. Lloyd's works, especially *Aristotelian Explorations*, which has an excellent recent (1996) bibliography and starts with a good discussion of changes in the interpretation of Aristotle's oeuvre by Lloyd and other scholars since the 1960s. The older tradition is well introduced by Charles Singer, *Greek Biology and Medicine* (Oxford, 1922), and D'Arcy Thompson, *Aristotle as Biologist* (Oxford, 1913).

For medicine, the best introduction is now L. Conrad, M. Neve, V. Nutton, R. Porter, and A. Wear, *The Western Medical Tradition* (Cambridge, 1995), especially Nutton's chapters (1–3) on the ancient world. This also contains a very useful chronological table on pp. 7–9, which locates in their historical context many ancient medical writers whose names may be unfamiliar to the reader. G. Majno's *The Healing Hand* (Cambridge MA, 1975) is a medical history written not by a scholar but by a pathologist with Greek and Latin; it reveals a pathologist's interest in the effectiveness (or otherwise) of ancient treatments, including testing the performance of some ancient drugs in laboratory experiments. It also considers Mesopotamia, Egypt, and India, and is as entertaining as it is educational. More specialized works or older useful surveys include A. J. Brock, *Greek Medicine* (London,, 1929), L. Edelstein, *Ancient Medicine* (Baltimore, 1967), M. Grmek, *Diseases in the Ancient Greek World* (Baltimore, 1989), R. Jackson, *Doctors and Diseases in the Roman Empire* (London, 1988), J. Longrigg, *Greek Rational Medicine* (London, 1993), E. Phillips, *Greek Medicine* (London, 1973), J. Scarborough, *Roman Medicine* (London, 1969), and O. Temkin, *Hippocrates in a World of Pagans and Christians* (Baltimore, 1991). One of the liveliest areas of modern work on ancient medicine, from both the methodological and the content perspectives, has been on women: methodologically because most of the ancient texts (including gynaecological treatises) were written by men, not women; and in terms of content, the development of women's studies and gender issues has prompted new questions and problems. L. Dean-Jones, *Women's Bodies in Classical Greek Science* (Oxford, 1994) and H. King, *Hippocrates' Woman* (London, 1998) offer excellent introductions to both aspects.

---

[132] Text ed. E. Oder and C. Hoppe, Leipzig, 1924 (vol. 1), 1927 (vol. 2): another text lacking an English translation (as far as I know), though French, German, and Spanish translations of parts of versions have been available since the C16 and C17. On the differences between (and problems with) different MSS of this corpus see Doyen 1981.

Principal primary sources in English translation:

Aristotle, *History of Animals etc.* There are many translations; the complete works are in the Loeb Classical Library, and in the Oxford translation which has been reprinted by Bollinger (Princeton) in 2 vols. In addition, new translations of individual works are appearing all the time.

Cato, *De agricultura.* Ed. and trans. W. D. Hooper, revised by H. B. Ash, Loeb, 1934.

Columella, *De re rustica.* Ed. and trans. H. B. Ash, E. S. Forster and E. H. Heffner, Loeb, 1941–55 (3 vols).

Galen, *On Prognosis.* Ed. and trans. V. Nutton (Berlin, 1979).

Galen, *On the Elements According to Hippocrates.* Trans. W. J. Lewis (plus 4 other Galen texts in English translation), **http://www.ea.pvt.k12.pa.us/ medant**

Galen, *Selected Works.* Trans. P. N. Singer (Oxford, 1997).

Herophilos, ed. and trans. H. von Staden (Cambridge, 1989).

Hippokrates: there is no complete English translation of the Corpus as yet, but the Loeb now makes most works available in 8 vols. The complete works are available with French translations by E. Littré in the Budé (1849, 10 vols).

Oppian, *Halieutica.* Ed. and trans. A. W. Mair, Loeb, 1928.

Pliny (the Elder), *Natural History.* Ed. and trans. H. Rackham, Loeb, 1938–63 (10 vols). Selection in Penguin Classics, trans. J. Healy.

Theophrastos, *Enquiry into [or History of] Plants.* Ed. and trans. Sir A. Hort, Loeb, 1916 (2 vols).

Theophrastos, *Causes of Plants.* Ed. and trans. B. Einarson and G. Link, Loeb, 1976–90 (3 vols).

Varro is in Loeb, bound with and listed under Cato's *De agricultura.*

EPILOGUE

In 1864 the biologist George Lewes wrote (p. viii) 'Numerous and exhaustive as are the works devoted to Aristotle's moral and metaphysical writings, there is not one which attempts to display, with any fullness, his scientific researches . . . Although Aristotle mainly represents the science of twenty centuries, his scientific writings are almost unknown in England. Casual citations, mostly at second hand, and vague eulogies, often betraying great misconception, are abundant; but rare indeed is the indication of any accurate appreciation extending beyond two works, the *De Anima*, and the *History of Animals*. The absence of translations is at once a cause and a sign of this neglect.'

Things have improved, a bit, in the intervening 135 years. Cohen and Drabkin brought together a large and diverse selection of English translations of ancient scientific works in 1948.[1] Every year for the last 25 years, on average, there has been a new edition or notification of the discovery of a new scientific text. Galen has been the focus of a recent scholarly project whose proportions reflect his corpus. Nevertheless, despite the 9,000 printed pages of that vast corpus already published, there are still unedited and untranslated treatises surviving in full in Arabic, and two-thirds of the corpus still awaits an English translation. The state of editions and translations of ancient scientific works as a whole remains scandalous by comparison with the torrent of modern works on anything unscientific – about 100 papers per year on Homer, for example.[2] And an embarrassingly large number of classicists are as (if not *more*) ignorant of Greek scientific works as their predecessors were in 1864.[3]

---

[1] *A Sourcebook in Greek Science*, reprinted in 1958. It is apparently still available from the USA, to order, at vast expense. Ask in your local bookshop.

[2] Over 100 are listed in *L'Année philologique* 1995, for example.

[3] See Lloyd 1985 p. 1. Cohen and Drabkin made similar points in their Preface of 1948. This ignorance continues. For example, a Canadian classicist and an Oxford classicist, writing about the finances of the Athenian empire, stated in a book edited by another Oxford classicist and published by OUP in 1990 that 'The Greek counting system was not decimal but sexagesimal'. Unsurprisingly they give no reference for this statement, and I assume that they did not bother to consult *any* book on ancient mathematics, where they would have read clearly and unambiguously that the Greeks worked with the decimal system, e.g. Thomas in the Loeb *Greek Mathematical Works*, vol. 1, English notes on arithmetical notation and operations, which opens with the statement: 'From earliest times the Greeks followed the decimal system of enumeration.' Those more familiar with Greek mathematics will know that sexagesimal notation, derived from the Babylonians, appears

One can study classics, ancient history, or classical civilization, at school and at university, at undergraduate and postgraduate level, without ever being introduced to ancient scientific texts or ideas. This phenomenon no doubt has many causes, which are not my concern here. But the result is that Greek science is relatively unknown to classicists today, to the detriment of both classics and historians of Greek science. An illustration: one Ptolemy studied the heavens and wrote the *Almagest*,[4] another Ptolemy rode with Alexander the Great and founded the Ptolemaic dynasty. The first Ptolemy's *Algamest* dominated the best European and Islamic minds for fifteen hundred years – five times as long as the second Ptolemy's family ruled Egypt (323–30 B.C.). But the second Ptolemy is widely known in the classical community, whereas the first is not.

Quite apart from the 'science for its own sake' argument, these texts can hugely benefit classicists and ancient historians pursuing their normal interests (whatever they may be), for they touch or delve into every aspect of ancient life. Some were written and not just read by 'educated laymen' of the ancient world, not professional philosophers making a living out of education (of whom there were relatively few). As Cohen and Drabkin pointed out, these works are 'a vital element of the *humanistic* tradition' (p. viii, emphasis added). They have a right to a place in a modern version of Hall's *Companion to Classical Texts*,[5] and classicists have a duty to include them in such a volume.

from the Hellenistic period on, in astronomy, usually for fractions (whole numbers continue to be expressed in ordinary Greek notation, producing a mixed system still used by astronomers today).

[4] And the *Analemma, Geography, Handy Tables, Harmonics, Hypotheses, Optics, Phaseis, Simple Sphere* and *Tetrabiblos*.

[5] This essential research tool in classics omits most of the scientific authors from chapter 8, 'MS authorities for the text of the chief classical writers' – even Galen, whose printed corpus constitutes about 10% of *all* surviving Greek literature up to 300 A.D., and bulks more than twice as large as his nearest rivals in volume of output, Aristotle and Plutarch (Nutton, 1999, p. 5). It has little to say even on those included, e.g. Theophrastos: item 1, The *Characters*, gets 15 lines; items 2–7, *Inquiry into Plants, Causes of Plants, On Stones, On Fire, On Sense and Sensibility*, and *Metaphysics*, get 7 lines between them. So while one of the 7 plates to the volume (and one of only two which picture people) features 'A Greek *physician* reading' (emphasis added), there is no reference to Hippokrates or Dioskorides or Galen in chapter 8.

BIBLIOGRAPHY

A. PRIMARY SOURCES

Aelian, *De natura animalium*. Ed. and trans. A. F. Scholfield, Loeb, 1958–9 (3 vols.).

Aesop, *Fables*. Trans. S. A. Handford, Penguin, 1954; also Vernon-Jones (New York, 1912).

Aiskhulos, *Libation Bearers*. Trans. H. W. Smyth, Loeb, 1946.

Anon., *Aetna*, in *Minor Latin Poets*. Ed. and trans. J. W. and A. M. Duff, Loeb, 1935. Text also, ed. F. R. D. Goodyear (Cambridge, 1965).

Anon., *Periplus of the Erythraean Sea*. Trans. W. H. Schoff (New York, 1912), also Huntingford (Hakluyt Soc., 1980).

Apollonios of Perga, *On Conic Sections*. Trans. T. B. L. Heath (Cambridge, 1896).

Aratos, *Phainomena*. Trans. D. Kidd (Cambridge, 1997); also A. W. Mair, Loeb.

Archimedes, *On Plane Equilibriums, On Floating Bodies, The Sand-Reckoner*: in T. B. L. Heath, *The Works of Archimedes* (Cambridge, 1897), with the *Supplement on the Method*, 1912, reprinted by Dover (no date).

Aristarkhos, *On the Sizes and Distances of the Sun and the Moon*. Trans. T. B. L. Heath (Oxford, 1913), reprinted by Dover 1981.

Aristophanes, *Birds, Clouds, Wasps*. Ed. and trans. J. Henderson, Loeb, 1998; *Wasps* also trans. A. H. Sommerstein (Warminster, 1983).

Aristotle, *Generation of Animals*. Ed. and trans. A. L. Peck, Loeb, 1943.

——*History of Animals*. Ed. and trans. A. L. Peck (vols 1 and 2) and D. M. Balme (vol. 3), Loeb, 1965–91.

——*Meteorology*. Ed. and trans. H. D. P. Lee, Loeb, 1952.

——*Movement of Animals*. Trans. E. S. Forster, Loeb, 1937.

——*Parts of Animals*. Trans. W. Ogle (Princeton, 1984).

——*Parva Naturalia* (a collective term for the short texts *Dreams; Length of Life; Memory; Prophecy in Sleep; Respiration; On the Senses; Sleep; Youth, Old Age, Life and Death* [one work]) published with *On the Soul*.

——*Physics*. Ed. and trans. P. Wickstead and F. Cornford, 1929, 2 vols.

——*Politics*. Ed. and trans. H. Rackham, Loeb, 1932.

——*Posterior Analytics*. Ed. and trans. H. Tredennick and E. S. Forster, Loeb, 1960.

——*Prior Analytics*. Trans. H. Tredennick, Loeb, 1938.

——*Progression of Animals*. Trans. E. S. Forster, Loeb, 1937.

——*On the Soul*. Ed. and trans. W. S. Hett, Loeb, 1957.

——*Topics*. Trans. E. S. Forster, Loeb, 1960.

[Aristotle], *On Breath* (published with Aristotle *On the Soul*).

—— *On Colours, On Things Heard, Mechanics, Physiognomics,* and *On Plants* in *Minor Works*. Ed. and trans. W. S. Hett, Loeb, 1936. *Mechanics* also trans. E. S. Forster (Princeton, 1984).

—— *Problems*. Ed. and trans. W. S. Hett, 1936–7 (2 vols).

Arrian, *Indika*. Ed. and trans. P. A. Brunt (in *Anabasis*, vol. 2), 1983.

—— *Periplous of the Euxine*. French trans. by A. Silberman, Budé, 1995.

Athenaeus, *Deipnosophistae*. Ed. and trans. C. B. Gulick, Loeb, 1927–41 (7 vols).

Augustine, *City of God*. Ed. and trans. G. E. McCracken *et al.*, Loeb, 1957–72 (7 vols).

Aulus Gellius, *Attic Nights*. Ed. and trans. J. C. Rolfe, Loeb, 1927–8 (3 vols).

Bede, *De temporum ratione*. Ed. C. W. Jones, *Bedae: Opera de Temporibus* (Cambridge, Mass., 1943).

Cato, *De agricultura*. Ed. and trans. W. D. Hooper, revised by H. B. Ash, Loeb, 1934.

Celsus, *De medicina*. Ed. and trans. W. G. Spencer, Loeb, 1935–8 (3 vols).

Cicero, *De natura deorum*. Ed. and trans. H. Rackham, Loeb, 1933.

—— *De re publica*. Ed. and trans. C. W. Keyes, Loeb, 1928.

—— *Tusculan Disputations*. Ed. and trans. J. E. King, Loeb, 1927.

Codex Constantinopolitanus. Ed. and trans. E. M. Bruins (Leiden, 1964), 3 vols.

Codex Theodosianus. Ed. T. Mommsen and P. M. Meyer (Berlin, 1905), 3 vols.

Columella, *De re rustica*. Ed. and trans. H. B. Ash, E. S. Forster and E. H. Heffner, Loeb, 1941–55 (3 vols).

The Digest of Roman Law. Ed. T. Mommsen (Berlin, 1920).

Dio, *Epitome of Roman History*. Trans. E. Cary, Loeb, 1914–27 (9 vols).

Diodorus Siculus, *The Library of History*. Ed. and trans. C. H. Oldfather *et al.*, Loeb, 1933–67 (12 vols).

Diogenes Laertius, *Lives of the Philosophers*. Ed. and trans. R. D. Hicks, Loeb, 1925 (2 vols).

Diophantos, *Arithmetika*. Trans. T. B. L. Heath (Cambridge, 1885, and New York, 1964).

Dioskorides, *De materia medica*. Trans. Goodyer, ed. Gunther (New York, 1933).

Euclid, *Elements*. Trans. T. B. L. Heath (Cambridge, 1926 and New York, 1956).

Galen, *Affections and Errors of the Soul; My Own Books; The Order of My Own Books*. Trans. P. N. Singer in *Galen: Selected Works* (Oxford, 1997).

—— *On the Natural Faculties*. Ed. and trans. A. J. Brock, Loeb, 1916.

—— *On the Sects for Beginners*. Trans. Frede (Indianapolis, 1985).

—— *Prognosis*. Ed. and trans. V. Nutton (Berlin, 1979).

Geminos, *Elements of Astronomy*. French trans. G. Aujac, Budé, 1975.

Herodotos, *Histories*. Ed. and trans. A. Godley, Loeb, 1920–4 (4 vols).

Hero, *Automatopoietikes* [Automaton-making]. Trans. in S. Murphy, 1995.

——*Belopoiika* [Artillery-construction]. Trans. in E. W. Marsden, 1971.

——*Pneumatics*. Trans. in B. Woodcroft, 1851.

Herophilos, *The Art of Medicine in Early Alexandria*. Ed. and trans. H. von Staden (Cambridge, 1989).

Hipparkhos, *The Geographical Fragments of Hipparchus*. Ed. and trans. D. Dicks (London, 1960).

Hippokrates, *Aphorisms*. Trans. W. H. S. Jones, in Loeb, *Hippocrates*, vol. 4, 1967.

——*The eighth-month child*. French trans. R. Joly, *Hippocrate*, vol. 11, Budé, 1970.

——Different books of *Epidemics* appear in different volumes of the Loeb series.

——*Haemorrhoids, Physician* and *Places in Man*. Ed. and trans. P. Potter, in Loeb, vol. 8, 1995.

——*On Joints*. Ed. and trans. E. T. Withington, in Loeb, vol. 3, 1927.

——*The Oath*. Trans. W. H. S. Jones in Loeb, vol. 1, 1923.

Isidore of Charax, *Parthian Stations*. Trans. W. H. Schoff (Philadelphia, 1914, reprinted 1989).

Justin, *Epitome of the Philippic History of Trogus*. Trans. J. C. Yardley (Atlanta, 1994).

Khairemon: P. W. van der Horst, *Chaeremon: Egyptian Priest and Stoic Philosopher. The Fragments Collected and Translated with Explanatory Notes* (Leiden, 1984).

Lucretius, *De rerum natura*. Ed. and trans. M. F. Smith and W. H. D. Rouse, Loeb, 1975.

Nicander, *Alexipharmaca, Theriaca*. Trans. A. S. F. Gow and A. F. Scholfield (Cambridge, 1953).

Oppian, *Halieutica*, Ed. and trans. A. W. Mair, Loeb, 1928.

Ovid, *Metamorphoses*. Ed. and trans. F. J. Miller, revised by G. Goold, Loeb, 1984.

Pausanias, *Guide to Greece*. Trans. W. H. S. Jones, Loeb, 1931–5 (6 vols).

Petronius, *Satyricon*. Ed. and trans. M. Hesletine, Loeb, 1969.

Philo, *Belopoiika*. Trans. in E. W. Marsden, 1971.

Philoponos, *Corollary on Void*. Trans. D. Furley (London, 1991).

Philostratos, *Imagines*. Ed. and trans. A. Fairbanks, Loeb, 1931.

Plato, *Gorgias*. Ed. and trans. W. R. M. Lamb, Loeb, 1925.

——*Laws*. Ed. and trans. R. G. Bury, Loeb, 1926 (2 vols).

——*Philebus*. Ed. and trans. H. N. Fowler, Loeb, 1925.

——*Republic*. Ed. and trans. P. Shorey, Loeb, 1935–7 (2 vols).

——*Sophist*. Ed. and trans. H. N. Fowler, Loeb, 1921.

Pliny (the Elder), *Natural History*. Ed. and trans. H. Rackham, Loeb, 1938–63 (10 vols).

Pliny the Younger, *Letters*. Ed. and trans. B. Radice, Loeb, 1969 (2 vols).

Plutarch, *Animals are Rational, The Causes of Natural Phenomena, Convivial Questions, On the Face of the Orb of the Moon, On the Principle of Cold, Whether Land or Sea Animals are Cleverer*, all in *Moralia*. Ed. and trans. F. C. Babbitt *et al.*, Loeb, 1928–76 (16 vols).

——*Life of Cato the Elder, Life of Marcellus, Life of Pompey, Life of Theseus*, in *Lives*. Ed. and trans. B. Perrin, Loeb, 1914–26 (11 vols).

Polybios, *Histories*. Ed. and trans. W. R. Paton, Loeb, 1914–40 (7 vols).

Posidonius, *The Fragments*. Edd. L. Edelstein and D. Kidd (Cambridge, 1972).

Posidonius, *The Translation of the Fragments*. By D. Kidd (Cambridge, 1999).

Proclus, *Commentary on the First Book of Euclid's Elements*. Trans. G. R. Morrow (Princeton, 1970).

Procopius, *Secret History* (also known as *Anecdota*). Trans. H. B. Dewing, Loeb, 1969.

Ptolemy, *Almagest*. Trans. G. Toomer (London, 1984).

——*Hypotheses*. Trans. and comm. B. Goldstein, *Transactions of the American Philosophical Society* 57.4 (Philadelphia, 1967).

——*Geography*. Trans. E. Stevenson (Mineola, 1991).

——*Optics*. Trans. and comm. A. M. Smith, *Transactions of the American Philosophical Society* 86.2 (Philadelphia, 1996).

——*Tetrabiblos*. Ed. and trans. F. E. Robbins, Loeb, 1980.

Pytheas, *On the Ocean*. Ed. and trans. C. Roseman (Chicago, 1994).

Saïd al-Andalusi, *Book of the Categories of Nations*. Ed. and trans. S. I. Salem and A. Kumar, 1991.

Seneca, *Epistles*. Ed. and trans. R. M. Gummere, Loeb, 1917–25 (3 vols).

——*Natural Questions*. Ed. and trans. T. H. Corcoran, Loeb, 1971–2 (2 vols).

Sophokles, *Rootcutters*: in *Fragments*. Ed. and trans. H. Lloyd-Jones, Loeb, 1996.

Strabo, *Geography*. Ed. and trans. H. L. Jones, Loeb, 1917–36 (8 vols).

Suetonius, *Caesar*. Ed. and trans. J. C. Rolfe, Loeb, 1914 (2 vols).

Tacitus, *Annals*. Ed. and trans. C. H. Moore, Loeb, 1931–7 (2 vols).

Tertullian, *De baptismo*. Ed. A. Reifferscheid and G. Wissowa, C.S.E.L. 20 (Leipzig, 1890) (no English trans.).

Theophrastos, *Causes of Plants*. Ed. and trans. B. Einarson and G. Link, Loeb, 1976–90 (3 vols).

——*Characters*. Ed. and trans. J. Rusten, Loeb, 1992.

——*On Fire*. Ed. and trans. V. Coutant (Assen, 1971).

——*On Fish*. Trans. R. Sharples in Fortenbaugh and Gutas, 1992, chapter 11.

——*Enquiry into [or History of] Plants*. Ed. and trans. A. Hort, Loeb, 1916 (2 vols).

——*Metaphysics*. Trans. W. D. Ross and F. H. Fobes (Oxford, 1929).

——*Meteorology*. Ed. and trans. by H. Daiber in Fortenbaugh and Gutas, 1992, chapter 8.

——*On Odours*, with *Enquiry into Plants*. Loeb, vol. 2.

——*On the Senses*. Ed. and trans. G. M. Stratton, *Theophrastus and the Greek Physiological Psychology* (London, 1917).

——*On Stones*. Ed. and trans. D. Eichholz (Oxford, 1965), also E. Caley and J. Richards (Columbus, 1956).

——*On Weather-signs*, with *Enquiry into Plants*. Loeb, vol. 2.

Thoukudides, *History of the Peloponnesian War*. Ed. and trans. C. F. Smith, Loeb, 1919–23 (4 vols).

Tzetzes, *Khiliades*. Ed. and trans. P. Leone, 1968.

Varro, *Rerum Rusticarum*: in Loeb with Cato, *De agricultura*.

Vegetius, *Epitome of Military Science*. Ed. and trans. N. P. Milner (Liverpool, 1993, 2nd ed. 1998).

Virgil, *Georgics*. Ed. and trans. H. R. Fairclough, Loeb, 1935.

Vitruvius, *De architectura*. Ed. and trans. F. Granger, Loeb, 1931–4 (2 vols).

B. SELECTIONS

A Sourcebook in Greek Science. Edd. and trans. M. R. Cohen and I. E. Drabkin (Cambridge MA, 1948).

Early Greek Philosophy. Ed. J. Barnes (London, 1987).

Galen: Selected Works. Trans. P. N. Singer (Oxford, 1997).

Greek Astronomy. T. B. L. Heath, 1932, reprinted by AMS Press (New York, 1969).

Greek Mathematical Works. Ed. and trans. I. Thomas, Loeb, 1939–41 (2 vols).

Greek Medicine: A Sourcebook. Trans. J. Longrigg (London, 1998).

The Presocratic Philosophers. Ed. and trans. J. Barnes (London, 1979).

C. MODERN WORKS

Aaboe, A. (1964): *Episodes from the Early History of Mathematics* (Washington).

Africa, T. (1968): *Science and the State in Greece and Rome* (New York).

Amundsen, D. W. (1996): *Medicine, Society and Faith in the Ancient and Medieval Worlds* (London).

Anglin, W. and Lambek, J. (1995): *The Heritage of Thales* (New York).

Authier, M. (1995): 'Archimedes: the scientist's canon', ch. 4 in Serres (ed.) (Oxford).

Bailey, K. C. (1929 and 1932): *The Elder Pliny's Chapters on Chemical Subjects*, 2 vols (London).

Balme, D. (1987): 'Aristotle's use of division and differentia' in A. Gotthelf and

J. Lennox (edd.), *Philosophical Issues in Aristotle's Biology* (Cambridge), 69–89.

Barlow, C. and Bryan, G. (1944): *Elementary Mathematical Astronomy*, 5th ed. revised by H. Spenser Jones (London).

Barton, T. (1994): *Ancient Astrology* (London).

Beagon, M. (1992): *Roman Nature* (Oxford).

Beavis, I. (1988): *Insects and Other Invertebrates in Classical Antiquity* (Exeter).

Benoît, P. and Micheau, F. (1995): 'The Arab intermediary' in Serres (ed.).

Berendes, J. (1902): *Des Pedanios Dioskurides aus Anazarbos Arzneimittellehre* (Stuttgart).

Berggren, J. L. (1991): 'The relation of Greek Spherics to Early Greek Astronomy' in Bowen (ed.), 227–48.

Berryman, S. (1998): 'Euclid and the Sceptic: a paper on vision, doubt, geometry, light and drunkenness', *Phronesis* 43, 176–96.

Berthon, S. and Robinson, A. (1991): *The Shape of the World* (London).

Betz, H. D. (ed.) (1996): *The Greek Magical Papyri in Translation*, vol. 1, 2nd ed. (Chicago).

Blatner, D. (1997): *The Joy of* π (London).

Boas, M. (1959): 'Structure of matter and chemical theory in the seventeenth and eighteenth centuries', in M. Clagett (ed.), *Critical Problems in the History of Science* (Madison).

Bowen, A. C. (ed.) (1991): *Science and Philosophy in Classical Greece* (London).

——(1999): 'The art of the commander and the emergence of predictive astronomy' in C. Tuplin and N. Fox (edd.), *Science and Mathematics in Ancient Greek Culture* (Oxford) (to appear).

Bowen, A. C. and Goldstein, B. R. (1989): 'Meton of Athens and astronomy in the late fifth century B.C.', in E. Leichty *et al.* (edd.), *A Scientific Humanist* (Philadelphia), 39–81.

Boyer, C. and Merzback, U. (1989): *A History of Mathematics*, 2nd ed. (New York).

Bunbury, E. H. (1879): *History of the Ancient Geography*, 2 vols (London, reprinted Amsterdam 1979).

Bunt, L., Jones, P. and Bedient, J. (1976): *The Historical Roots of Elementary Mathematics* (New Jersey, reprinted New York, 1988).

Buchanan, R. (1976): 'The Promethean Revolution', *History of Technology* 1, 73–83.

Buchner, E. (1982): *Die Sonnenuhr des Augustus* (Mainz).

Byl, S. (1980): *Recherches sur les grands traités biologiques d'Aristote* (Brussels).

Cajori, F. (1928–9): *A History of Mathematical Notations*, 2 vols (Chicago).

Cameron, A. (1976): *Circus Factions* (Oxford).

Cas, R. and Wright, J. (1987): *Volcanic Successions* (London).

Cherfas, J. (1988): *The Hunting of the Whale* (London).

Cherniss, H. (1945): *The Riddle of the Early Academy* (Berkeley and New York, 1980).

Clagett, M. (1955): *Greek Science in Antiquity* (New York).

Cohen, D. (1992): *Athenian Economy and Society, a Banking Perspective* (Princeton).

Colish, M. L. (1990): *The Stoic Tradition* I (Leiden).

Conrad, L., Neve, M., Nutton, V., Porter, R., and Wear A. (1995): *The Western Medical Tradition* (Cambridge).

Cosens, C. (1998): 'The experimental foundations of Galen's teleology', *Stud. Hist. Phil. Sci.* 29, 63–80.

Cosgrove, D. (1993): in B. Bender (ed.), *Landscape: Politics and Perspectives* (Oxford), ch. 9.

Cowan, R. (1996): Presidential Address to the Society for the History of Technology, *Technology & Culture* 37, 572–82.

Crombie, A. C. (1994): *Styles of Scientific Thinking in the European Tradition* (London), 3 vols.

Cronin, P. (1992): 'The authorship and sources of the *Peri semeion* ascribed to Theophrastus' in Fortenbaugh and Gutas (edd.), ch. 10.

Crowe, M. (1990): *Theories of the World from Antiquity to the Copernican Revolution* (New York).

Davidson, J. (1997): *Courtesans and Fishcakes* (London).

Davies, M. and Kithramby, J. (1986): *Greek Insects* (Oxford).

Dean-Jones, L. (1994); *Women's Bodies in Classical Greek Science* (Oxford).

Derkse, W. (1993): *On Simplicity and Elegance*, Ph.D. Diss. (University of Amsterdam).

Dilke, O. A. W. (1971): *The Roman Land Surveyors* (Newton Abbot).

——(1985): *Greek and Roman Maps* (London).

——(1987): *Mathematics and Measurement* (London).

Dixon, K. R. and Southern, P. (1992): *The Roman Cavalry* (London).

Doyen, A-M. (1981): 'Les textes d'hippiatrie greque', *L'Antiquité Classique* 50, 258–73.

Drachmann, A. G. (1948): *Ktesibios, Philon and Heron* (Copenhagen).

——(1963): *Mechanical Technology of Greek and Roman Antiquity* (Copenhagen).

DuBois, P. (1991): *Torture and Truth* (London).

Duncan-Jones, R. (1990): *Structure and Scale in the Roman Economy* (Cambridge).

Düring, I. (1944): *Aristotle's Chemical Treatise* (Goteborg).

Engels, D. W. (1978): *Alexander and the Logistics of Macedonian Imperialism* (Berkeley).

Farrington, B. (1944 and 1949): *Greek Science*, 2 vols (London).

——(1947): *Head and Hand in Ancient Greece* (London).

Field, J. V. (1996): 'European astronomy in the first millennium: the archaeological record' in C. Walker (ed.), *Astronomy before the Telescope* (London).

Fischer, K. D. (1988): 'Ancient Veterinary Medicine: a survey of Greek and Latin sources and some recent scholarship', *Medizinhistorisches Journal* 23, 191–209.

Flegg, G. (ed.) (1989): *Numbers through the Ages* (London).

Fortenbaugh, W. and Gutas, D. (edd.) (1992): *Theophrastus: his Psychological, Doxographical and Scientific Writings.* Rutgers University Studies in Classical Humanities 5 (London).

——and Sharples, R. (edd.) (1988): *Theophrastean Studies.* Rutgers Studies in Classical Humanities 3 (London).

Fowler, D. (1990): *The Mathematics of Plato's Academy*, 2nd corr. ed. (Oxford).

——(1992): 'Logistic and fractions in early Greek mathematics: a new interpretation' in *Histoire de fractions, fractions d'histoire*, edd. P. Benoît, K. Chemla and J. Ritter (Berlin), 133–47.

Foxworthy, B. and Hill, M. (1982): *Volcanic Eruptions of 1980 at Mount St Helens: the First 100 Days.* Geological Survey Professional Paper 1249 (Washington).

Fraser, P. (1969): 'The career of Erasistratus of Ceos', *Rendiconti dell' Istituto Lombardo.* Classe di Lettere e Scienze Morali e Storiche 103, 518–37.

Frede, M. and Striker, G. (1996): *Rationality in Greek Thought* (Oxford).

French, R. (1994): *Ancient Natural History* (London).

Goody, J. and Watt, I. (1968): 'The consequences of literacy', in *Literacy in Traditional Societies* (Cambridge).

Gotthelf, A. (ed.) (1985): *Aristotle on Nature and Living Things* (Bristol).

——(1988): 'Historiae I: plantarum et animalium', in Fortenbaugh and Sharples, 100–35.

Gottschalk, H. B. (1965): *Strato of Lampsacus: Some Texts.* Ed. with commentary, *Proceedings of the Leeds Philosophical and Literary Society*, Lit. & Hist. Section, vol. xi, part vi, pp. 95–182 (Leeds).

——(1980): *Heracleides of Pontus* (Oxford).

Gow, J. (1884): *A Short History of Greek Mathematics* (New York).

Gray, J. (1987): 'The discovery of non-Euclidean geometry', in E. R. Phillips (ed.), *Studies in the History of Mathematics* (Washington), 37–60.

Green, P. (1986): 'Hellenistic technology: eye, hand and animated tool', *Southern Humanities Review* 20, 101–13.

Greene, K. (1994): 'Technology and innovation in context: the Roman background to mediaeval and later developments', *Journal of Roman Archaeology* 7, 22–33.

Hahn, R. (1995): 'Technology and Anaximander's cosmical imagination: a case study for the influence of monumental architecture on the origins of western philosophy/science', in J. Pitt (ed.), *New Directions in the Philosophy of Technology* (Dordrecht), 95–138.

Hakfoort, C. (1991): 'The missing syntheses in the historiography of science', *History of Science* 29, 207–16.

Hall, F. W. (1913): *Companion to Classical Texts* (Oxford).

Hankinson, R. (1995): 'The growth of medical empiricism', in D. Bates (ed.), *Knowledge and the Scholarly Medical Traditions* (Cambridge), ch. 4.

Hansen, M. H. (1976): *Apagoge, Endeixis and Ephegesis against Kakourgoi, Atimoi and Pheugontes* (Odense).

Hanson, N. R. (1973): *Constellations and Conjectures*, ed. W. C. Humphreys Jr (Dordrecht).

Harris, W. (1989): *Ancient Literacy* (Cambridge MA).

Harrison, A. R. W. (1971): *The Law of Athens*, vol. 2 (Oxford).

Harrison, F. (1913): *Roman Farm Management* (New York).

Heath, T. B. L. 1897 = *The Works of Archimedes*.

—— 1913 = *Aristarchus of Samos*.

—— (1920): *Archimedes* (London).

—— (1921a): *History of Greek Mathematics*, 2 vols. (Oxford, reprinted New York, 1981).

—— (1921b): 'Mathematics and Astronomy', in R. Livingstone (ed.), *The Legacy of Greece* (Oxford), 97–136.

—— (1932 and 1969): *Greek Astronomy* (New York).

—— (1949): *Mathematics in Aristotle* (Oxford).

Heiberg, J. L. (1922): *Science and Mathematics in Classical Antiquity* (Oxford).

Heilbron, J. L. (1996): 'An institute for the history of science', *Lychnos*, 9–24.

Hine, H. M. (1981): *An Edition with Commentary of Seneca Natural Questions Book 2* (Ayer).

Hodson, F. (ed.) (1974): *The Place of Astronomy in the Ancient World* (London).

Høyrup, J. (1996): 'Changing trends in the historiography of Mesopotamian mathematics: an insider's view', *History of Science* 34, 1–32.

—— (1997): 'Hero, Ps-Hero, and Near Eastern Practical Geometry', *Antike Naturwissenschaft und ihre rezeption* 7, 67–93.

Hurwit, J. (1985): *The Art & Culture of Early Greece* (Ithaca).

Hyland, A. (1990): *Equus* (London).

Ifrah, G. (1985): *From One to Zero*, trans. L. Bair (London).

Jackson, R. (1990): 'Roman doctors and their instruments: recent research into ancient practice', *Journal of Roman Archaeology* 3, 5–27.

Jennison, G. (1937): *Animals for Show and Pleasure in Ancient Rome* (Manchester).

Jones, A. (1996): 'On Babylonian astronomy and its Greek metamorphoses', in *Tradition, Transmission and Transformation*, edd. J. J. Ragep and S. P. Ragep (Leiden), 139–55.

Jones, B. (1995): *Night Sky Identifier* (London).

de Jong, J. J. (1989): 'Greek mathematics, Hellenistic architecture and

Vitruvius' *De Architectura*', in H. Geertman and J. J. de Jong (edd.), *Munus non ingratum* (Leiden), 100–13.

Karasszon, D. (1988): *A Concise History of Veterinary Medicine* (Budapest).

Kaufmann, W. (1994): *Universe*, 4th ed. (New York).

Keaveney, A. and Madden, J. A. (1982): 'Phthiriasis and its victims', *Symbolae Osloenses* 57, 87–99.

Keyser, P. (1990a): 'Alchemy in the ancient world: from science to magic', *Illinois Classical Studies* 15, 353–78.

——(1990b): 'J. L. Heiberg' in Briggs and Calder III (edd.), *Classical Scholarship: A Biographical Encyclopaedia* (London).

Kidd, D. (1988): *Posidonius: the Commentary*, 2 vols (Cambridge).

——(1997): *Aratus* Phainomena, ed. and trans. with commentary (Cambridge).

King, H. (1998): *Hippocrates' Woman* (London).

Klein, J. (1968): *Greek Mathematical Thought and the Origin of Algebra*, trans. E. Brann (Cambridge MA, reprinted New York, 1992).

Kline, M. (1972): *Mathematical Thought from Ancient to Modern Times* (Oxford).

Knorr, W. (1975): *The Evolution of the Euclidean Elements* (Dordrecht).

——(1986): *The Ancient Tradition of Geometric Problems* (Dordrecht).

——(1991): 'What Euclid meant', in Bowen (ed.), ch. 7.

Kudlien, F. (1970): 'Medical education in classical antiquity', in C. O'Malley (ed.), *The History of Medical Education* (Berkeley).

——(1981): 'Galen's religious belief', in V. Nutton (ed.), *Galen: Problems and Prospects* (London), 117–30.

——'Galen', *DSB*, vol. 5.

Lang, M. (1957): 'Herodotus and the abacus', *Hesperia* 26, 271–87.

——(1964): 'The abacus and the calendar', *Hesperia* 33, 146–67.

——(1965): 'The abacus and the calendar II', *Hesperia* 34, 224–47.

Lennox, J. (1991): 'Between data and demonstration', in Bowen (ed.), *Science and Philosophy in Classical Greece*, ch. 12.

——(1994): 'The disappearance of Aristotle's biology: a Hellenistic mystery', in T. D. Barnes (ed.), *The Sciences in Greco-Roman Antiquity* (Edmonton), 7–24.

Lewes, G. H. (1864): *Aristotle: A Chapter from the History of Science including Analysis of Aristotle's Scientific Writings* (London).

Lewis, M. (1992): 'The south-pointing chariot in Rome', *History of Technology* 14, 77–99.

Lindberg, D. (1992): *The Beginnings of Western Science (600 B.C. to A.D. 1450)* (Chicago).

Lloyd, G. E. R. (1982a): *Early Greek Science: Thales to Aristotle* (London).

——(1982b): *Greek Science after Aristotle* (London).

——(1983): *Science, Folklore and Ideology* (Cambridge).

—— (1985): 'Science and morality in Greco-Roman Antiquity', Inaugural Lecture (Cambridge).

—— (1991): *Methods and Problems in Greek Science* (Cambridge).

—— (1992): 'Democracy, philosophy and science in ancient Greece' in Dunn (ed.), *Democracy: the Unfinished Journey* (Oxford), ch. 3.

—— (1995): 'Epistemological arguments in early Greek medicine in comparativist perspective', in D. Bates (ed.), *Knowledge and the Scholarly Medical Traditions* (Cambridge), 25–40.

—— (1996a): *Aristotelian Explorations* (Cambridge).

—— (1996b): *Adversaries and Authorities* (Cambridge).

Lobban, C. and Harrison, P. (1994): *Seaweed Ecology and Physiology* (Cambridge).

Longrigg, J. (1993): *Greek Rational Medicine* (London).

Lynch, J. P. (1972): *Aristotle's School* (Berkeley).

Macve, R. (1985): 'Some glosses on "Greek and Roman accounting"', in P. Cartledge and D. Harvey (edd.), *Crux* (Exeter), 233–64.

Maddison, F. (1963): 'Early astronomical and mathematical instruments. A brief survey of sources and modern studies', *History of Science* 2, 17–50.

Majno, G. (1975): *The Healing Hand* (Harvard).

Major, J. and Scott, K. (1988): *Volcaniclastic Sedimentation in the Lewis River Valley, Mount St Helens, Washington – Processes, Extent, and Hazards*. US Geological Survey Bulletin 1383-D, US Govt. Printing Office (Washington).

Marsden, E. W. (1971): *Ancient Greek Artillery*, 2 vols (vol. 1 texts with trans. and commentary, vol. 2 historical development) (Oxford).

Maxwell-Stuart, P. (1996): 'Theophrastos the traveller', *Par. del Passato* 51, 241–67.

Meiggs, R. (1982): *Trees and Timber in the Ancient Mediterranean World* (Oxford).

Métraux, G. P. R. (1978): *Western Greek Land-use and City-planning in the Archaic Period* (London).

Murphy, S. (1995): 'Heron's *Automatopoietikes*', *History of Technology* 17, 1–44.

Needham, J. (1962): *Science and Civilisation in China*, vol. 4, Part 1 (Cambridge).

Neugebauer, O. (1975): *History of Ancient Mathematical Astronomy*, 3 vols. (Berlin).

Nitske, W. R. and Wilson, C. M. (1965): *Rudolf Diesel* (Oklahoma).

Nixon, L. and Price, S. (1992): in O. Murray (ed.), *The Greek City* (Oxford).

Nutton, V. (1972): 'Galen and medical autobiography', *PCPS* n.s. 18, 50–62, also in Nutton (1988), ch. 1.

—— (1973): 'The chronology of Galen's early career', *CQ* 23, 158–71, also in Nutton (1988), ch. 2.

—— (1985a): 'Murders and miracles: lay attitudes to medicine in classical antiquity', in R. Porter (ed.), *Patients and Practitioners*, (Cambridge) 23–53, also in Nutton (1988), ch. 8.

Nutton, V. (1985b): 'The drug trade in antiquity', *Journal for the Royal Society of Medicine* 78, 138–45, also in Nutton (1988), ch. 9.

——(1988): *From Democedes to Harvey* (London).

——(1995): Chapters 1–3 in Conrad *et al.*, *The Western Medical Tradition* (London).

——(1997): 'Galen on Theriac: Problems of authenticity', in A. Debru (ed.), *Galen on Pharmacology* (Leiden), 133–51.

——(1999): 'Ancient Medicine: Asclepius transformed', in Tuplin and Fox (edd.), *Science and Mathematics in Ancient Greek Culture* (Oxford) (to appear).

Oleson, J. (1984): *Greek and Roman Water Lifting Devices* (Toronto).

O'Neill, J. (1998): 'Practical reason and mathematical argument', *Stud. Hist. Phil. Sci.* 29, 195–205.

Osborne, C. (1987): *Rethinking Early Greek Philosophy* (London).

Owens, J. (1991): 'The Aristotelian conception of the Pure and Applied Sciences', in A. C. Bowen (ed.), *Science and Philosophy in Classical Greece* (London), ch. 3.

Paisley, P. B. and Oldroyd, D. R. (1979): 'A classical theory of volcanic activity', *Centaurus* 23, 1–20.

Pederson, O. and Pihl, M. (1974): *Early Physics and Astronomy* (London).

Pickstone, J. V. (1995): 'Past and present knowledges in the practice of the history of science', *History of Science* 33, 203–24.

Plantzos, D. (1997): 'Crystals and lenses in the Greco-Roman world', *AJA* 101, 451–64.

Plommer, H. (1973): *Vitruvius and later Roman Building Manuals* (Cambridge).

Porter, R. (1983): 'The history of medicine: past, present and future'. Lecture given at Uppsala University, Sweden, in 1982 (Uppsala).

Preus, A. (1988): 'Drugs and psychic states in Theophrastos' *Historia plantarum* 9.8–20', in Fortenbaugh and Sharples, ch. 6.

Pritchett, W. (1963): *Ancient Athenian Calendars on Stone* (Berkeley).

——(1965): 'Gaming tables and I.G.I.[2] 324', *Hesperia* 34, 131–47.

Pullan, J. (1970): *The History of the Abacus*, 2nd ed. (London).

Purcell, N. (1996): 'Rome and the management of water: environment, culture and power', in G. Shipley and J. Salmon (edd.), *Human Landscapes in Classical Antiquity* (London), ch. 8.

Ramsey, J. T. and Licht, A. L. (1997): *The Comet of 44BC and Caesar's Funeral Games*, American Philological Association Classical Studies 39 (Atlanta).

Richards, J. L. (1988): *Mathematical Visions. The Pursuit of Geometry in Victorian England* (London).

Richardson, W. (1985): *Numbering and Measuring in the Classical World* (Bristol).

Richmond, J. (1973): *Chapters on Greek Fish-lore* (Wiesbaden).

Riddle, J. (1985): *Dioscorides on Pharmacy and Medicine* (Austin).

——(1992): *Contraception and Abortion from the Ancient World to the Renaissance* (Harvard).

Rihll, T. E. (1993): 'War, slavery and settlement in early Greece', in *War and Society*, edd. J. Rich and G. Shipley (London), 77–107.

——and Tucker, J. V. (1999): 'Practice makes Perfect', in Tuplin and Fox (edd.), *Science and Mathematics in Ancient Greek Culture* (Oxford) (to appear).

Riley, M. (1995): 'Ptolemy's use of his predecessors' data', *TAPhA* 125, 221–50.

Roccatagliata, G. (1986): *A History of Ancient Psychiatry* (London).

Rosenfeld, A. (1965): *The Inorganic Raw Materials of Antiquity* (London).

Rosenmeyer, T. G. (1989): *Senecan Drama and Stoic Cosmology* (Berkeley).

Rottländer, R. (1986): 'The Pliny Translation Group of Germany', in R. French and F. Greenaway (edd.), *Science in the Early Roman Empire: Pliny the Elder, his Sources and Influence* (London), ch. 2.

Saccheri, G. (1733): *Euclides ab omni naevo vindicatus* (reprinted with trans. and comm. by G. B. Halsted, 1920).

Sallares, R. (1991): *Ecology of Ancient Greece* (London).

Samuel, A. (1972): *Greek and Roman Chronology* (Munich).

Sandbach, F. H. (1975): *The Stoics* (London).

Scarborough, J. (1977): 'Nicander's toxicology I: Snakes', *Pharmacy in History* 19, 3–23.

——(1979): 'Nicander's toxicology II: Spiders, scorpions, insects and myriapods', *Pharmacy in History* 21, 3–34.

——and Nutton, V. (1982): 'The *preface* of Dioscorides' *Materia Medica*', *Trans. and Studies of the College of Physicians of Philadelphia* n.s. 4, 187–227.

——(1986): 'Pharmacy in Pliny's *NH*: some observations on substances and sources', in French and Greenaway (edd.), *Science in the Early Roman Empire: Pliny the Elder, his Sources and Influence* (London), ch. 5.

——(1991): 'The pharmacology of sacred plants, herbs and roots', in C. Faraone and D. Obbink (edd.), *Magika Hiera* (Oxford), ch. 5.

Serres, M. (ed.) (1995): *A History of Scientific Thought*, originally published as *Élements d'histoire des Science* (Bordas, 1989) (Oxford).

Shapiro, A. (1994): 'Artists' colors and Newton's colors', *Isis* 85, 600–30.

Sharples, R. (1988): 'Some aspects of secondary tradition of Theophrastus' *Opuscula*', in Fortenbaugh and Sharples, ch. 4.

——(1992): 'Theophrastos' *On Fish*' in Fortenbaugh and Gutas (London), ch. 11.

——(1996): *Stoics, Epicureans and Sceptics* (London).

Sheikh 'Ibada al-Nubi (1997): 'Soldiers', in S. Donadoni (ed.), *The Egyptians* (Chicago), ch. 6.

Sherwin-White, S. (1978): *Ancient Cos* (Göttingen).

Simms, D. L. (1995): *History of Technology* 17, 45–111.

Simon, B. (1978): *Mind and Madness in Ancient Greece* (London).

Singer, C. (1922): *Greek Biology and Medicine* (Oxford).

Singh, S. (1997): *Fermat's Last Theorem* (London).

Sleeswyk, A. (1990): 'Archimedes' odometer and water-clock', in *Ancient Technology* (Finnish School at Athens), 23–37.

de Solla Price, D. (1957): 'Precision instruments to 1500', in Singer *et al.* (edd.), *A History of Technology*, vol. 3 (Oxford), 582–619.

——(1974 and 1975): *Gears from the Greeks, Transactions of the American Philosophical Society* 64.7 (Philadelphia and New York).

Solmsen, F. (1960): *Aristotle's System of the Physical World* (New York).

——(1975): *Intellectual Experiments of the Greek Enlightenment* (Princeton).

Sorabji, R. (1993): *Animal Minds and Human Morals* (New York).

von Staden, H. (1989): *Herophilus* (Cambridge).

Stahl, W. (1971): *Martianus Capella and the Seven Liberal Arts* (New York).

Stannard, J., 'Asklepiades', *DSB* vol. 1.

de Ste Croix, G. (1956): 'Greek and Roman Accounting', in A. Littleton and B. Yamey (edd.), *Studies in the History of Accounting* (London), 14–74.

Stothers, R. B. and Rampino, M. R. (1983): 'Volcanic eruptions in the Mediterranean before A.D. 650 from written and archaeological sources', *Journal of Geophysical Research* 88, 6357–71.

Temkin, O. (1973): *Galenism* (Ithaca).

Thomas, R. (1992): *Literacy and Orality in Ancient Greece* (Cambridge).

Thompson, D'Arcy (1895): *Glossary of Greek Birds* (Oxford).

——(1913): *Aristotle as Biologist* (Oxford).

——(1947): *Glossary of Greek Fishes* (Oxford).

Thomson, J. O. (1948): *History of Ancient Geography* (Cambridge).

Thorndike, L. (1923): *History of Magic and Experimental Science*, vol. 1 (New York).

Tod, M. N. (1950): 'The alphabetic numeral system in Attica', *Annals of the British School at Athens* 45, 126–39.

Touwaide, A. (1991): 'Greek medical manuscripts: a bibliography', *Newsletter of the Society for Ancient Medicine* 19, 8–33.

Toynbee, J. (1973): *Animals in Roman Life and Art* (Ithaca).

Tuplin, C. and Fox, N. (edd.) (1999): *Science and Mathematics in Ancient Greek Culture* (Oxford) (to appear).

Unguru, S. (1979): 'History of ancient mathematics: some reflections on the state of the art', *Isis* 70, 555–65.

Vickers, M. (1992): 'The metrology of gold and silver plate', in T. Linders and

B. Alroth (edd.), *The Economics of Cult in the Ancient Greek World* (Uppsala), 53–72.

van der Waerden, B. (1983): *Geometry and Algebra in Ancient Civilisations* (Berlin).

Wellmann, M. (1897): *Krateuas* (Berlin).

Wertheim, M. (1997): *Pythagoras' Trousers* (London).

Whitney, E. (1990): *Paradise Restored: The Mechanical Arts from Antiquity through the Thirteenth Century. Transactions of the American Philosophical Society* 80.1 (Philadelphia).

White, K. D. (1993): '"The base mechanic arts"? Some thoughts on the contribution of science (pure and applied) to the culture of the Hellenistic Age', in P. Green (ed.), *Hellenistic History and Culture* (London).

Wilson, C. A. (1999): 'Distilling, sublimation and the Four Elements: the aims and achievements of the earliest Greek chemists', in C. Tuplin and N. Fox (edd.), *Science and Mathematics in Ancient Greek Culture* (Oxford) (to appear).

Wolff, M. (1987): 'Philoponus and the rise of preclassical dynamics', in R. Sorabji (ed.), *Philoponus and the Rejection of Aristotelian Science* (London).

Woodcroft, B. (1851): *Hero's* Pneumatics. M. B. Hall reprinted this translation with an introduction in 1971 (London).

ABOUT THE AUTHOR

Dr Rihll was born in Swansea in 1960, and educated at Swansea, Exmouth, Exeter, the University of Kent, and the University of Leeds. After a Post-Doctoral Fellowship held jointly in the Schools of History and Geography at Leeds, she became lecturer in Ancient History in the Department of Classics at the University of Wales Lampeter 1990–95, and then at the University of Wales Swansea from 1995. She has published articles on various Greek topics, including Homer, Athenian constitutional history, slavery, simulation modelling of archaic Greek settlement patterns, and ancient science and technology. She is married to J. V. Tucker and has two children, Elizabeth and Henry.

INDEX OF NAMES, SUBJECTS, AND PASSAGES

Aaboe, A., 18 n. 53, 60

abacus, 49–50

Academy, 3 n. 11, 5, 39, 77

accuracy, 12, 32, 39 n. 4, 42, 47–8, 50 + n. 51, 65, 70 + n. 31, 74, 80, 95 + n. 43, 100–1, 103 + n. 71, 104, 111, 127

Aelian of Praeneste (late C2–early C3 A.D.), 111 + n. 29; *De natura animalium* (8.16) 115 n. 43; (12.43) 113 n. 38; (13.21) 12 n. 35, 110 n. 23; (15.2) 111 n. 31; (17.6) 112 n. 36

Aesop (*c.* 600 B.C.), 33, 106

Aetna – see also Vesuvius and volcano – 92–5, 104; (224–46) 68; (294–9) 35 + n. 33

Africa, T., 22

Agatharkides of Knidos (C2 B.C.), 90 n. 26

Agripps, Marcus Vipsanius (63–12 B.C.), 83–4, 102

Aiskhulos of Athens (525–455 B.C.), iv n. 5, 5 n. 15, 77–8, 89, 110

al-Andalusi, Saïd (C11 A.D.), xii n. 9, 17 n. 52

alchemy, iv n. 3, 2 + n. 4, 26 n. 8, 111 n. 59

Alexander of Aphrodisias (late C2–early C3 A.D.), 37 + n. 35, 38

Alexander the Great of Macedon (356–323 B.C.), 39, 48, 83, 84 n. 11, 85, 87, 89, 112 n. 35, 122, 125, 134, 138

Alexandria, 6, 11 n. 35, 27 n. 15, 64 n. 7, 108 n. 19, 122, 129 n. 106

algebra, 3, 40 n. 41, 42 n. 17

amateurs/ism, 5–6, 78, 88, 90, 117, 121, 132, 138

Amundsen, D. W., 122 n. 76

anatomy, 12, 106, 120, 123, 128–30

Anaxagoras of Klazomenai (*c.* 500–428 B.C.), 9 n. 29, 33

Anaximander of Miletos (*c.* 610–545 B.C.), 6 n. 17, 83

Anaximenes of Lampsakos, 6 n. 23

Andreas of Alexandria (*fl.* 240–200 B.C.), 14, 126

anaesthetics 128 + n. 104, 129–31

Anglin, W. and Lambek J., 40 n. 9

anonymity, 3, 18, 19 + n. 54, 71 n. 35, 85

anthropocentricity, 73, 107

Apollodoros of Alexandria (C3 B.C.), 127 n. 96

Apollonios of Perga (C2 B.C.), iv, 5, 43 n. 22, 43 n. 24, 60

Apollonios Mus of Alexandria (C1 A.D.), 125

Aratos of Soli (Cyprus) (late C4–early C3 B.C), *Phainomena*, 65 n. 15, 81, 127 n. 97; (26–44) 68

Arkhagathos of Sparta (*fl.* 220 B.C.), 123

Archimedes of Syracuse (287–212 B.C.), iv, 6 + n. 19, 14 + n. 41, 16 n. 49, 29–30, 33–5 + n. 31, 38–9, 60, 63 n. 4, 70, 102 n. 68; *Measurement of a circle* 42 n. 18; *On floating bodies* 26, 30–2; *On plane equilibriums* (Prop. 7) 12 n. 37; *On sphere-making* 69 n. 28; *The sand-reckoner* 43 n. 24, 80 n. 56, 81

Arkhytas of Tarentum (*c.* 400–350 B.C.), 5 n. 16, 59

Aristarkhos of Samos (*c.* 320–250 B.C.), 19 n. 54, 65, 71 n. 35, 72 + n. 39, 73, 77–8, 80 + n. 56, 97; *On the sizes and distances of the sun and moon*, 73–6, 81

Aristophanes of Athens (*fl.* 427–388 B.C.), *Birds* (1001–5), 39 n. 3, 64 n. 7; *Wasps* (656–64), 45; *Clouds*, 63 n. 7, 72, 99, 134; (200–4), 102; (771–3), 69

Aristotle of Stagira (384–322 B.C.), iii, x, 2 n. 3, 3, 5, 9 n. 29, 10–13 + n. 38, 15, 17, 19 n. 56, 20 + nn. 57, 58, 21 + n. 62, 27–8, 34 + n. 26, 37, 93, 100, 107 + n. 14, 108–9, 111 n. 31, 114 n. 43, 115 + n. 44, 136–8 + n. 5; *Generation of animals*, 109, 110 n. 22, 116; *History of animals*, x, 11, 109, 127, 133; (487b, 548–9), 114 n. 43; (538a, 570a), 110; (591a, 602b), 111; (584a–b), xi n. 2; *Meteorology*, 25, 26 n. 8, 38, 69 n. 27, 104; (1.9), 99 n. 59; (1.14), 99 n. 57; (2.3), 92 n. 35; (2.5), 99 n. 60; (2.7–8), 92 nn. 33, 36; *Movement of animals*, 109; *On the senses*, 109; *On the soul*, 107 n. 11, 109; (418b–19a), 115 n. 45; *Parts of animals* (644b30), 108–9 + n. 20; (659), 113–14; (669a), 114 n. 41; (681a), 107 + n. 10; *Physics*, 28, 54; *Posterior Analytics* (1.31), 17 n. 51; *Prior Analytics* (1.23.41a26, 1.44.55.a27), 59; *Progression of animals*, 109; *Topics*, 17 n. 51

[Aristotle], *Athenaion Politeia* (43.2), 64 n. 8; *Mechanics* (1, 21, 25, 28, 32–4), 35–6; *On breath*, 109; *On colours* (793a–b), 24, 28; *On plants*, 107, 108 n. 17; (824a15–26), 92 n. 34; *On things heard* (801a), 120–1; *Physiognomics*, 106, 131; *Problems*, 7; (10.41), xi n. 2; (15.3), 52 n. 56; (15.7), 76; (26.61), 100 n. 63; (32.2, 3, 5, 11), 114

arithmetic, iv n. 3, 35 + n. 29, 39, 41 + n. 14, 43 n. 22, 53–4, 56, 59, 100

arithmetical error, 50 + nn. 50, 51, 63

Arrian, Flavius Xenophon, of Nicomedia (*c.* A.D. 90–175), 84 n. 11; *Indika* (30), 112 n. 36; *Periplous of the Euxine*, iv n. 3, 84 n. 11.

Asklepiades of Prusias (C1 B.C.), 123

Asklepiads of Kos, Knidos, Rhodes, 121 + n.74
Asklepiodotos (C1 B.C), 98–9
astrology, 1, 2 + nn. 2, 3, 11, 22 n.63, 62 + n.1,
    71 n.33, 97 + n.54
astronomy, 1, 2, 11, 15, 16 + n.46, 17–18, 39,
    82, 88, 93 n.39, 99–103, 137 n.3, Chapter 4
    passim; naked eye, 69, 72
Athenaeus of Naukratis (Egypt) (*fl.c.* 200
    A.D.), 125
atomism, 9–10, 28, 123
Attalus III (King of Pergamum 138–33 B.C.), 4
    n.13, 126
Augustine, Saint Aurelius, of Thagaste (Numi-
    dia, Africa) (A.D. 354–430), 97 n.54; *City of
    God* (5.3), 70 n.33; (22.24), 15 n.45
Augustus (Octavian) (63 B.C.–A.D. 14), 64 +
    n.10, 89, 102 n.66, 134
Authier, M., 5 n.15
axial rotation of the earth, 19 n.54, 70–3, 78

Babbage, Charles, 27
Babylon, 17–18, 42 n.19, 43 n.21, 98–9, 137
    n.3
Bailey, K. C., xi n.4
Balme, D., 109 + n.21
Barlow C. and Bryan, G., 80
Barnes, J., 3 n.8, 91 n.30
Barton, T., 64 n.13, 81
Beagon, M., 124 n.86
Beavis, I., 106 n.7, 107 n.13, 107 n.15
Bede, the Venerable, of Yarrow (England)
    (A.D. 673–735), 46 + n.32
Benoit, P. and Micheau, F., iv n.2
Berggren, J. L., 54
Berryman, S., 25 n.5
Berthon, S. and Robinson, A., 101 n.64
Betz, H. D., 119 n.58
biology, 25, 63 + n.3, Chap 6 *passim*
Blatner, D., 39 n.1
Boas, M., 19 n.56
botany, 2 n.2, 12 n.36, 93 n.39, 108, 116–18
Bowen, A. C., 62 n.2
Bowen, A. C. and Goldstein, B. R., 1 n.22, 64
    n.7
Boyer, C. and Merzback, U., 3 n.72
Brock, A. J., v n.8, 135
Brodersen, K., 104
Bruins, E. M., 43 n.24
Bunbury, E. H., 87, 89 n.24, 104
Bunt, L., Jones, P. and Bedient, J., 42 n.19, 60
Burton, H., 38
Byl, S., 20 n.57

Caesar, Gaius Julius (100–44 B.C.), 63, 64 +
    n.10, 90, 117 n.54
Caesar comet, 94 n.41
Cajori, F., 41 n.15

calculatores 44 + n.26, 120 n.61
calendars, 63 + n.7, 64 + nn.8–10
Caley, E. and Richards, J., xii, 104
Cameron, A., 134 n.127
Capella, Martianus Minneus Felix, of Madaura
    (Africa) (*c.* C5 A.D.), 87 + n.17
Cary M. and Warmington, E. H., 105
Carpenter, R., 105
Cas, R. and Wright, J., 94 n.41, 95 n.42
Cato, Marcus Porcius, of Tusculum (234–149
    B.C.), 6 n.21, 117 + n.54, 122 n.76, 123–4,
    De agricultura, 136; (141), 133 n.121; (154),
    112 n.33
cautery, 123–5 + n.90, 130–1, 132 n.118
Celsus, Aulus Cornelius (C1 A.D.), 96 n.50,
    121; *De medicina*, 121 n.72; (3.10.2), 128;
    (3.21.9), 125 n.90; (5.26.33–4), 130 n.109;
    (5.27.2), 130 n.113; (5.27.13, 7.7.15k), 130
    + n.113; (5.27.2, 5.28.1b, 5.28.3, 6.19.3,
    7.7.15f–k, 7.12.1), 130 n.110; (5.28.1b),
    131 n.114; (7.Proo.4), 128; (8.20.4), 14
    n.41
chemistry, 2 n.2, 25 + n.7
Cherfas, J., 112 n.32
Cherniss, H., 3 n.11, 80–1
Cicero, Marcus Tullius, of Arpinum (106–43
    B.C.), 5 n.15, 41 n.12, 64 n.10, 82, 96, 123,
    127 n.97, 117 n.54; *De Natura Deorum*
    (2.50), 15 + n.44; (2.88), 69 n.28; *Rep.*
    (1.21–2), 102 n.68; (1.28), 69 n.28; *Tusc.
    Disp.* (1.63), 69 n.28; (2.61), 96 n.52; (5.2),
    15 n.44; (5.23), 6 n.19
Clagett, M., 22, 97 + n.54
Codex Constantinopolitanus (77r), 43 n.24
Codex Theodosianus, published in A.D. 438, a
    codification of all imperial laws since Con-
    stantine, 132 n.119
Cohen, D., 44 n.29
Cohen, M. R. and Drabkin, I. E., xii, 2 n.3, 20
    + n.59, 21 + n.61, 81, 91 n.29, 95 n.43, 137
    + nn.1, 3, 138
Colish, M. L., 96 n.51
colour, 7 n.25, 24, 30, 34, 115 n.45
Columella, Lucius Junius Moderatus, of Cadiz
    (Spain) (C1 B.C.–A.D.), 64 n.12, 117 +
    n.54, 133 + n.124, 136; (2.14), 118; (6.11,
    6.12.5, 7.5.18, 7.10.5, 7.13.2), 132 n.118;
    (6.19, 6.26, 6.37.10, 7.12.14), 133; (7.3.16),
    133 n.122; (7.9.12, 8.2.3), 130 n.112, 130 +
    n.112
comprehensiveness of ancient texts, 14 +
    nn.40, 41; 25, 30, 35–6, 46 n.31, 77, 90–1
competitiveness of ancient scientists, x, 4 +
    n.14, 6 n.23, 8, 10, 13, 17–18, 21 n.61, 22
    n.63, 28, 65–6, 71 n.35, 72 n.39, 77–80, 82,
    93 n.39, 120, 122–4

computation, 18, 30, 43 + n. 24, 44–8, 50 + n. 50, 51–4, 65, 73, 74 + n. 73, 78, 80, 100–1
Conrad, L., Neve, M., Nutton, V., Porter, R. and Wear, A., 135
Copernicus, Nicolaus (A.D. 1473–1543), 37, 62, 73
Corcoran, T. H., 33, 37
Corpus Agrimensorum Romanum, a compilation of treatises and commentaries upon them and extracts from mathematical and legal works relevant to Roman surveyors, ranging in date from C1 A.D., 105
Cosens, C., 7 n. 25
Cosgrove, D., 87
Cowen, R., 13 n. 39
Crassus, Marcus Licinius (*c.* 115–53 B.C.), 123
Crombie, A. C., 1 + n. 1, 16
Cronin, P. 91 n. 31
Crowe, M., 80

Daedalus, 15
Daiber, H., 91 n. 32
Darius I (King of Persia 521–486 B.C.), 45, 89
data, 11 + n. 34, 12 + n. 36, 65–6, 74 n. 43, 85, 99–101, 103–4, 107–10, 114, 117–18
Davidson, J., 110 n. 24
Davies, M. and Kithramby, J., 107 nn. 13, 14, 15
Dean-Jones, L., 135
Delphi, 5 n. 15, 87
Demetrios of Phaleron (Athens) (*c.* 350–270 B.C.), 6 + n. 20
Demokritos of Abdera (*fl.* 465–400 B.C.), 9, 28, 114 n. 41
dentists, 36
Derkse, W., 13 + n. 38
description, 85, 93, 95 + n. 43, 101, 109–10, 117
Dicks, D., 99 n. 60
Diesel, Rudolph, 27 + n. 16
Digest of Roman Law, a collection of legislation and commentaries by earlier jurists, esp. Gaius, Paulus and Ulpian, compiled under Justinian, emperor A.D. 527–65 (18.1.35.2, 48.8), 126 + n. 93; (27.1.15.5), 44 n. 26
Dilke, O. A. W., 60, 64 n. 11, 84 n. 9, 87, 88 n. 19, 102 n. 69, 104
Dio Cassius, of Nicaea (*c.* A.D. 165–235), 108 n. 19
Diodorus Siculus (of Agyrium in Sicily) (C1 B.C.) (2.29.6), 4 n. 14; (12.36.2–3), 63 n. 7
Diogenes the Cynic (dog), of Sinope (*c.* 400–323 B.C.), 15
Diogenes Laertius (C3 A.D.), 6 n. 20, 6 n. 23, 12 n. 36, 29 n. 19, 68, 102, 117 n. 49, 123 n. 80

Diophantos of Alexandria (*c.* C2 A.D.), iv n. 3, 60; *Arithemetica* (2.8), 40 n. 8
Dioskorides of Anazarbus (Cilicia) (*c.* A.D. 40–80), v n. 9, x, 4 n. 13, 11, 126–7, 138 n. 5
divers, diving bell, 7, 113–14, 117
Dixon, K. R. and Southern, P., 132 n. 120
Dogmatists, 122
Drachmann, A. G., 14 n. 41, 35 n. 31, 38
drugs, 6 n. 18, 11, 79, 106 + n. 7, 107 n. 15, 108, 117 + n. 52, 119 n. 58, 121, 123–8, 132 n. 118, 133 n. 125
DuBois, P., 130 n. 111
Duff, J. W. and A. M., 68, 92 n. 37, 95, 104
Duncan-Jones, R., 44 n. 26
Düring, I., 26 n. 8, 38
dynamics, 34, 93

earthquakes, 91–2 + n. 36
eclipses, 17, 62 + n. 2, 70, 73 n. 42, 78
Ekphantos of Syracuse (*c.* 400 B.C.), 72 n. 39
Edelstein, L., 135
Edelstein, L. and Kidd, D., 96 n. 48, 96 n. 52, 106 n. 8
Egypt, 17, 42 n. 19, 84, 88, 91 n. 30, 119 n. 58, 128, 135
Eichholz, D., 104
Einarson, B. and Link, G., 136
Empedokles of Akragas (*c.* 495–35 B.C.), 5 n. 16, 19 n. 56, 21, 28, 33, 80
Empiricists, 122
Engels, D., 48 nn. 41, 42
entomology, 107–8
Epikouros of Samos (341–270 B.C.), 28, 123
Erasistratos of Keos (*c.* 350–300 B.C.), 122, 129 + n. 106
Eratosthenes of Kyrene (C3 B.C.), 47 + n. 40, 78 n. 55, 85, 87 n. 17, 91 + nn. 29, 30
errors in ancient observations/calculations (see also arithmetical error), 63 n. 4, 65 n. 15, 70 + n. 31, 97, 101, 103–4, 110–11
Etna – see Aetna
Euclid of Alexandria (late C3–early C2 B.C.), iv, 5 n. 15, 9 + n. 27, 39, 40 n. 8, 42 n. 19, 44, 55, 60–2, 70, 129 n. 106; *Elements*, 14 n. 41, 54–6, 58–60; *Optics*, 38; *Phainomena*, 54, 66 + n. 16
Eudoxos of Knidos (408–355 B.C.), 5 n. 16, 54, 56, 59, 65 + n. 15, 66 + nn. 16, 18, 127 n. 97
Eunapios of Sardis (A.D. 345–*c.* 414), 6 n. 23
Euripides of Athens (*c.* 485–406 B.C.), iv n. 5, 77
experiment, 4 + n. 13, 28–30, 33, 35 + n. 29, 92, 103, 110 n. 23, 112
explicit transliteration, 40–2

Fairbanks, 92
Farrington, B., 16 n. 49, 22, 96 n. 48, 121 n. 72

Faventius (*c.* A.D. 300), 30 n. 20
Fermat, Pierre de (A.D. 1601–65), 40 + n. 8
Field, J. V., 102 + n. 70
finger-counting, 45–6
fire extinguishers, 35 n. 30, 98 n. 55
Fischer, K. D., 21 n. 60, 130, 132 + nn. 117
    118, 134 nn. 128, 130
Flegg, D., 51 n. 54
folklore, 11, 16 n. 48, 22 n. 63, 99 + n. 60, 100
Forster, E. S., 136
Fortenbaugh, W., 116 n. 48
fossils, 91 + n. 30
four-elements theory, 19 n. 56, 21 + n. 61, 27–
    8, 108 n. 17, 123
Fowler, D., 39 n. 6, 41 n. 12, 42 nn. 17, 18, 43
    nn. 22, 23, 44 n. 27, 53 + n. 59, 58 n. 73, 59 +
    n. 74
Foxworthy, B. and Hill, M., 95 n. 44
Fraser, P., 129 n. 106
Frede, M. and Striker, G., 16 n. 47
French, R., 3 n. 6, 22, 83, 87
Freudenthal, G., 37
Frontinus, Sextus Julius (*fl.* A.D. 30–104), 6 +
    n. 22
Furley, D., 11–12, 14 n. 41, 34, 37

Galen of Pergamum (A.D. 129–*c.* 205), iv n. 2,
    v + n. 8, xii n. 9, 6 + n. 23, 7 n. 25, 11–12, 14
    n. 41, 54, 106, 108 n. 19, 119 n. 59, 120, 123–
    4 + n. 84, 125–6, 128 n. 99, 136–7, 138 n. 5;
    Affections and errors of the soul (2.5), 46 +
    n. 31; *Antidotes* (1.1), 4 n. 13; *Compound
    drugs arranged by kind,* 127; *Compound drugs
    arranged by location* (1.8), 125 n. 89, 127;
    Mixtures and properties of simples, 127; *On
    anatomical procedures,* 129 + n. 105; *On my
    own books,* 120 n. 65, 124 n. 84; *On simples,*
    120 n. 68; *On the sects for beginners,* 123 n. 83;
    Prognosis, 7, 120 n. 68; *The order of my own
    books,* 120 n. 64
Galileo, Galilei, 34 + n. 27
Gates, Bill, 27
Gellius, Aulus (*c.* A.D. 123–165), 117 n. 49
Geminos of Rhodes (C1 B.C.), 96 n. 48; *Ele-
    ments of astronomy* (8), 63 n. 7
genre, 29–30, 32–3, 40 + n. 10, 76–7, 88–9
geography, Chapter 5 *passim*
geology, 24 + nn. 1, 2, 3, 91, 92 n. 33, 98–9 +
    n. 57
geometry, 5 n. 17, 14 n. 41, 15, 17–18, 26 n. 13,
    35, 39, 41 + n. 14, 42 n. 17, 44 n. 25, 53, §3.4
    passim, 64 n. 7, 65, 76
Geoponica, by Cassianus Bassus (C10 A.D.),
    133–4
gods, 9–10, 17, 20, 29, 63 + n. 7, 64, 77, 83,
    106, 130 n. 107
Apollo, 3, 17; Asklepios, xi n. 2, 120; Athena,

46–7; Gaia, 83; Hera, 17; Ouranos, 83; Pan,
    106 n. 4; Poseidon, 17, 83 + n. 7; Tartaros/
    Pluto, 83, 93; Zeus/Jupiter, 17 + n. 50, 83,
    83, 93–4
Goldstein, B., 81
Goody, J. and Watt, I., 16 n. 49
Goodyear, F. R. D., 92 n. 37
Gotthelf, A., 109 n. 21, 116 n. 47
Gottschalk, H., 29 n. 19, 38, 70 n. 32
Gow, J., 5, 43 n. 22, 53 n. 57, 60
gravity, 77
Gray, J., 56 n. 63
Green, P., 35 n. 32
Greene, K., 27 n. 14
Grmek, M., 135
Grote, G., 5
Gunther, R., v n. 9

Hadrian, Publius Aelius (A.D. 76–138), 84
    n. 11, 134
Hahn, R., 6 n. 17, 16 n. 49
Hakfoort, C., 43 n. 20
Hall, F. W., 138 + n. 5
Hankinson, R., 4 n. 14
Hansen, M. H., 126 n. 94
Hanson, N. R., 16 n. 46, 72 n. 40
Harris, W., 43 n. 23
Harrison, A. R. W., 46 n. 35, 126 n. 94
Harrison, F., 133 n. 123
Healy, J., xii n. 6, 136
Heath, T. B. L., xi n. 4, 5, 31 + n. 22, 32 nn. 23,
    24, 38, 40 + nn. 9, 11, 41 + n. 16, 42 n. 18, 43
    n. 22, 53 n. 57, 58 n. 73, 60–1, 65 nn. 15, 16,
    19, 73 n. 42, 81
Heiberg, J. L., xi n. 4, 14 n. 41, 43 n. 24, 82 n. 4,
    119 n. 59, 124 nn. 84, 86
Heilbron, J. L., xii n. 7
Hekataios of Miletos (*c.* 550–490 B.C.), 89 +
    n. 24
heliocentric theory, 19 n. 54, 72
Herakleides of Herakleia (Pontus) (*c.* 390–310
    B.C.), 19 n. 54, 70, 71 n. 35, 72 n. 39, 73
Hero of Alexandria (C1 A.D.), xi n. 4, 14 n. 41,
    26 + n. 10, 29 n. 19, 35 + n. 31, 38, 119 n. 59
heroes, Chap. 1§5 *passim,* 27 n. 16, 122
Herodotos of Halikarnassos (484–420 B.C.),
    12, 17, 82, 86–7; (1.62), 110; (2.12), 91
    n. 30; (2.36.2, 7.187), 49 + n. 46; (4.42), 88
    + n. 21; (4.44), 89; (4.98), 45; (4.105), 106;
    (5.49–50), 102; (5.52–3), 83; (7.129), 92
    n. 33; (7.187), 50 + n. 50
Herophilos of Khalkedon (C3 B.C.), 63 n. 6,
    120 n. 63, 122, 129 + n. 106, 136
Hesiod of Askra (*c.* 700 B.C.), 11, 66, 70
Hett, W. S., 24, 36
Hiketas of Syracuse (C3 B.C.), 19 n. 54, 72
    n. 39

Hine, H. M., 87, 98 n. 56
Hipparkhos of Nicaea (c. 190–120 B.C.), 63
    n. 4, 68, 70, 99 n. 60, 127 n. 97; star cata-
    logue, 66; chord table, 74 n. 43; *Commentary
    on the Phainomena of Aratus and Eudoxus*, 65
    n. 15, (1.4.1), 66 + n. 18
Hippokrates of Kos (c. 460–380 B.C.), xi, 136,
    138 n. 5; *Aphorisms* (7.87), 124; *Epidemics*
    (1.1), 100 n. 61; *Haemorrhoids* (2), 131;
    Joints (11), 130 n. 110; *Physician* (5), 128
    n. 103; *Places in man* (39), 122 n. 76, (40),
    130 n. 108; *The Oath*, 121 + n. 74
Hippocratics, 8, 99, 120, 122 + n. 78, 131
Hippolutos, Bishop of Portus Romanus (C3
    A.D.), 91 + n. 30
Hodson, F., 81
Homer (c. 700 B.C.), 20, 41 n. 12, 68 n. 22, 78,
    87, 110, 137 + n. 2
Horst van der, P. W., 62 n. 1, 81
Hort, A., iv n. 4, 117 n. 50, 136
Høyrup, J., 14 n. 41, 41 n. 14, 43 n. 43
Hyland, A., 134 n. 126

'Ibada al-Nubi, 84 n. 12
Ifrah, G., 51 n. 55, 53 n. 56
implicit translation, 37, 40–2, 46, 59 + n. 74, 80
industrial revolution, 26–7
innovation/invention, 18, 27
instruments – see also machines, 32, 63 nn. 4, 5,
    6, 64 + n. 10, 69 + n. 28, 70 + n. 29, 102 +
    n. 68, 110, 114, 120, 122 n. 77, 128 + n. 101
irrational numbers, 41, 53 + n. 57, 56, 59
Isidore of Charax (Babylonia) (c. late C1 B.C.–
    early C1 A.D.), 84 n. 14

Jackson, R., 122 n. 77, 128 n. 101, 135
Jones, A., 17
Jones, B., 67 n. 19
Jones, H., 102
Jones, W., 124
Jong, J. J. de, 54
Judson, L., 37
Justin (C3 A.D.), 4 n. 13, 98–9, 126 n. 91
Justinian, Peter Sabbatius, of Tauresium
    (c. 482–563 A.D.), 85, 134

Karasszon, D., 130 n. 107, 132 n. 117, 133
Karneades of Kyrene (c. 213–129 B.C.), 6 n. 21
Kaufmann, W., 71 nn. 36, 37, 38
Keaveney, A. and Madden, J., 110 n. 26
Keyser, P., 2 n. 4, 26 n. 8, 119 n. 59
Khairemon (C1 A.D.), 62 n. 1, 81, 96 n. 49
Khrusippos, of Soli (c. 280–206 B.C.), 106
Kidd, D., 68 n. 20, 68 n. 22, 81, 96 n. 52, 97
    nn. 53, 54
King, H., 135

Kleanthes, of Assos (Troad) (c. 331–232 B.C.),
    72, 77–8
Klein, J., x + n. 1, 7 n. 25, 58 n. 72
Kleomedes (C1 A.D.), *De motu circulari* (2.6),
    73 n. 42
Knorr, W., 3 + n. 7, 14 n. 41, 40 + nn. 10, 11,
    53 + n. 60, 58 n. 73, 59
Kolaios of Samos (late C7 B.C.), 87
Krateuas (C1 B.C.), 4, 126
Ktesibios of Alexandria (fl. 275–260 B.C.), 5,
    26, 35 + nn. 30, 32, 129 n. 106
Kudlien, F., 120 nn. 65, 123 n. 82, 124 n. 84

Lang, M., 49 n. 47, 50
Lee, H. D. P., 104
Leibniz, 37
Lennox, J., 27 n. 15, 109 n. 21
Leukippos, of Abdera or Elea or Miletos (C5
    B.C.), 9, 28
Lewes, G., 21 n. 62, 137
Lewis, M., 26 n. 12
Lewis, E., 38
Lewis, W. J., 136
Lindberg, D., 22, 43 n. 20, 87 + n. 17
Lindsay, J., 38
literacy, 16 n. 49, 43 + n. 23
Lloyd, G. E. R., 4 n. 14, 7 + n. 24, 7 n. 26, 8–9 +
    n. 29, 11 + n. 32, 14, 16 nn. 48, 49, 22, 23, 34
    n. 26, 36 n. 34, 107 n. 10, 109 n. 21, 115 n. 43,
    119 n. 60, 121 n. 73, 135, 137 n. 3
Lobban, C. and Harrison, P., 117 n. 52
Longrigg, J., 123 n. 80, 135
Lucretius, Titus Carus, of Rome (c. 99–55
    B.C.), 28, 123
Lyceum, 3 + n. 9, 17 + n. 52, 76, 102, 116, 122
Lynch, J. P., 3 n. 11

machines, 14 + n. 41, 26, 35, 102 n. 68, 122,
    133; air-gun, 35; Antikythera mechanism, 26
    + n. 11, 69–70 + n. 30; clocks, 35, 63 + nn. 5,
    6; diving bell, 7, 114; Horologium Augusti,
    64 + n. 10; pumps, 35 + n. 30; south-pointing
    chariot, 26 + n. 12
Macve, R. 44 n. 28
Maddison, F., 69 n. 29
Mago of Charthage (C4 B.C.), 133
Mair, A. W., 68 n. 24, 81, 106 n. 3, 112, 116,
    136
Majno, G., 119 n. 59, 135
Major, J. and Scott, K., 95 n. 47
manuscript tradition, xii n. 9, 21 + n. 60, 29
    n. 19, 40, 50 n. 51, 59 + nn. 74, 75, 85, 92
    n. 37, 108 n. 17, 111 n. 29, 118 + n. 56, 127
    n. 97, 135 n. 132
Marcus Aurelius (A.D. 121–180), 7, 84, 126
Marsden, E. W., 27 n. 15, 35 nn. 28, 29, 38

Martial, Marcus Valerius, of Bilbilis (Spain (*c.* A.D. 40–104), 130 n. 111

mathematics, Chapter 3 *passim*, 13, 14 n. 41, 18, 26 + n. 13, 31 n. 23, 34, 62, 66, 78 + n. 54, 79–80 + n. 56

Maxwell-Stuart, P., 12 n. 36

measurement, 10, 29, 32–3, 41 n. 12, 44 + n. 25, 47, 49, 63 n. 6, 69–70, 73, 92, 99

medical ethics, 4

medicine, 2 n. 2, 4 + n. 14, 79, 106–9, 118–31 *passim*, 132 + n. 118, 134

Meiggs, R., 107 n. 12, 117 n. 50

Menelaos of Alexandria (*c.* A.D. 100), 74 n. 43

Mesopotamia, 17, 41, 135

metals, 24–5, 29, 84, 90, 92, 94–5, 98, 111–12, 115, 128

meteorology, 25, 69 n. 27, 91

Methodists, 123

Meton of Athens (C5 B.C.), 39 n. 3, 63 n. 7, 70, 99

Metraux, G., 102 n. 67

Milner, N., 121 n. 72, 134 n. 128

Mithridates VI (King of Pontus 120–63 B.C.), 3, 4 + n. 13, 96 n. 52, 122 n. 76, 126

Morrow, G. R., 61

Murphy, S., 26 n. 10

natural motion, 34, 71 + n. 34, 77–9, 93

natural place, 77, 79

Nearkhos of Crete (C4 B.C.), 112 + n. 35

Needham, J., 3 n. 8, 102 n. 65

Nero, Lucius Domitius Ahenobarbus (A.D. 37–68), 32, 84, 134

Neugebauer, O., 64 n. 8, 65 n. 13, 66 nn. 17, 18, 80

Newton, Isaac, 2 n. 3, 36

Nicander of Kolophon (C2 B.C.), 108 n. 16, 117 n. 52, 127 + n. 97

Nigidius, Figulus (*c.* 100–45 B.C.), xi, 70 n. 33

Nitske, W. R. and Wilson, C. M., 27 n. 16

Nixon, L. and Price, S., 47 n. 37

numbers, 10, 39, 41 + n. 12, 42–3 + n. 24, 49–54, 56 + n. 64, 76 n. 50, 80 n. 56, 99, 101

numeracy, 43, 44–54

Nutton, V., xii n. 9, 5 n. 16, 6 n. 23, 7, 119 n. 59, 120 + nn. 61, 62, 66, 67, 121 + nn. 71, 73, 124 + n. 84, 125 n. 88, 128 n. 99, 135–6, 138 n. 5

observation, 10, 11, 16–17, 62, 63 n. 4, 65 + n. 15, 69, 70–3, 80, 88, 91 n. 30, 93, 98, 99 n. 57, 100, 108–12, 123, 127–8

Oleson, J., 35 n. 30

O'Neill, J., 14 n. 41

Oppian of Anazarbus (late C2–early C3 A.D.), 111 + n. 31, 115 n. 43, 136; *Halieutica* (1.9–12), 99; (1.82–5), 99, 113; (4.647–84), 111;

(5.131–51), 111–12 + Fig. 6.1; (5.458–520), 106 n. 3; (5.612–74), 115–16

optics, 25 n. 5, 69, 77, 83 n. 5

organic/inorganic, 25

Origen, of Egypt (*c.* A.D. 185–254), 96 n. 49

Oreibasios (*c.* A.D. 325–400), 14 n. 41

Osborne, C., 7 n. 25

Ovid, Publius Naso, of Sulmo (43 B.C.–A.D. 17), 92 n. 33

Owens, J., 2 n. 5

Paisley, P and Oldroyd, D., 93 n. 40

Palladius, Rutilius Taurus Aemilianus (after A.D. 450), 30 n. 20

Parmenides of Elea (Italy) (C5 B.C.), 27

Paul of Aigina (C7 A.D.), 119 n. 59

Pausanias of Lydia (*fl.c.* A.D. 150), 6 n. 23

Pederson, O. and Pihl, M., xii, 37, 73 n. 42

Pelagonius (C4 A.D.), 46 66; *Ars Veterinaria*, 59 n. 75, 134 + n. 129

Perikles of Athens (C5 B.C.), 46, 66

Peripatos/peripatetic – see Lyceum

Periplous of the Erythraian Sea, 90, 104

Petronius (C1 A.D., 130 n. 111

pharmacology – see drugs

Phillips, E., 135

Philip II of Macedon (*c.* 382–336 B.C.), 49 n. 45, 98, 125

Philo of Byzantium (late C3–early C2 B.C.), 25 + n. 4, 27 n. 15, 35 + n. 29, 38

Philolaos of Kroton (C5 B.C.), 5 n. 16

Philoponos, Johannes, of Caesarea (C6 A.D.), 34 + n. 27, 37 + n. 35, 38

Philostratos of Lemnos (*c.* C3 A.D.) (two authors of the same name, same family, same century, writing the two different works), *Imagines* (2.17), 91–2 + n. 33; *Lives of the Sophists*, 6 n. 23

physics, Chapter 2 *passim*, 77, 82, 96, 123 + n. 80

Pickstone, J. V., iv n. 1

Pindar of Thebes (518–*c.* 446 B.C.), 77–8

Plantzos, D. 69 n. 26

Plato of Athens (*c.* 429–347 B.C.), 9 n. 29, 10, 13, 15, 16 n. 49, 39 + n. 4, 59, 124; *Laws* (737e, 738a), 39 n. 5; (817e–820), 44 n. 25; *Philebus* (56d–57d), 44 + n. 25; *Republic* (7.521c–31c), 39 n. 6, (529d–e), 15; *Sophist* (219–221), 113 + n. 38

Pliny the Elder, Gaius Secundus, of Comum (A.D. 23–79), xii, 6, 15, 25 n. 7, 95 + n. 43, 96 + n. 50, 107 n. 12, 111, 118 n. 54, 124, 133, 135; *Natural History* (2.99.216), 98; (2.202), 99; (2.234), 115 n. 45; (3.17, 6.181), 84; (6.61.4), 83; (7.40), xi n. 2; (7.66), xi; (7.85), 89 n. 25; (7.205), 89 n. 23; (7.112) 96 n. 52; (8.63), 133;

(9.5.15), 108 n. 19; (9.86, 9.111), 114 n. 42; (9.148), 115 n. 43; (10.75), 92 n. 34; (13.140), 112; (25.7), 4; (25.9), 125; (25.116), 111; (26.66), 117 n. 52; (28.5), 128 n. 100; (28.9), 122 n. 76; (29.13), 123; (33.133), 41 n. 12

Pliny the Younger, Gaius Caecilius Secundus, of Comum (c. A.D. 61–113), 95 n. 43

Plommer, H. 30 n. 20

Plutarch of Khaironeia (c. A.D. 46–120), 5 n. 15, 16 n. 49, 65, 87, 106–7 + n. 9, 110, 138 n. 5; *Animals are rational* (Mor. 985d–992e), 107 n. 9; *Caesar* (59), 64 n. 10; *Cato* (22–23), 6 n. 21, 123; *Causes of natural phenomena* (Mor. 911–919), 110 n. 23, (12), 115 n. 45; *Marcellus* (14.5), 6 n. 19; *On the face in the orb of the moon* (Moralia 922f–25d) §4.4 *passim*, 81; *On the principle of cold* 13 (Mor. 950b), 115 n. 45; *Pompey* (42.5), 96 n. 52; *Theseus* (1), 104; *Whether land or sea animals are cleverer* (= *The cleverness of animals* Mor. 959–85), 107 n. 9, 110 n. 23

politics, 6 + n. 21, n. 22, 9 + n. 29, 11, 15, 27 n. 15, 44–6, 49–51 + n. 55, 63–4 + nn. 7–10, 84, 89, 96, 101–3, 106 + n. 2, 117 n. 54, 119–20 + n. 61, 122 + n. 78, 125–6, 129

Polubios of Megalopolis (c. 200–118 B.C.), 5 n. 16, 6 n. 21, 9 n. 29, 49 n. 45, 90

polymaths, xi + n. 4, 11, 14, 46 n. 31, 77–8 + n. 54, 82–4, 88–92, 116, 117 n. 54

Pompey, Gnaeus Magnus (106–48 B.C.), 4, 96 + n. 52, 117 n. 54

poison, 4 + n. 13, 108, 111, 125–6, 127 n. 96

Porter, R., 102 n. 60

Poseidonios of Apamea (c. 135–51 B.C.), 6 n. 21, 9 n. 27, 14 + n. 40, 15, 69 n. 28, 73, 82 + n. 4, 96–9, 106; *On the Ocean*, 82, 96 nn. 48, 52; *On divination*, 97 n. 54

Potter, P., 131

precession of the equinoxes, 68–9 + n. 25

pregnancy, x, xi

Preus, A., 117 n. 53

Price, D de Solla, 26 n. 11, 70 nn. 29, 30

Pritchett, W. K., 49 n. 47, 64 + nn. 8, 9

Proclus of Constantinople (c. A.D. 410–485), 9 n. 27, 26 n. 13, 61

Procopius of Caesarea (c. A.D. 500–562), 85

professionals/ism, 5 + nn. 15, 16, 17, 6, 119–21, 138

psychiatry, 131

Ptolemy, Claudius of Ptolemais (fl. A.D. 121–151), iv, v, 2 n. 3, 17–18, 60, 69–72, 81, 86, 100, 103; star catalogue, 66; size and distance of the moon from earth, 73; chord table, 74 n. 43; mathematical geography, 82, 91, 138 + n. 4; *Almagest*, iv + n. 6, 14, 62; (1.7), 71; (1.11), 51 n. 53; (1.12, 5.1, 5.12, 8.3), 70;

(3.1), 63 n. 4; (7.3), 70 n. 31; *Geography*, iv, 101, 104; *Optics*, iv, 25 n. 5, 38; (2.5), 115 n. 45; *Tetrabiblos*, v, 62; (1.2.1–3), 97–8

Pullan, J., 49 n. 47

Purcell, N., 87

Pythagoras of Samos (C6 B.C.), 18, 39, 40 n. 8, 59, 92 n. 33

Pythagoras' theorem, 18, 55–8, 75 n. 48

Pythagoreans, 53, 72 n. 39, 73, 76

Pytheas of Massilia (France) (fl. 325–300 B.C.), 66 n. 18, 87–8 + n. 20, 104

Rackham, H., 112, 136

Ramsey, J. and Licht, A., 94 n. 41

ratio, 32, 34–5, 49, 53, 56, 59, 74–6

Rationalists, 122

religion – see gods

research, 4, 8, 11, 27

rhetoric/persuasion, 12–13, 22, 36, 39 n. 7, 80, 123–4

Richards, J. L., 54 n. 61

Richardson, W., 41 n. 12, 60

Richmond, J., 110 n. 24

Riddle, J., 4 n. 13, 11 n. 33, 107 n. 12, 122 n. 75, 128

Rihll, T. E., 84 n. 13

Rihll, T. E. and Tucker, J. V., 7 n. 25

Robbins, F., 81, 98

Roccatagliata, G., 131 + n. 116

Rosenfeld, A., 24 nn. 1, 3

Roseman, C., 66 n. 18, 88 n. 20, 104

Rosenmeyer, T. G., 83 n. 8

Rottländer, R., xii n. 6

Rusten, J., 88 n. 22

Saccheri, G., 55–6

Sallares, R., 87

Sambursky, S., 37

Samuel, A., 65 n. 14

Sandbach, F., 83 n. 8

Sarton, G., 16 n. 49

'save the phenomena', 11 + n. 32, 62, 78

Scarborough, J., 2 n. 2, 108 n. 16, 119 n. 59, 121 n. 69, 124 n. 87, 127 n. 97, 135

Scarborough, J. and Nutton, V., v n. 9, 15 n. 45

scepticism, 10

Schoff, W. H., 84 n. 14, 90 + n. 28, 104

schools/sects, 3–5, 10 n. 31, 12, 20, 121–3

scientific revolution, 26–7

Seleukos of Babylon (c. 150 B.C.), 19 n. 54, 71 n. 35, 72 n. 39, 97

self-sufficiency, 124–5

Seneca the Younger, Lucius Annaeus, of Cordoba (Spain) (c. 4 B.C.–A.D. 65), 32, 37, 82, 83 + n. 8, 91, 92 n. 37, 118 n. 54, 121; *Epistles* (33.9), 10; (90.7–13), 15 + n. 43; (90.20–30), 14 n. 40; *Natural Questions* (1 pref

Seneca the Younger (*cont.*):
    7–11), 103; (1.6.5, 1.15.7), 69; (1.16, 3.17–
    18, 4A pref 17, 6.1–2, 7.31), 82 n.5; (2.9.2–
    3), 36–7; (2.26.4–6), 98–9; (2.32.7), 62 n.1;
    (2.42–6), 17 n.50; (3.25.5–6), 33; (3.29.3),
    21 n.59; (5.15.1–4, 6.21.1), 98 + n.56;
    (6.23.4), 83 n.7; (6.4–31), 92 n.33
Serres, M., 43 n.20
sexagesimal numbers, 46–7 + n.38, 137 n.3
Shapiro, A., 7 n.25
Sharples, R., 10 n.31, 83 n.8, 111 n.28, 114
    n.41, 118 n.56
Sherwin-White, S., 122 n.78
Silius Italicus (*c.* A.D. 35–100), 6 n.19
Simms, D., 35 n.31
Simon, B., 131 n.115
Simplicius (C6 A.D.), 37 + n.35, 38, 119 n.59
Singer, C., 135
Singer, P., v n.8, 136
Singh, S., 40 n.8
Skulax of Karuanda (C6 B.C.), 89
slaves, slavery, 9, 16 n.49, 33, 88, 116–17, 130
    n.111, 132
Sleeswyk, A., 35 n.31
Smith, A. M., 25 n.5, 38, 81, 115 n.45
Sokrates of Athens (*c.* 469–399 B.C.), 5, 9
    n.29, 10, 28, 72, 124 n.84, 126
Solmsen, F., 7 n.25, 37
Solon of Athens (late C7–early C6 B.C.), 19
Sophokles of Athens (*c.* 496–405 B.C.), iv n.5,
    77, 79, 124 n.85
Sorabji, R., 37 + n.35, 107 n.9
Sosigenes of Alexandria (C1 B.C.), 63
specific gravity, 29–33
spontaneous generation, 110 + n.26
Staden, H. von, 120 n.63, 127 n.97, 129
    n.106, 136
Stahl, W., 39 n.7, 87 n.17
Stannard, J., 123 n.81
statics, 34
status of scientists, 5, 6, 27 n.15, 35, 117
Ste Croix, G. de, 41 + n.13, 44 n.28, 48 +
    n.44, 60
Stevenson, E., 104
stoicism, 10, 76, 83 + n.8, 96 + n.51, 106, 122
    n.76
Stothers, R. and Rampino, M., 95 n.47
Strabo of Amaseia (Pontus) (*c.* 65 B.C.–A.D.
    19), 82 + n.4, 86, 89 + n.25, 90, 96, 101,
    104; *Geography*, 89; (1.1.11), 83; (1.1.21),
    102; (1.2.1), 85; (1.2.6), 89 n.23; (1.1.16),
    84; (1.3.3), 85, 102 n.68; (1.3.4–5), 91 n.30,
    99 n.57; (1.3.9), 99; (1.3.12), 82 n.4;
    (1.3.16–20), 92 n.33; (2.2.1, 2.3.8), 82 n.4;
    (2.3.6), 99; (2.5.8), 84 n.11, 102; (2.5.10–
    11), 103 n.71; (3.2.9, 3.4.15), 98; (3.5.8–9),

97; (6.2), 93 n.38; (6.2.11), 98; (7.5.8), 98;
    (11.1.6), 96 n.52; (13.1.67, 16.1.15), 98
Strato of Lampsakos (*fl.* 287–69 B.C.), 20, 28,
    29 + n.19, 38, 91 n.30, 122
Suda, The, a Greek lexicon/encyclopaedia
    compiled at the end of the C10 A.D., xii
    n.9, 89 n.23
Suetonius, Gaius, Tranquillus (*c.* A.D. 69–
    140), 117 n.54
suicide, 4, 122 + n.76

Tacitus, Cornelius (*c.* A.D. 55–118), 95 n.43,
    126 n.91
Tannery, P., 58 n.73
Taub, L., 104
technology/technological analogies – see also
    machines and instruments, 5 + n.17, §1.3
    passim, 16 n.49, 19, 26 + n.10, 35–8, 94–5,
    98 n.55, 99, 112, 115
Temkin, O., 124 n.84, 135
Tertullian, Quintus Septimius Florens, of
    Africa (*c.* A.D. 160–230), 35 n.33
Thales of Miletos (*c.* 624–548 B.C.), 6 n.17, 68
Theaitetos of Athens (*c.* 415–369 B.C.), 59
Theodoros of Kyrene (C5 B.C.), 6 n.17, 59
Theophrastos of Eresos (Lesbos) (371–287
    B.C.), v, 5, 11, 12 + n.36, 20 + n.58, 82,
    93 n.39, 102, 107 n.12, 108, 110, 111 n.30,
    116–18 + nn.48, 49, 121, 123 n.80, 126,
    136, 138 n.5; *Causes of plants*, v, 116, 82, 107
    n.12; *Characters*, v; (5.9, 21.4, 21.9), 88 +
    n.22; *History of Plants*, v, x, 82, 107 n.12,
    116–17, 124; (2.7.4), 118 n.55; (4.6.5), 114
    n.43, 117; (4.6.4, 4.6.8, 4.7.2, 6.3.2, 7.1.3,
    7.5.4, 8.7.7, 8.9.1, 9.8.2), 117–18; (9.16.7),
    126; (9.18), iv n.4; *Metaphysics*, 7; *Meteorol-
    ogy*, 91 + n.32; *On animals which change
    colour*, 111 n.28; *On creatures that remain on
    dry land*, 114 n.41; *On Fire*, v, 7, 28, (37)
    130; *On Fish*, 111 n.28, (3) 114 n.41; *On
    Metals*, 91; *On Stones*, v, xii, 7, 91, 104; *On
    things turned to stone*, 91 n.30; *On Water*, 91;
    On Weather-signs, v, 91 + n.31, 100 n.62,
    104
Theopompos of Khios (*c.* 377–320 B.C.), 6
    n.23
'they say' [φασί], 12 + n.37
Thomas, I., iv n.5, xi n.4, 31 n.23, 32 n.24, 42
    n.18, 58 n.71, 60, 81, 137 n.3
Thomas, R., 43 n.23
Thomson, J. O., 85 + n.15, 86, 104
Thompson, D'Arcy, xi n.4, 63 n.3, 107 n.15,
    110 nn.24, 25, 111 n.31, 115 n.43, 135
Thorndike, L., 25 n.7
Thoukudides of Athens (C5 B.C.), 5 n.15, 82,
    106 n.6
tides, 62, 90–1, 97–8

Timokharis of Alexandria (early C3 B.C.), 69, 70 + n. 31
Tod, M. N., 44 n. 28
Toomer, G., iv n. 6, 71, 81
Touwaide, A., 21 n. 60
toxicology, 4, 108, 125–6
Toynbee, J., xii n. 8
trade/traders, 35, 44 + n. 27, 46, 68, 84, 86, 88, 90, 100, 112 n. 33, 126
Tzetzes (C12 A.D.), *Khiliades* (8.972–3), 39 n. 4, (12.723–8), 110 n. 22

Unguru, S., 40 n. 11
use/utility, 5 n. 17, 6 + nn. 18, 22, 14–15, 26 + n. 13, 35–6, 44–50, 53–4, 63–4, 81, 83–5, 88, 107, 115 + n. 44, 117 + nn. 52, 53, 120–1, 123–7

Varro, Marcus Terentius, of Reate (116–27 B.C.), 96 n. 50, 117 n. 54, 133 + nn. 123, 125, 136
vegetarianism, 4
Vegetius, Flavius Renatus (late C4 A.D.), *Epitome of military science* (1), 121 n. 72; (2.7, 2.19), 48; (2.20, 3.15, 4.30), 49; (4.42), 98; *Mulomedicina*, 134 + n. 128
Vesuvius – see also Aetna and volcano, 6, 86 n. 16, 92–3, 95 + nn. 43, 46
veterinary science, xii n. 8, 6 n. 18, 21 n. 60, 59 n. 75, 108, 121 n. 72, §6.5 *passim*

Vickers, M., 47 n. 39
Virgil, Publius Maro, of Mantua (70–19 B.C.), 92 n. 37, 133
Vitruvius, Marcus Pollio (C1 B.C.), 14, 32, 38; *On architecture* (9 pref. 9–12), 29–30
vivisection, 4, 129–30
volcano – see also Aetna and Vesuvius, 35 + n. 33, 91, 92 + n. 36, 95 + n. 43, 98–9

Waerden, B. van der, 40 n. 9, 58 n. 73
Warmington, E. H., 105
Wellmann, M., 4 n. 13
Wertheim, M., 13 n. 39
whaling, 111–13 + Fig. 6.1
White, K. D., 27 n. 14, 38
Whitney, E., 14, 15 + n. 42, 15 n. 45
Wilamowitz, U. von, 124 n. 84
Wilson, C. A., 26 + n. 9
Wolff, M., 34 n. 27
Woodcroft, B., xi n. 4, 38

Xenophanes of Kolophon (*c.* 570–480 B.C.), 91
Xenophon of Athens (late C5–early C4 B.C.), 5 n. 15
Xerxes (King of Persia 486–465 B.C.), 50

Zeno of Sidon (C2 B.C.), 9 n. 27
zero, 51, 51 + n. 53
zoology, 63 n. 3, 106–8, §6.2 *passim*